7|18

NEAR-DEATH EXPERIENCES

Near-Death Experiences . . .
and Others

ROBERT GOTTLIEB

Farrar, Straus and Giroux   New York

Farrar, Straus and Giroux
175 Varick Street, New York 10014

Owing to limitations of space, illustration credits can be found on page 351.

Library of Congress Cataloging-in-Publication Data
Names: Gottlieb, Robert, 1931– author.
Title: Near-death experiences . . . and others / Robert Gottlieb.
Description: First edition. | New York : Farrar, Straus and Giroux, 2018.
Identifiers: LCCN 2017035982 | ISBN 9780374219918 (hardcover) |
    ISBN 9780374717919 (ebook)
Subjects: LCSH: Performing arts—United States—Reviews. |
    Entertainers—Miscellanea.
Classification: LCC PN2266.5 .G68 2018 | DDC 791.097309/04—dc23
LC record available at https://lccn.loc.gov/2017035982

Designed by Abby Kagan

Our books may be purchased in bulk for promotional, educational, or business use.
Please contact your local bookseller or the Macmillan Corporate and Premium Sales
Department at 1-800-221-7945, extension 5442, or by e-mail at
MacmillanSpecialMarkets@macmillan.com.

www.fsgbooks.com
www.twitter.com/fsgbooks • www.facebook.com/fsgbooks

1   3   5   7   9   10   8   6   4   2

CONTENTS

PREFACE

LAS, NOT EVERYTHING A WRITER WRITES seems worthy of being collected—even to the writer. Choosing what to put into this book, I've tried to be disinterested, but no doubt I've included at least a few pieces that might have been left un-resuscitated. Such is parental love—or ego.

Most of the essays in the first, and longer, part of the book appeared originally in *The New York Review of Books*. Others appeared in *The Atlantic*, *The New Yorker*, *The New York Times Book Review*, the *Los Angeles Times Book Review*, *The New York Observer*, and *The Wall Street Journal*. The piece on the Trumps was published in the *Observer* in September 2000: There was no compelling reason to reprint it in my first collection, *Lives and Letters*, seven years ago; today there's a compelling reason. A few other pieces that painfully got left behind then for reasons of space have been rescued because they seem, at least to me, to be worth rescuing.

The main difference between this book and *Lives and Letters* is the inclusion in it of twenty-odd of the three hundred or so dance reviews I've published in the *Observer* since 1999—reviews that I hope have some more than immediate interest. My great friend Janet Malcolm has been urging me to reprint these for years, which is both flattering and unnerving—doesn't she like the rest of my work? If you don't appreciate their appearance here, blame Janet—it's *that* girl's fault.

NEAR-DEATH EXPERIENCES

Near-Death Experiences

I'VE NEVER HAD A NEAR-DEATH EXPERIENCE and don't know anyone who has, but according to a poll that's quoted throughout the NDE literature, at least five percent of Americans have returned from one and told the tale. That may be a small percentage, but it's a lot of people—given today's population, over fifteen million. Other estimates are lower, but they're still huge. And most of these people seem to be writing books.

The current front-runner is the omnipresent *Heaven Is for Real*, by Todd Burpo "with" Lynn Vincent—and don't underestimate that "with": Lynn Vincent has been, among other things, the ghostwriter for Sarah Palin's *Going Rogue*, and she knows what she's doing. (I imagine that after dealing with Palin, dealing with Colton Burpo—who, before he turned four, almost died of a ruptured appendix, went to heaven, and came back with a detailed report—must have been a piece of cake.) Actually, she's not little Colton's collaborator, she's his dad's: It's Todd, Colton's father, who tells the story.

Todd Burpo is the pastor of the Crossroads Wesleyan Church in Imperial, Nebraska, population approximately two thousand. He also owns a company that installs garage doors, and is a wrestling coach for junior high and high school students and a volunteer with the Imperial fire department. His wife, Sonja, works as an office manager, has a master's in library and information science, and is a certified teacher. When Colton, their second child, suffers his burst appendix—his condition has been misdiagnosed—the family undergoes an agonizing period of suspense during the time he's close to death before making a full recovery. Lynn Vincent jerks every tear in recounting this frightening story—"*Daddy! Don't let them take meeee!*"—but has room for touches of humor, too. At a crucial moment: "That night might be the only time in recorded history that eighty people [Todd's parishioners] gathered and prayed for someone to pass gas!" ("Within an hour, the . . . prayer was answered!")

Colton's remarkable story is really two stories. One is his account of what he sees when, under anesthesia, he looks down from the hospital room ceiling and observes the doctors working on his body, his Mommy praying and talking on the telephone in one room, and his Daddy praying in another. When, days later, he casually mentions this to his father, "Colton's words rocked me to the core. . . . *How could he have known?*" Actually, this kind of out-of-body experience—in which the presumably unconscious person still has the faculties of sight, hearing, and memory—turns out to be a fairly common phenomenon.

The other story is what Colton experienced in heaven while he was being operated on, a story that emerges only four months later when, under Todd's gentle questioning, Colton's parents learn that their boy had met "nice" John the Baptist and the angel Gabriel, who's also nice. And because "a lot of our Catholic friends have asked whether Colton saw Mary, the mother of Jesus," the answer is yes. "He saw Mary kneeling before the throne of God and at other times, standing beside Jesus. 'She still loves him like a mom,'" Colton reports. What's more, Colton sat in Jesus's lap observing his clothes (white with a purple sash) and his "markers"—Colton's term for the stigmata. Everyone but Jesus had wings: "Jesus just went up and down like an elevator."

What most startled the Burpos was Colton's suddenly saying, "Mommy, I have two sisters." There's not only his older sister, Cassie, but "You had a baby die in your tummy, didn't you?" As Vincent puts it, "At that moment, time stopped in the Burpo household, and Sonja's eyes grew wide." Sonja: "Who told you I had a baby die in my tummy?" "She did, Mommy. She said she had died in your tummy." "Emotions rioted across Sonja's face." "It's okay, Mommy. She's okay. God adopted her." "Don't you mean Jesus adopted her?" "No, Mommy. His Dad did!" Before returning to earth, Colton also witnessed the battle of Armageddon and saw Jesus victorious and Satan defeated and thrown into hell. His entire trip to heaven, he reports, took place in three minutes.

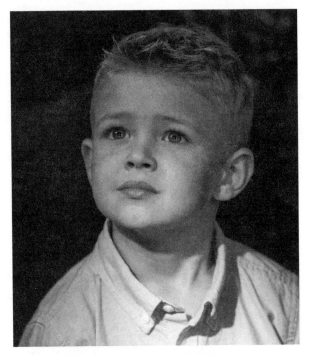

Connor Corum as Colton Burpo in *Heaven Is for Real*

The tale of Colton Burpo, so slickly told and efficiently exploited, poses an immediate question, of course: Are the Burpos sincere, or is this a fraud? Despite all the commercialization, I believe that *they* believe; that little Colton said things he thought to be true and that were shaped into this artful narrative by an astute collaborator.

WITH EIGHT MILLION COPIES SOLD since its publication in 2010, *Heaven Is for Real* was number one on the trade nonfiction best-seller list for well over a year and recently opened successfully as a movie, starring Greg Kinnear as Todd Burpo. The movie is pretty, pious, and at times plausible—not as an account of a trip to a greeting-card pastel heaven but as an account of parents dealing with their faith, their child, and their bank account. (One of the themes of both the book and the movie is the Burpos' constant struggle with bills.) The film benefits from restrained performances, Kinnear never seeming embarrassed by what he's been given to do and the little boy who plays Colton not only an amazing look-alike for the real Colton but simple and unaffected. You believe the actor if not his story.

The most interesting thing about the movie is how Hollywood has modeled it after a familiar genre that has nothing to do with the book: the ordinary good guy who stands up for what he believes against the naysayers. The church elders, who have been close friends and devoted supporters of the Burpos, suddenly, without our being prepared, decide they may have to replace Todd, since all the fuss about Colton is making their church too much of a roadshow attraction. But Todd is allowed to give one last sermon to set things straight, which he proceeds to do in a montage of spoken clichés so confused and banal that it's almost impossible to follow them. No matter: The genuine all-American guy of high intentions is instantly a hero again. Mr. Deeds has come to town, Mr. Smith has come to Washington—it's Capracorn at its most virulent. And indeed there's a final image of Kinnear hugging his family while everyone brims with goodwill that's a direct steal from the famous shot of Jimmy Stewart at the end of *It's a Wonderful Life*. What's odd is that none of this dramatic conflict is in the book. When the chips are down, Hollywood relies on itself, not Revelation.

NEAR-DEATH EXPERIENCES became a subject of wide-ranging public discussion and dispute in 1975, when a doctor named Raymond Moody Jr. published *Life After Life*—a book that in the subsequent literature on the phenomenon more or less holds the place of the Bible, its authority constantly cited and Moody's imprimatur constantly sought. Its hold on the reading public is also remarkable: Thirteen million copies have been sold. But considering its sensational effect, the book itself is painstakingly unsensational. It's a circumspect report on what the young doctor had been hearing from some of his patients—and then from others whom he sought out, more than a thousand in all—about experiences they had when near death. In fact, it was Moody who coined the phrase "near-death experience."

What his book did was validate the subject. As he wrote in a recent memoir, *Paranormal: My Life in Pursuit of the Afterlife*, "People no longer had to keep it in the closet or worry about people thinking they were crazy. It gave us legitimate consolation." But in a revised edition of his *Life After Life* published in 2001, he writes: "Sadly, the avalanche of books on the subject includes many that, to my personal knowledge, have been fabricated by unscrupulous self-promoters cynically seeking notoriety or financial gain rather than true advancement in knowledge."

If Raymond Moody is the godfather of the near-death movement, the godmother—or grandmother—was Elisabeth Kübler-Ross, who demands attention because of *On Death and Dying* (1969), her influential book on the five stages of grief. In a later book, *On Life After Death*, she turns to more speculative matters, speaking with absolute (and unsupported) authority: "What the church tells little children about guardian angels is based on fact. There is proof that every human being, from his birth until his death, is guided by a spirit entity." Among her other pronouncements: "it is a blessing to have cancer" and "a minimum of 30 percent of our population" have been sexually abused in their childhood.

When Kübler-Ross herself emerged from a self-induced out-of-body experience, she tells us, "my bowel obstruction was healed, and I was literally able to lift a hundred-pound sugar bag from the floor without any discomfort or pain. I was told that I radiated, that I looked twenty years younger." Why am I not surprised that her early ambition was to be a doctor in India the way Albert Schweitzer was in Africa, and that Mother Teresa "is one of my saints"? But she found even more important work to do than healing. "My *real* job," she explains, "is to tell people that death does not exist. It is very important that mankind knows this, for we are at the beginning of a very difficult time. Not only for this country, but for the whole planet earth."

WHAT EXACTLY CONSTITUTES A NEAR-DEATH EXPERIENCE? Jeffrey Long, in *Evidence of the Afterlife*, sums up:

> Researchers have concluded that NDEs may include some or all of
> the following twelve elements:

1. Out-of-body experience (OBE): Separation of consciousness from the physical body
2. Heightened senses
3. Intense and generally positive emotions or feelings
4. Passing into or through a tunnel
5. Encountering a mystical or brilliant light
6. Encountering other beings, either mystical beings or deceased relatives or friends
7. A sense of alteration of time or space
8. Life review
9. Encountering unworldly ("heavenly") realms
10. Encountering or learning special knowledge
11. Encountering a boundary or barrier
12. A return to the body, either voluntary or involuntary

And indeed, as you trawl through the personal narratives of those who report their NDEs, these are the notes that are sounded again and again.

Such experiences are hardly new—there are numerous examples of them, or something similar to them, throughout history. Like many others, Moody cites the story of Er, as told in *The Republic* (Plato "was one of the greatest thinkers of all time"). Er (an ancient Greek cousin to Lazarus) was a warrior who rose from his funeral pyre and described what he had experienced while "dead." It does sound as if Er had undergone a genuine NDE, but because the NDE vocabulary is so fluid, it's sometimes hard to distinguish one particular experience from other, related ones—visions, hallucinations, dreams.

A very detailed report of an NDE was left us in a memoir by General William Booth, founder of the Salvation Army, who, when a young man, was seized by a sudden fever and in just a few hours "was brought to the very brink of death.... A strange faintness seized me. I lost consciousness. My next sensation was altogether beyond description. It was the thrill of a new and celestial existence. I was in heaven."

Many of today's familiar tropes are present: the flashback through his past life, the angelic spirits, the glorious music. Jesus appears to Booth, a radiant yet stern presence, and speaks:

Go back to earth. I will give thee another opportunity. Prove thyself worthy of My name. Show to the world that thou possessest My spirit by doing My works, and becoming, on My behalf, a savior of men. Thou shalt return hither when thou hast finished the battle, and I will give thee a place in My conquering train, and a share in My glory.

And so the Salvation Army.

Many other great names are cited throughout the literature: Plotinus, Meister Eckhart, Blake, Swedenborg, Dostoevsky. Did they have visions? Out-of-body experiences? NDEs? More recent witnesses include Carl Jung, who in his *Memories, Dreams, Reflections* reports what was clearly an NDE. At the age of sixty-eight, while suffering a long, life-threatening illness, he found himself floating in space, which was "bathed in a gloriously blue light." And then his physician, "or, rather, his likeness"—"in his primal form"—floated up from Europe, where Jung's physical body lay. "He had been delegated by the earth to deliver a message to me, to tell me that there was a protest against my going away. I had no right to leave the earth and must return"—proof of, if nothing else, Jung's monumental ego. His visions and experiences, he reports, "were utterly real; there was nothing subjective about them; they all had a quality of absolute objectivity."

And would Elizabeth Taylor lie? After the death of her husband Mike Todd, she "went to that tunnel, saw the white light, and Mike. I said, 'Oh Mike, you're where I want to be.' And he said, 'No, Baby. You have to turn around and go back because there is something very important for you to do.'" No doubt he was thinking of the important things she would go on to achieve for AIDS relief and other causes, not the making of *Cleopatra*. Among the other stars who have reported NDEs are Peter Sellers, Donald Sutherland, Chevy Chase, Burt Reynolds, and Lou Gossett Jr., who has had five of them. (He also recalls a previous incarnation as a pirate with a harem off the coast of Morocco.)

THE NUMBER-TWO BOOK in the heaven genre, as I write, is considerably more sophisticated, tendentious, and disagreeable than *Heaven Is for*

Real. It's *Proof of Heaven: A Neurosurgeon's Journey into the Afterlife*, by Eben Alexander, the work of a doctor who tells us that his "conclusions are based on a medical analysis of my experience, and on my familiarity with the most advanced concepts in brain studies and consciousness studies." In other words, he's his own expert witness. What happened to Dr. Alexander? One night when he was fifty-four, he reports, "a rare illness" threw him into a seven-day coma, during which time his "entire neocortex—the outer surface of the brain, the part that makes us human—was shut down." His twenty-year-old son "was looking at what he knew was, essentially, a corpse. My physical body was there in front of him, but the dad he knew was gone."

Gone, but not gone. That dad was undergoing a rich yet not atypical NDE experience: "I was flying, passing over trees and fields, streams and waterfalls, and here and there, people. There were children, too, laughing and playing. The people sang and danced around in circles, and sometimes I'd see a dog, running and jumping among them, as full of joy as the people were." There's a beautiful girl: "Golden-brown tresses framed her lovely face." There are millions of butterflies all around. He reaches the Core, where everything "came instantly in an explosion of light, color, love, and beauty that blew through me like a crashing wave . . . in a way that bypassed language." "I understood that I was part of the Divine and that nothing—absolutely nothing—could ever take that away," and so "was granted full access to the cosmic being I really am (and *we* all are)."

In heaven Alexander learned that we are eternal. And he brings back important tidings: "Each and every one of us is deeply known and cared for by a Creator who cherishes us beyond any ability we have to comprehend. That knowledge must no longer remain a secret." And: "I see it as my duty—both as a scientist and hence a seeker of truth, and as a doctor devoted to helping people—to make known to as many people as I can that what I underwent is true, and real, and of stunning importance. Not just to me, but to all of us." He's a prophet as well as a surgeon.

He's also a man who's had a troubled life, tormented by the knowledge that he'd been adopted as an infant, giving way to profound depression, alcoholism, despair. Only when he eventually meets the teenage couple who had had to give him away, and discovers that he had been loved by them, does he recover from the feeling that "subconsciously, I had believed that I *didn't deserve* to be loved, or even to exist." No wonder the crucial message he receives in heaven is *"You are loved and cherished."* And no wonder he encountered that golden-brown-tressed girl: A snapshot proves that she's a birth sister who had died before he was reunited with his birth family.

On first reading this narrative I was struck by both its grandiosity and its obvious elements of wish fulfillment, but I took for granted the lofty medical credentials Alexander stresses. However, as a lethal exposé by Luke Dittrich in *Esquire* recently revealed, Alexander's successful career has been stained by an extraordinary chain of unpleasant departures from prestigious institutions, by malpractice suits (five in one ten-year stretch—all settled out of court), and by loss of surgical privileges—he's been without official credentials since 2007. (The Virginia Board of Medicine once ordered him to take continuing education classes in ethics and professionalism.) None of this, needless to say, is alluded to in *Proof of Heaven*.

Dittrich also raises questions about Alexander's veracity. Most damning are the tempered remarks he quotes from Dr. Laura Potter, who was on duty in the ER the night Alexander was brought in. Alexander tells us that his coma was caused by a case of E. coli bacterial meningitis, neglecting to mention that the coma was actually induced by Dr. Potter, in order to keep him alive until he was in a condition to be treated. Through the seven days of coma, whenever they tried to wake him, he was, Potter reports, in an agitated state—"just thrashing, trying to scream, and grabbing at his tube." At those moments, she says, he was delirious but conscious. (A central point in Alexander's argument is that throughout this entire week, his brain was incapable of creating a hallucinatory conscious experience.) When Alexander showed Dr. Potter the passages in his manuscript referring to her, she told him that they didn't reflect her recollection. He then said to her, as she reported to Dittrich, that it was a matter of "artistic license," and added that parts of his book were "dramatized, so it may not be exactly how it went, but it's supposed to be interesting for readers."

Certainly, readers have found it so. Last year alone, almost 950,000 copies of *Proof of Heaven* were sold. A movie is coming, a follow-up book is on the way, and according to Dittrich, "Anyone can pay sixty dollars to access his webinar guided-meditation series, 'Discover Your Own Proof of Heaven.'" What's more, you can pay to join the doctor on a "healing journey" through Greece. As for Dittrich's revelations, Alexander told him, "I just think that you're doing a grave disservice to your readers to lead them down a pathway of thinking that any of that is, is relevant." All that should matter is the message he returned with from heaven.

(In an official, if unspecific, response to Dittrich, Dr. Alexander proclaims that the *Esquire* article "is a textbook example of how unsupported assertions and cherry-picked information can be assembled at the expense of the truth.")

It's up to us to decide for ourselves whether Alexander is dishonest, delusional, a fantasist—or even telling the truth, at least as he sees it. Dittrich takes the long view: "Dr. Eben Alexander looks less like a messenger from heaven and more like a true son of America, a country where men have always found ways to escape the rubble of their old lives through audacious acts of reinvention."

TODD BURPO AND EBEN ALEXANDER couldn't be more different, but the message they, and all the others, deliver is the same one, a message mankind has always been happy to receive: You can go on living after you die—in the short run, by returning from death or near-death; in the long run, up in heaven. In fact, once you get to heaven it's so wonderful there you don't *want* to return. In account after account the narrator begs to be allowed to stay on, but someone on high—Jesus, God, Saint Patrick, an angel—insists that he go back to earth. ("Mark! You must go back!" "Go back? No! No! I can't go back!" . . . "You must return; I have given you [a] task, you have not finished." "No, no, please God, no! Let me stay.") They all obey, however, and so we get *Heaven Is for Real; Proof of Heaven; To Heaven and Back; Nine Days in Heaven; 90 Minutes in Heaven; A Glimpse of Heaven; My Time in Heaven; When Will the Heaven*

Begin?; *Waking Up in Heaven*; *AfterLife: What You Really Want to Know About Heaven, the Hereafter, and Near-Death Experiences*; *A Vision from Heaven*; *My Journey to Heaven*; *Flight to Heaven*; *Appointments with Heaven*; *Hello from Heaven!*; *The Boy Who Came Back from Heaven*; *Revealing Heaven*; plus others whose titles don't include the H word—*I Saw the Light, Saved by the Light, Embraced by the Light*.

But if these books all take us to heaven and back, they're by no means all alike. Some are just risible. Mary Stephens Landoll had *A Vision from Heaven* while in bed with a bad chest cold. In her vision, she was dressed in "a white satin (huge puffed up shoulders) file gown with chip diamond sparkles all over it. . . ." As for Jesus, he "certainly looked Jewish. . . . His neck was real muscular and wide like a calf—strong as an animal. He was not a wimp. He was healthy." Kat Kerr, in *Revealing Heaven*, not only sees John, her late husband, playing golf with Jesus but also watches a heavenly movie with John Wayne.

Most of these narratives, however, despite details that may strike one as bizarre or just plain silly, are clearly sincere, and a number of them are cogent and convincing. That is, the reader—or at least this reader—is convinced that they represent a reality the author experienced and remembered. The range of backgrounds is very wide, the life stories and lifestyles dramatically divergent, and the tone of most of them generally unruffled and confident. And though accounts of heaven tend to pall after one has read thirty or so of them, the real-life stories of the narrators are frequently absorbing and often moving.

Don Piper, whose *90 Minutes in Heaven* is one of the most widely read of these books, "died" in a car crash; had a typical near-death experience of heaven; was in the hospital for 105 days; lay in bed at home for thirteen months; and "endured thirty-four surgeries." What he most wants to convey is that he survived because so many people prayed for him: "You prayed; I'm here."

Crystal McVea—sexually abused at the age of three; a violent stepfather; bulimia and abortion in high school; suicide attempts—nevertheless survived and flourished. We feel she's telling the truth in her memoir *Waking Up in Heaven* when she writes that, after her NDE, she "really *missed* God. I longed to be with Him again. . . . I mean, it wasn't like I had met the president or a celebrity or something. This was the Creator of the universe! The Lord God of Israel!"

Betty J. Eadie, author of the much-loved *Embraced by the Light*, speaks of

> the unconditional love of God, beyond any earthly love, radiating from him to all his children. . . . But above all, I saw Christ, the Creator and Savior of the earth, my friend, and the closest friend any of us can have. I seemed to melt with joy as I was held in his arms and comforted—home at last. I would give all in my power, all that I ever was, to be filled with that love again—to be embraced in the arms of his eternal light.

Uniquely, she reports on "the Lord's sense of humor, which was so delightful and quick as any here—far more so. Nobody could outdo his humor."

Particularly moving is the account of Jeff Olsen in *I Knew Their Hearts*. He was driving, nodded off, and when his car plunged off the road, his wife and baby son were killed and seven-year-old Spencer was trapped but saved. Olsen's account of his almost four months in the hospital, eighteen major surgeries, one leg lost, right arm almost gone, skin grafts—and of his guilt and remorse—is direct, modest, and sensible. He doesn't go to heaven, but on the first night, in terrible pain, he floats through the hospital and wanders down the halls, coming upon his own broken body. Because of Spencer he rejects the idea of suicide: "Having a child is like having your heart leave your body and walk around in the world. . . . I just didn't know how to be there for him with my own heart still broken in so many ways." In a dream God says to him, "Choose joy," and eventually he repairs himself emotionally, becomes a successful advertising director, remarries, adopts two sons, lives a life. His book inspires, not through the God part but through his strength and fortitude as a man.

BECAUSE ASPECTS OF THE MORE ARTLESS NDE NARRATIVES are so available to ridicule, it's hard to remember that even some of the seemingly absurd byways of the literature can be genuine reflections of serious concerns. Gary Kurz, a fundamentalist Christian who is a strict Biblicist—that is, he believes that every word of the Bible must be taken literally—has devoted three books to the place of pets in the afterlife: *Cold Noses at the Pearly Gates*, *Wagging Tails in Heaven*, and *Furry Friends Forevermore*. They repeat themselves, but they're good-natured, even funny, and from a Biblicist point of view, they have a certain logic to them.

Kurz is anti-evolution. ("I am not a mammal. I am not an animal. I am a man.") He dismisses the idea of departed pets coming back to visit, and he's adamant that animals will not be included in the final Rapture. He's also fierce on the subject of the heaven narrative: "As a Christian and Biblicist, I reject erroneous claims about Heaven, the 'I visited there myself' claim in particular. The Bible teaches clearly, that short of the rapture [which would mean the return of Jesus to earth], the only way to get to Heaven is to die." In fact, when Kurz comes upon certain descriptions of heaven: "Pleeeeeeease! When I hear something like that I repeat what I have said so many times before. 'Pass the bread, the baloney has already been around.'"

On the other hand, Kurz wonders whether "animals aren't just another order of angels or perhaps directed by angels to serve and protect humankind." And indeed reports bear out that animals can come to our rescue in much the way guardian angels do. *USA Today*, for instance, published an account of Gary, from Columbus, Ohio, who trained his cat, Tommy, to use the telephone. Sure enough, when Gary fell out of his wheelchair and his osteoporosis and mini-strokes kept him from getting up, Tommy dialed 911 for help. "The cat was lying by a telephone on the living room floor when the officer went in. Tommy saved Gary's life!" There's a considerable library of books that provide scores—hundreds—of comparable stories about angels, including a particularly engaging one about a bank employee who helps a man retrieve his lost Filofax and whose name turns out to be . . . Dawn Angel!

Anecdotes like these are the bread and butter of the tabloids, and they have their entertainment value. Their absurdities, however, reflect the naive but potent hunger for the kind of reassurance that the more substantial NDE narratives also provide. Yes, these scenarios of visits to heaven may seem preposterous to the skeptical reader (like myself). And yes, the comforting messages brought back from heaven have often been delivered before—but through prophecy, revelation, the Word. The recent spate of NDE books offers something more concrete: contemporary first-person reportage. If their authors are not liars, something happened to these people. But what? Can what they report, however unlikely it sounds, be reconciled with science, so that we can respect the phenomenon while rejecting its literal manifestations?

II

THE INCREASING FOCUS OF SCIENCE TODAY on the study of the brain has spilled over into considerations of what exactly may be happening to people who experience out-of-body and near-death experiences. In *Erasing Death*, a stimulating book published in 2013, Dr. Sam Parnia recapitulates recent arguments that there may well be a continuation of consciousness after what we conventionally think of as death. He's one of a number of physicians and scientists who have been reconsidering the mainstream definition of death, concluding that it isn't the single event of cardiac arrest but is a process. In other words, the heart stops but the brain doesn't, so that visions, hallucinations, dreams—or NDEs—may take place after we're officially labeled dead. In other words, these are in fact ADEs: *actual* death experiences.

Much of Dr. Parnia's discussion rests on the extraordinary progress made over the last twenty years in the art of resuscitation—and, as he emphasizes, of post-resuscitation. (He's been a leader in this field.) The central procedure involved is the use of hypothermia—cooling the body to slow the heart. In a provocative sidelight, he invokes the *Titanic*. Rewatching James Cameron's movie after a number of years, he concluded that if the people on the rescue ship *Carpathia*, which arrived on the scene less than two hours after the disaster, had been aware of the benefits of hypothermia, many of the 1,514 drowned victims found bobbing in the sea might have been brought back to life:

Today we would not have necessarily declared those people dead—at least not in the irreversible and irretrievable sense. Although I agree they were dead, they were nonetheless salvageable. Their bodies would have been largely preserved by the icy cold waters, and two hours is not much time at all. In short, they were potentially completely viable.

Erasing Death takes us through the histories of a number of patients not only "dead" for several minutes or hours but who have existed in years-long comas or other states of unconsciousness before suddenly reviving and even resuming a more or less normal life. (I have direct knowledge of one such case.) These people were not clinically dead, because their hearts were beating, but they were presumed to be brain-dead . . . until they weren't. So what is happening to brains in this "dead" or unconscious condition? In what way can they and do they function? Do they retain some level of awareness? Are they dreaming? Are they having near-death experiences? We don't know.

What adds to the confusion is that the vocabulary in which such things are discussed is (and no doubt has to be) vague: Parnia, among others, refers to consciousness, the self, the mind, the psyche, the soul, as if these things were almost interchangeable.

In his consideration of NDEs, Parnia sets forth a series of explanations that various reputable scientists have proposed in recent years: temporal lobe epilepsy; the effect on the dying brain of certain drugs; a change in the levels of carbon dioxide in those who are dying; a surge of electrical activity in the brain in the minutes preceding death; a lack of oxygen in the brain during the death process that may "cause uncontrolled activity in the brain areas responsible for vision," thus triggering the illusion of experiencing a light and/or a tunnel—this is known as the "dying brain" hypothesis; and more. He summarizes these theories with apparent disinterestedness, but in his tempered dismissal of them I sense a certain satisfaction. What he's hoping for, I infer, is a larger answer, or at least the answer to a larger question: Is it possible that what we call the mind may be "a separate, undiscovered scientific entity" that isn't the result of the brain's usual processes? This is a revolutionary proposition, and one that he seems to be straining to see confirmed.

What emerges, finally, from Parnia's book is that it's not simply the science that concerns him. His core issue is finding "a spiritual or metaphysical perspective on the survival of our consciousness beyond death." He concludes:

> Today, the tantalizing question for science is, If the human conscious-ness or soul does indeed continue to exist well past the traditional marker that defines death, does it really ever die as an entity? Our new studies will continue to explore this and other significant ethical questions. For now, though, we can be certain that we humans no lon-ger need to fear death.

A comforting conclusion, but several readings of Parnia's text have left me baffled about the evidence he's marshaled and the logic he's em-ployed to reach it.

MIDWAY THROUGH HIS BOOK, Dr. Parnia refers in passing to a 2006 study by Dr. Kevin Nelson on the possible relationship between NDEs and sleep patterns. Nelson isn't mentioned elsewhere, even in the bibli-ography, which is hard to understand because two years before *Erasing Death* was published, Nelson published a carefully thought-out and per-suasive book called *The Spiritual Doorway in the Brain*. In it, he suggests what seems to me a possible, even plausible, explanation of what may actually be happening to people who are experiencing NDEs. Nelson was inspired by something a woman reported decades earlier to Raymond Moody, author of the groundbreaking book *Life After Life*—a woman who after suffering cardiac arrest found herself fully conscious of the world around her but paralyzed and unable to signal to the doctors that she was alive. What natural physiological process, Nelson asked him-self, could have caused her precipitous, total, yet temporary paralysis?

It came to him that there was a clear connection here to what we experience every night when sleeping—"when our eyes move rapidly beneath our lids, as if watching events before us. It is called the rapid eye movement stage of sleep, familiar to everyone who studies the brain. We call it the REM state of consciousness." REM activity would explain the light beckoning to eternity that is one of the most salient features of most NDEs:

> With death approaching, what if we were overtaken by REM paralysis, our visual system stimulated to produce light, and the dreaming apparatus in our brains triggered—all while we were consciously awake and in a state of medical crisis? REM consciousness and wakefulness blending into each other as death approached could explain many of the major features of near-death experiences.

The research that Nelson and his colleagues have been doing on this theory as well as on what he terms a variety of related spiritual events— "out-of-body experiences, feelings of rapture or nirvana, mystical 'oneness,' and visions of saints or the dead"—has, not surprisingly, stimulated controversy:

> On one hand, the link I have made between REM and the near-death experience upsets those who see such experiences as a revelation of the afterlife or proof of an underlying web of consciousness or the existence of God. For these people, my work puts near-death experiences uncomfortably close to dreams—in other words, experiences that aren't real. On the other hand, my work also irks some die-hard atheists, because it inextricably links spirituality with what it means to be human and makes it an integral part of all of us, whether our reasoning brain likes it or not.

He himself is searching for answers:

> Are spontaneous and authentic spiritual experiences nothing more than "experiments of nature" telling us how the brain works? . . . Do these cold, hard clinical facts suck the divine nectar from our spiritual lives? My answer is an emphatic NO!

We are, he believes, "poised on the threshold of a new era that holds tremendous promise for a new level of spiritual exploration." But his faith in spiritual experiences isn't really explained. And his scrupulosity leads him to remark that "basing one's spirituality on science is as foolhardy as basing one's science on spirituality."

Nelson's ideas on near-death experiences make sense, at least to me, but, as with Parnia, I find it difficult to join him in his "optimistic" belief that "understanding the brain as a spiritual organ strengthens our quest for meaning and complements a mature spirituality."

UNFORTUNATELY, THESE PROFOUND ISSUES are being turned into battlefields in the culture wars. Dr. Eben Alexander, the author of *Proof of Heaven*, puts it this way:

> Science—the science to which I've devoted so much of my life—doesn't contradict what I learned up there [in heaven]. But far, far too many believe it does, because certain members of the scientific community, who are pledged to the materialist worldview, have insisted again and again that science and spirituality cannot coexist.

"Certain members" is the language of the witch hunt, and the mutual exclusivity of spirituality and materialism exists primarily in the eye of this particular beholder: As we have seen, men of science like Parnia and Nelson (and, among others, Freeman Dyson) are deeply interested in the spiritual, and seek to reconcile it with their purely scientific insights. What's really happening here is that the words "materialism" and "spirituality" are being used by Alexander as code for "atheism" and "religion."

By far the most contentious and rancorous of the books I've been considering is *Life After Death: The Evidence*, by the right-wing politico Dinesh D'Souza, who "remained lukewarm" in his religious beliefs until he became religiously engaged, leading to a new career as a Christian propagandist (*What's So Great About Christianity*, *What's So Great About God*), complementing his ongoing career as a disputatious patriot

(*What's So Great About America*, *The Roots of Obama's Rage*, and his 2014 best seller, *America: Imagine a World Without Her*). *Life After Death* isn't really about life after death—it's a zealous assault on atheism. "I want to engage atheism and reductive materialism on their own terms, and to beat them at their own game."

D'Souza goes about it by leading us through step-by-step "logical" arguments that might just convince naive school kids, his specious logic matched by his smug certainties and his conviction that he has proved his thesis: "We have repelled the atheist case against the believers. . . . By examining the arguments for and against life after death, we have concluded that there is a strong intellectual and practical case for belief." In other words, he agrees with himself. (Recently, this self-proclaimed patriot and Christian has not only been forced to resign his position as president of a small Christian college following an ugly sexual scandal that cost him his marriage, but has also pleaded guilty to charges of using straw donors to make illegal contributions to a United States Senate campaign, in violation of the federal campaign finance law, and to making false statements in this regard.)

D'Souza's discussion of NDEs is as skewed as the rest of his book, directed not at understanding them or explaining them scientifically but at using them as another weapon against atheism: "While the critics of NDEs have raised some interesting possibilities—it might be this and it might be that—on balance, near death experiences do suggest that consciousness can and sometimes does survive death. By itself this is a very damaging conclusion for those who deny the afterlife." Who those "critics" may be, I have no idea. People who do not accept NDE narratives as literal truth? The deployment of such straw men is typical of D'Souza's methodology throughout.

AS THESE VARIOUS BOOKS SUGGEST, then, two struggles are taking place simultaneously. One is the grappling of the neuroscientists with their new discoveries about the brain and about death—an endeavor that is clearly only in its early stages. The other is political and cultural, between skeptics and defenders of the faith. Because this latter struggle is so fierce, and because the discoveries of the neuroscientists are so challenging and even threatening, hyperbole, delusion, and anger dominate far too much of what should be disinterested discourse. After all, death and the possibility of an afterlife are matters that concern everyone and demand serious rather than overwrought consideration. Whom can we turn to for informed, rational reflection on the subject of NDEs?

One obvious choice is the sometimes controversial but always illuminating Oliver Sacks, himself a leading neuroscientist (and an admirer of Kevin Nelson's *The Spiritual Doorway in the Brain*). In a 2012 article he considers the question of out-of-body experiences and religious epiphanies:

> Both OBEs and NDEs, which occur in waking but often profoundly altered states of consciousness, cause hallucinations so vivid and compelling that those who experience them may deny the term hallucination, and insist on their reality. And the fact that there are marked similarities in individual descriptions is taken by some to indicate their objective "reality." But the fundamental reason that hallucinations—whatever their cause or modality—seem so real is that they deploy the very same systems in the brain that actual perceptions do.

NDEs tend to occur, he tells us, in some measure echoing Nelson, in the "transitional stages, where consciousness of a sort has returned, but not yet fully lucid consciousness." As for Eben Alexander's *Proof of Heaven*, "to deny the possibility of any natural explanation for an NDE, as Dr. Alexander does, is more than unscientific—it is antiscientific." Sacks's conclusion:

> Hallucinations, whether revelatory or banal, are not of supernatural origin; they are part of the normal range of human consciousness and experience. This is not to say that they cannot play a part in the spiritual life, or have great meaning for an individual. Yet while it is understandable that one might attribute value, ground beliefs, or construct narratives from them, hallucinations cannot provide evi-

dence for the existence of any metaphysical beings or places. They provide evidence only of the brain's power to create them.

Assuming, then, that in some way those who have experienced NDEs have unconsciously created their own scripts, why *these* scripts? We're told by Moody and others that people from Asia and elsewhere have recounted NDEs reflecting patterns of behavior and belief very different in detail from those we've come upon in recent American narratives, but none of the books I've read has provided any such foreign accounts. In fact, there's an extraordinary sameness to our native NDEs—a unanimity of experience that has been proposed as confirmation of their genuineness: *This* vision of heaven corroborates this *other* vision of heaven, give or take the obvious differences in sophistication between, say, Colin Burpo and Eben Alexander.

It was not like this in earlier days. In *Life After Life* (1975), Raymond Moody went to great pains to tell us, "I am not trying to prove that there is life after death. Nor do I think a 'proof' of this is presently possible." And he goes out of his way to insist that none of the experiences he's been told of involve Jesus, God, or heaven—"Through all of my research . . . I have not heard a single reference to a heaven or a hell anything like the customary picture to which we are exposed in this society." But somewhere along the way, his cautious approach to the near-death experience—even so, dismissed by some professionals as purely anecdotal and highly unscientific—has been transformed by the Christian narrative.

Or by that part of the Christian narrative that is basic to fundamentalist or evangelical believers—and more than twenty-six percent of Americans belong to an evangelical church. Almost all the writers of today's NDE narratives have had a Christian upbringing, although a few came to religion later in life. They're certainly all believers—if they weren't, they would report surprise at finding themselves in heaven. (Or hell: several narrators stop by there, too.) They have known of Jesus and God and heaven from their earliest days as children in Sunday school and weekly churchgoing, from their parents, from TV evangelism. The appurtenances, the images, the surroundings, must be deeply engrained in both their conscious and unconscious minds.

So it should come as no surprise that for such people of powerfully held religious belief and lifelong acquaintanceship with Christian doctrine and chronicles, their dreams, or hallucinations, or visions—or NDEs—should take the form of visits to Christ in heaven. If people can believe that they're possessed by the spirit of Christ in a church (and millions of evangelicals *do* believe they are), why should they not be equally convinced that their dreams are the reality? And since we're dealing with faith here, there's no point in arguing or denying, or calling on science to refute belief. After all, a large number of Americans don't accept the idea of evolution.

The recent rash of books on NDEs and connected matters is further witness, if we require further witness, to the extraordinary power of the evangelical vision of life. It withstands science, it withstands the reality principle. A majority of Americans simply insist on the reassurance of life after death, and many, many religious authorities—both before and after the heyday of Billy Graham, now ninety-five, who, with his mix of good sense and jingoistic motivational language, seems to me the most impressive of them all—have offered that reassurance. Besides, however much we skeptics may scoff, is there any real danger in Betty Eadie's seeming "to melt with joy" as she was held in Christ's arms and comforted? Perhaps rather than being derided or censured, she should be envied.

The New York Review of Books
OCTOBER 23–NOVEMBER 6, 2014

A Trio of Go-Getter Trumps

TRUMP, THE TOWER! Trump, the Plaza! Trump, the Palace! Trump, the Castle! And let's not forget Trump, the candidate, and Trump's *The Art of the Deal*, and Trump's Ivana and Trump's Marla. And here's to the ill-fated Trump Shuttle (with its in-flight magazine, *Trump's*), and the Trumping of the Plaza Hotel and Marjorie Merriweather Post's Palm Beach extravaganza, Mar-a-Lago, and Adnan Khashoggi's $30 million yacht (on which the new owner never spent a night, even after renaming it *Trump Princess*), and the rescue of Wollman Rink, and the near-bankruptcy in Atlantic City, and the feud with Mayor Ed Koch, and the endless battles over Westpride. Let's celebrate, too, the authentic Trump voice: "That woman is a fat pig"; "Fuck Hyatt. I have them signed, now I can do what I want"; "I would never buy Ivana any decent jewels or pictures. Why give her negotiable assets?"; "You have the palace and you have the castle, hence you have the kingdom."

Now, reading Gwenda Blair's convincing and instructive book *The Trumps: Three Generations That Built an Empire,** we can relive our decades with "the Donald" in just a few hours—a big step in the right direction.

Blair begins with a common strategic error: thinking she has to start off with a bang. Her bang of choice is a day in 1989 when Trump is signing copies of Trump: The Game, at F.A.O. Schwarz. This gives her a chance to pile on the clichés and the hype—Donald Trump is not only "the most famous man in America, if not the world," but also someone who has "hobnobbed with the glitterati" (no wonder the media "were slavering at his feet"). Once she's dutifully exploited this

---

*Recently reprinted with a new preface and a new subtitle: *Three Generations of Builders and a President.*

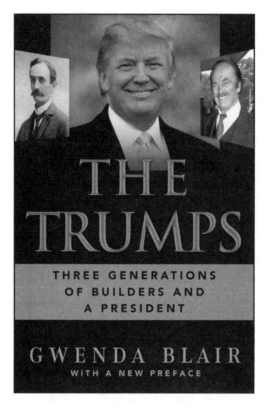

grotesque scene—the crowd shouting, "Donald, how much money do you make a minute, anyway?"; a cocktail pianist crooning, "Big bucks will never seem the same / After you've played Trump: The Game / If you should forget that Trump's his name / You'll see it 553 times in the game"—she gets down to business, the business of telling the fascinating story of the three generations of go-getters who made the Trump name and the Trump fortunes.

In the beginning was Friedrich, who in 1885, at the age of sixteen, alone and with no prospects, made his way from Kallstadt, his village in southwestern Germany, to "the giant, throbbing metropolis" of New York. It's the classic American immigrant story, except that, for Friedrich, the streets did turn out to be paved with gold. He began as a barber, but quickly decided that his main chance lay out West—and by 1891 he had started his first enterprise, a modest dairy restaurant in Seattle. Next stop was a mining town called Monte Cristo, but he had no intention of mining: Instead, he put up a boardinghouse and began "mining the miners." There were complications over the title of the land this establishment was built on, but as Blair puts it, "the type of people who would be attracted to Monte Cristo were not the type to pay attention to fiddling details like legal titles." (Later Trumps would skirt other laws with equal insouciance.) By Monte Cristo standards, Friedrich prospered, and in the 1896 election (in which William Jennings Bryan lost a bid for the presidency) he was elected justice of the peace. The margin of victory was thirty-two votes to five; Friedrich was twenty-seven years old.

Then came the Alaska gold rush, and Friedrich was off to the Yukon. Far from having to eat his shoes and laces like Chaplin in *The Gold Rush*, he struck it rich—first in the tent restaurant business ("A frequent dish was fresh-slaughtered, quick-frozen horse"), and then as the proprietor of a hotel-cum-bordello and restaurant. In 1901, after making his pile, he returned to Kallstadt to take a wife; a few years later he decided to settle there for good. Worth $350,000 in today's money, he was a rich man, and Kallstadt welcomed him. But there were strict laws in Germany for dealing with presumed draft-dodgers, even if they were now American citizens, and Friedrich wasn't forgiven. Appeals to the Kaiser were rebuffed, and by the summer of 1905 he was back in New York permanently: "The Trumps were to be Americans, after all."

Friedrich (now Frederick) was the pioneer. His oldest son, Fred, born three months after the return to America, would be the consolidator. "I always wanted to be a builder," Fred was to say. "It was my dream as a boy, just as some kids want to be firemen." He worked at menial jobs, at carpentering; he studied engineering and estimating; he put up family money to begin constructing homes in Queens (his father had died when he was twelve). By the time he was twenty-one, he had built—and sold—a score of houses. (One satisfied customer remembers that "Fred Trump was too young to be at the closing, so his mother came.") By 1938, his hard work, his passion for detail, his grasp of opportunities both large and small, and his political smarts had made him, according to the *Brooklyn Eagle*, "the Henry Ford of the home-building industry." He quickly learned to work profitably with the New Deal's

Federal Housing Authority as well as with New York's all-powerful master builder, Robert Moses; he became an intimate of Brooklyn's leading pols and lawyers, and he dealt at less than arm's length with the local mob; he hired a public-relations firm—unusual for a real estate operation then—and he gave prodigally to charities. ("Mindful of the growing prominence of Jews in the real estate industry and local politics, he became so active in Jewish philanthropies that people often assumed he belonged to that faith.")

In other words, Fred Trump was a master of realpolitik. But he was also genuinely in love with building (even if, according to one of his architects, "everything always came down to money, money, money"), and his love of building led him to put a little extra something into whatever he built, from those first modest Queens houses to the huge Trump Village in Coney Island. (Yes, plastering the Trump name on things runs in the family.) And nothing ever really interrupted Fred's success story. There may have been trouble along the way—for instance, public hearings in 1966 questioned his windfall profits on a government project; "outrageous," "unconscionable," "greedy," one commissioner proclaimed—but there was no indictment.

At that point, Donald was twenty years old. He had absorbed his father's obsessive work habits, his genius for spotting and grasping opportunity, and his ruthless determination to prevail. But he was a very different kind of man.

From the start, he was competitive, hardworking, and boastful (as a senior at New York Military Academy, "dropping the usual Trump family reticence about their wealth, he pegged his father's worth at $30 million and bragged that the number doubled every year"). Donald went on to Fordham and the Wharton business school (where, he has said, "[real estate] was the only thing I could see studying"), and then plunged into the family business. At twenty-six, he had sealed his first multimillion-dollar deal. When his father made him president of the company, he immediately dropped the various innocuous corporate names used by Fred and renamed the whole thing the Trump Organization.

And he moved to Manhattan. Friedrich had made his pile out

West; Fred had been content with Brooklyn and Queens and a few out-of-town venues. But for Donald, as one observer of his early years put it, "the purpose wasn't the money. It was to be famous." Whereas Fred had been driven to build and to succeed, Donald was driven to deal and to win, and on the largest scale. He had the ability. He had the charm. He had the conviction. He had the backing of his father and his father's powerful connections. He had the desperate need to prevail that motors so many stars. And he wasn't encumbered by the kind of scruples that make one hesitate or regret—his only regret was at losing. The Manhattan of the seventies and eighties proved to be the perfect setting for such a personality.

His string of early successes was remarkable—and made to seem more remarkable by his constantly exaggerating his triumphs and disclaiming his failures. He had mastered the big things, like tax abatement, and the little things, like "creative floor numbering" to make tall buildings seem even taller. He had mastered, of course, the art of the deal, and he had mastered the art of getting away with it—surviving three FBI probes, for instance, and a press that turned violently against him, labeling him a vulgarian, a sorehead, a conniver, a racist, a liar. He was a supreme salesman because, as Blair makes clear, he was selling himself—eventually "he would be his own marketing gimmick, charging premium prices for condos and rentals in buildings bearing his name." Where Friedrich provided services and Fred built things, Donald projected image.

Blair, a journalist whose previous book was about the television reporter Jessica Savitch, is relentless in examining and anatomizing Donald Trump's business dealings—she has the assiduousness and grasp (though not the power) of Robert A. Caro, her obvious role model. She makes you believe that this is how things worked in New York in the final third of the 1900s: the new glamour and glitz as fig leaf for the old backroom deal-making and corner-cutting.

She's also convincing on Donald Trump's private life (she doesn't even try to imagine his inner life, and nothing in her account suggests that he has one). He may have gone around with one blonde after another on his arm, but "a kind of gauche flashiness . . . did not endear

Trump to women. His dates, which consisted of a ride in a limo, a visible table at a chic restaurant or club, and an expansive monologue about his plans to remake the Manhattan skyline, had the flavor of a sales pitch." She cleverly proposes first wife Ivana as "his twin as a woman": "They shared the same flashy aesthetic, the same boundless appetite for more marble, more mirrors, more shiny brass, more dramatic lighting." But they competed with rather than complemented each other ("The developer did not want a queen, he wanted a concubine"), and for all her determination, Ivana was left behind. As for poor, pregnant Marla Maples, Trump kept "asking family and friends about whether tying the knot would help or hurt his business prospects." When he finally did say "I do," he had given *Entertainment Tonight* exclusive video rights to the rehearsal and sold the wedding photos (supposedly to benefit charities).

The story is all here, from the near-collapse of the empire to the rebound; from the "amphetamine-like substances" and the phobias (worried about germs, he "avoided shaking hands whenever possible and when it was not possible, he washed his hands afterward"—a real drawback if you're thinking of running for office), to the paranoias (bulletproof window shades). From first to last, he has been comfortable only with his family, clearly closer to his parents and siblings and children than to anyone else. (The family had its own dysfunctions, too, most conspicuously Donald's older brother, who failed to live up to his name—Fred Jr.—and self-destructed at forty-two, his closets reportedly "stuffed with empty liquor bottles.")

For decades, the Trumps' family minister was "God's salesman," Dr. Norman Vincent Peale, author of the immense best seller *The Power of Positive Thinking.* But positive thinking hadn't helped Fred Jr.; and despite all the money and the glitz and the notoriety, the bigness of the deals and the buildings and the headlines—despite the Tower and the Plaza and the Palace and the Game—Donald Trump doesn't come across in this account as a happy man. Even if you're the supreme positive thinker of your day, positive thinking takes you only so far.

The New York Observer
SEPTEMBER 18, 2000

"The Most Beautiful Girl in the World"

DIANA COOPER

WHAT CAN IT HAVE BEEN LIKE to have been Lady Diana Cooper, "the most beautiful girl in the world," "the only really glamorous woman in the world," the most celebrated debutante of her era, the daughter of a duke, the wife of a famous diplomat (and so the British ambassadress to Paris), an internationally acclaimed actress, a character in at least half a dozen novels (by writers as unalike as Evelyn Waugh, Nancy Mitford, Arnold Bennett, D. H. Lawrence, and Enid Bagnold), a dedicated nurse to wounded and dying soldiers in World War I, and a pig farmer?

It's a question we can answer, given the vast literature about her, beginning with her enchanting three volumes of memoirs,* and including biographies of both her and her husband, Duff Cooper; *his* much-admired memoirs, as well as his uninhibited (to say the least) diaries; an ample collection of their mostly rapturous letters to each other; an ample collection of her take-no-prisoners correspondence with Waugh; the letters of her dearest friend, Conrad Russell; and the frank autobiography of her son, the historian John Julius Norwich. And most recently we have a volume of her letters to that son. It's called *Darling Monster*, although there's nothing monstrous about her beloved John Julius, and there's nothing monstrous in her passionate but practical attachment to him. The apparent stability of their relationship suggests that she was as good a mother as she was a society figure, nurse, actress, wife, writer, hostess, ambassadress, farmer, and perhaps most of all, friend.

Lady Diana Manners (her name until she married Duff), born in

---

* *The Rainbow Comes and Goes, The Light of Common Day, Trumpets from the Steep.*

1892, was the last child of the Duke and Duchess of Rutland, or at least she was the duchess's last child: It was commonly assumed that her biological father was the brilliant, charming man-about-town (and serial seducer) Harry Cust, with whom Violet, the duchess, had a passionate affair. No one seemed to mind—not the duke, who politely (and affectionately) stood by as the baby's official father, or the duchess, or Diana herself. "I am cheered very much by *Tom Jones* on bastards," Diana wrote to a friend, "and like to see myself as a 'Living Monument of Incontinence.'" Harry Cust—"very beautiful, I thought him," she would write in her memoirs—was "a man I loved with all my heart."

You might think she had inherited her looks from this paragon, but Violet herself had been a great beauty (as well as an accomplished artist, her sculpture admired by Rodin, among others). "The most beautiful thing I ever saw," said Mrs. Patrick Campbell, and a favorite of Queen Victoria's. The duchess's notion was that Diana should marry Edward, Prince of Wales, but Diana had no use for him and the prince liked hard, sophisticated older women. Otherwise it would not have been an impossible match. Victorian dukes were almost as esteemed as royalty, and the Manners family owned something like sixty-five thousand acres of land, abundant coal mines, and Belvoir (pronounced Beaver) Castle, one of the grandest of ducal residences. The duke himself was a genial and well-liked if far from outstanding man, whose principal interests, as Philip Ziegler put it in his indispensable biography of Diana, "were dry-fly fishing and fornication; pursuits requiring much dexterity but not intellectually demanding."

DIANA WAS MOSTLY HAPPY IN HER HOME LIFE. She was very attached to her four older sisters, admired her two brothers, adored her mother (except when they drove each other crazy), and enjoyed life, both in London and up at the castle. She didn't have much formal educating, but there were governesses and lots of reading—a lifetime passion. At ten she almost died of a rare form of paralysis called Erb's disease. Fully expecting to die, she stayed firmly stoical. Her mother never suspected that Diana suffered from depressions, or "melancholias" as she called them. "If she had," Ziegler writes, "she would have been uncomprehending and unsympathetic. Only housemaids moped."

At first Diana was thought to be plain and lumpish, but by the time

Virago Modern Classics

Enid Bagnold

The Loved and Envied

Diana Cooper, by J. J. Shannon

she was fourteen, she had grown into a renowned beauty—only a few years later, Winston Churchill and a friend were determining which of the new crop of young dazzlers deserved the accolade as "the face that launched a thousand ships," and only two made the grade: Clementine Hozier, whom Churchill would marry, and Lady Diana Manners. When she was staying with friends in Norfolk in her early teens, she fell in with a group of young men from nearby Oxford, whom she enchanted and who enchanted her. The group named themselves "the Coterie" and the men became her faithful and ardent swains. Only the one she cared most for—Raymond Asquith, son of the prime minister—was ineligible: He was ten years older than the rest, and married. Even so, she grew intimate with both him and his wife, Katharine; his death in the war was one of the great traumas of her life, and she remained close to Katharine throughout their lives.

The years leading up to World War I were filled with fun and high jinks: balls, flirtations, jaunts around Europe. (When she went abroad with her mother, it was third class all the way: The duchess never liked to spend.) She had become a celebrity, her comings and goings avidly reported by the press, to her (secret) gratification. She was not only a beauty but an exotic, creating a somewhat outré style of dressing, getting in and out of highly publicized scrapes—she had a desperate desire to be conspicuous, to be acknowledged as different, original, singular. The boys in the Coterie were pursuing her relentlessly with self-consciously passionate and flattering letters and handsome gifts—her lifelong habit of gleefully accepting if not soliciting presents was already in play. She was restless and daring, and in no hurry to settle down. Yet she was still being chaperoned, and she was technically chaste.

Not everyone was amused by her carryings-on. Whereas the prime minister was all too markedly attached to her, his formidable wife, Margot, was one of the holdouts: "What a pity that Diana, so pretty and decorative, should let her brain rot! . . . [Her] main faults are that she takes money from men and spends her day powdering her face until she looks like a bled pig."

"She loved to be told that she was beautiful," Ziegler writes, "but never really understood what all the fuss was about." She was pale, blond, oval-faced—"sheeplike," one of the rare dissenters called her. And she was wretchedly aware of her lack of formal education, certain that she was stupid and uninteresting. What she didn't grasp was that she possessed an incandescence that animated and delighted almost every person she met. "When she came into a room it was plain it was a spirited person who entered, a person with an extra dose of life," Enid Bagnold wrote of her in her 1951 novel *The Loved and Envied*. "It was apparent on all sides how people were affected. They had a tendency to rise to their feet to be nearer her, not of course in her honour, but to be at the source of amusement, to be sure not to miss the exclamation, the personal comedy she might make of the moment of life just left behind." Typically, when Bagnold's book was published, Diana wrote to her that she was "much relieved and insanely happy that you should see me as you have, a beautiful, serene woman and unblemished, noble, interested, brave and good, instead of a raw, aged hypochondriac, fretted with panics and pains, funking the future with no pride or curiosity or enthusiasm."

ALL DIANA'S YOUNG MALE ADMIRERS, who were also her best pals, were quickly swept up in the war. All but one. Duff Cooper, two years her senior, was working in the Foreign Office, and so was kept from enlisting. Although he had many other women on his mind (and in his bed), he was determined to capture Diana. His background was suitable—his mother, Agnes, was the sister of the Duke of Fife, who was married to Louise, the Princess Royal. On the other hand, Agnes had barely survived the scandal of two elopements and a divorce and took to nursing until she married a prominent society doctor who specialized in the most intimate of surgeries. He liked to remark that between them, he and his wife "had inspected the private parts of half the peers of London."

If Duff's lineage and background—Eton, Oxford—were acceptable to Diana's family, nothing else about him was. He was already notorious for his drinking, his gambling, his womanizing. But to Violet, a far greater impediment was his impecuniousness: Apart from his very modest salary at the Foreign Office, he had an income of only a few hundred pounds a year, and no expectations. Diana couldn't have cared less. Slowly, steadily, as their heated correspondence reveals, she came to rely on him for both stimulation and stability. His brilliance was incontestable. And his passion for her was balanced by his understanding of her volatile and needy nature. From early childhood Diana had known what her needs were. She remembered sitting under the piano while her mother played, thinking, "O, I'm glad I'm a girl. I'm glad I'm a girl. Somebody will always look after me," a sentiment echoed in a letter from a later period: "There is no joy so lazy and delicious as to find one is a woman who *depends*."

Soon, the young men closest to Diana and Duff were dying. Duff would one day write to Diana, "Our generation becomes history instead of growing up." (With their world collapsing, she and Katharine Asquith overindulged in morphine and chloroform. "I hope she won't become *morphineuse*," commented Duff. "It would spoil her looks.") By the last year of the war, when he was finally allowed to join up, Duff was the only one left. Their ardent friendship had deepened into a serious love affair as they consoled each other. With regard to her parents' opposition, Diana wrote to her brother John: "For many years I have wanted to marry Duff because I know that when I am with him I am perfectly happy, that his mind I adore, that his attitude towards me and love and understanding are only equalled by mine towards him."

The increasing physical intimacy between them is charted in their letters, with Duff ever importuning and Diana ever adamant about retaining the final barrier. And indeed when they were finally married in 1919—Duff having survived the war, having won the DSO for bravery under fire, and Diana having at last broken her mother's resistance— she was still a virgin. Just. The wedding was a journalistic sensation, especially in regard to the presents: The list required eighty-eight pages of a large notebook and included a blue enamel and diamond brooch from the King and Queen (bearing their own initials); a diamond-and-ruby pendant from Queen Alexandra; a diamond ring from the Princess of Monaco; a gold sugar sifter from King Manuel of Portugal; and from among the scores of non-royals, a check from the Aga Khan, an automobile from Lord Beaverbrook, and a writing table from Dame Nellie Melba.

It wasn't only the rules of proper behavior that had kept her a virgin, or the bothersome but ineffectual chaperones. She was a loving woman but never a deeply sexual one: She craved embraces, cuddles, caresses, compliments, but as she would write, "Like most well-brought-up girls of my generation I was not much interested in it—sex I mean."

Duff, on the other hand, was not only exceptionally amorous but a relentless, compulsive seducer—his first infidelity took place in Venice, on their honeymoon. And the infidelities never stopped. Throughout his life his mistresses came and went (and sometimes came and stayed). Just a few of them: the Singer sewing machine heiress Daisy Fellowes; two nieces of Diana's, the beautiful Paget sisters; a beauty named Gloria Rubio, later Gloria Guinness—"I don't think I have ever loved anyone physically so much or been so supremely satisfied"; the young Susan Mary Patten, wife of an American diplomat, on whom he fathered a child; and, perhaps most seriously, the well-known writer Louise de Vilmorin, who became Diana's adored friend as well. Louise—a suspected collaborator—often took up residency in the Paris embassy when the Coopers reigned there, and when Duff turned his attentions from her to Susan Mary, it was Diana who had to comfort her. In middle age Duff was still as driven a fornicator—like both her fathers—as he had been at twenty.

Diana didn't look the other way, she just stood aside, perhaps unhappy but unprotesting: What mattered to her was not Duff's faithfulness but his love, of which she was completely certain. ("They were the flowers, but I was the tree.") "Did my mother know?" wrote John Julius. "Of course she did. And did she worry? Not in the least. 'So common to mind,' she used to say." When Lady Cunard asked the same question, Diana replied, "*Mind!* I only mind when Duffie has a cold." As Duff's excellent biographer, John Charmley, put it, what she wanted was "a father-figure to take care of her, and a romantic adoration; Duff provided both of these for his 'darling baby.'" Besides, from the very start of their marriage she put Duff's needs and pleasures ahead of her own. Not everyone was charmed, but those closest to them, including John Julius, accepted the situation with equanimity. And she herself, given her low-level libido, did only a little flirting, and perhaps after Duff's death, indulged in the odd fling.

WHEN DUFF DECIDED TO LEAVE the Foreign Office to become a politician, how were they to pay the costs of a campaign? Diana, who had always been stagestruck, made (for a handsome fee) two movies that were respectable but hardly a launching pad for a major film career. Her chance to earn serious money came when the illustrious Austrian director Max Reinhardt decided to revive his famous religious spectacle *The Miracle* and offered her the central role of the Madonna for the extended American tour he was planning. She had to stand for well over an hour—speechless, motionless—pretending to be a stone statue cradling an infant, before descending the steps from her niche in the cathedral to take the place of an errant nun who has been seduced. (Eventually, she would alternate roles and play, equally effectively, the sinning nun.) No words were spoken in *The Miracle*, but the theater was transformed into a cathedral—in the original production there were two thousand extras and a rose window that was three times the size of the one at Chartres.

Diana's radiant beauty and sublime composure thrilled and moved audiences everywhere—*The Miracle* toured America for six months of every year between 1924 and 1928, then went on to triumphs on the Continent and in England. All in all, and on and off, she played the Madonna to standing ovations for ten years. She had demanded a large salary so that Duff's coffers could be constantly replenished. As Charmley writes:

> Where she was eating macaroni cheese and persuading hoteliers to let her have her room for free, Duff was dining off oysters and champagne at Bucks, or flitting over to Paris for a weekend at the gaming tables and the whores. . . . The simple fact was that Duff was incapable of thrift and as unrestrained in his financial behaviour as he was in his sexual appetites.

Fortunately, it turned out that Diana was a real trouper, cheerfully sharing in the seedy life of rooming houses and relentless travel. She enjoyed it all—she was always attracted to what she called bohemian life. Duff hated it: Comfort and luxury came first with him. Not that Diana failed to appreciate good clothes, jewels, furs, as long as she didn't have to pay for them.

When Duff in due course ran for a seat in Parliament, she was there electioneering with him—a huge attraction to an electorate who had been fascinated by her for years. She proudly writes of how much she loved working up enthusiasm for him among a crowd of mill girls, promising that if her husband was elected she would come back and do a clog dance for them. He was—and she did.

After an acclaimed maiden speech, Duff quickly advanced into the government, eventually becoming First Lord of the Admiralty. In 1938 he achieved world prominence when, on the day after Neville Chamberlain signed the notorious Munich Agreement with Hitler, he resigned from the Cabinet: "War without honour or peace with dishonour, but war with dishonour—that was too much." When his and Diana's old friend Winston became prime minister, Duff re-entered the Cabinet, but he chafed at his job as chief of war information until, in 1943, he was made the official liaison with the Free French, then located in Algeria, with the ambassadorship to Paris guaranteed as soon as the city was reconquered. It was a hellish job, given the mutual loathing of the two prima donnas—the rampageous Churchill ("Ducky") and the ultra-prickly de Gaulle ("Wormwood"). But Duff turned out to be a born diplomat, more or less patching things up when the two men would defy and insult each other in outbreaks of misunderstanding and petulance.

Both in Algiers and in the Paris embassy after the Liberation, Diana, with her great talents as a hostess, made everything work smoothly, winning over everyone who came near her. The Coopers were so popular that even when the Conservatives were defeated in 1945, the Labour government kept them on for an extra year. The gruff new foreign minister, Ernest Bevin, became a huge admirer of Duff's and a slave of Diana's. When, inevitably, they were replaced, Nancy Mitford wrote to her great friend Evelyn Waugh, "They're gone at least for the moment and Paris is going to be dreary without them and my feet are cold and I'm on the verge of tears." The comedy of Mitford's novel *Don't Tell Alfred* is largely based on a Diana stand-in—"the most beautiful woman in the world"—simply refusing to evacuate her part of the embassy even after her successors have moved in. When she finally chooses to depart, "the hall presented a scene like a picture of the Assumption: a mass of up-turned faces goggling at the stairs down which, so slowly that she hardly seemed to be moving, came the most beautiful woman in the world. She was dressed in great folds of white satin; she sparkled with jewels; her huge pale eyes were fixed, as though upon some distant view, over the heads of the crowd. . . . When Lady Leone got to the bottom of the stairs [the guests] divided into two lanes; she shook hands, like a royal person, with one here and there as she sailed out of the house forever."

Duff had achieved a great deal in his official capacity. Against all kinds of opposition, he induced his country and France (still the impossible de Gaulle) to sign an official alliance. And he was already working indefatigably to bring Western Europe together, decades before it actually happened. As he had been prescient about the Nazi threat and the Munich Agreement, he was prescient about the future of the West. As early as the late fall of 1941, he wrote to the Foreign Office from Singapore, where he was on an official mission, doubting whether "vast populations of industrious, intelligent, and brave Asiatics" were likely to go on forever acknowledging "the superiority of Europeans." His fascination with diplomacy and world strategy went back to the still admired biography of Talleyrand that he had written in 1932, when he was temporarily out of government. His large ideas and tactical skills were certainly apparent to Churchill, who wrote to Anthony Eden: "We must not underestimate Duff Cooper. . . . He has great qualities of courage. He is one of the best speakers in the House of Commons. He has the root of the matter in him." (Even so, Eden—a longtime rival of Duff's— was soon disparaging him as a "lecherous little beast!")

What would Duff and Diana do, once they were free of their Paris responsibilities? They were already spending their weekends in a small but charming rented château not far away, and now they moved there and went on with their life of entertaining. The world came to them— to a considerable extent, and somewhat naughtily, distracting *le tout Paris* from the official residency and its new residents. During this period of exile Duff wrote his much-admired memoirs, *Old Men Forget*. And in 1952 he was created Viscount Norwich, to the irritation of Diana, who refused to be known by the title Lady Norwich—merely the wife of a peer: a comedown from Lady Diana, the daughter of a duke. She wasn't a snob, but there were limits.

MUCH AS SHE HAD ENJOYED HER LIFE in the embassy, she had enjoyed just as much her life in the modest cottage at Bognor, on the Sussex coast, which her mother had once given her. During the early years of the war she spent most of her time there, Duff coming down whenever he would get away from London, flinging herself into farming, rattling around her few acres of garden, raising goats and pigs, milking the cow, dealing with her beehive, making (and selling) cheeses. She was also, of course, entertaining guests—from the Duchess of Westminster and Lady Cunard to Cecil Beaton and Waugh, all of whom were expected to pitch in.

Bognor was also where she spent her happiest times with her beloved friend Conrad Russell (nephew of the Duke of Bedford, cousin of Bertrand Russell). When in 1933 they met at Katharine Asquith's, there was an instant affinity between them. During the war years he would travel down from his home on Katharine's estate—exhausting wartime trips in jam-packed railway cars—so that he could help out on the farm and spend long quiet evenings alone with Diana over simple food and Algerian wine while they read aloud to each other and basked in each other's (completely platonic) affection.

They wrote to each other constantly. "Everything I do with you is always amusing, always just the things I like best," he wrote to her in July 1941, "like feeding pigs, paper-hanging, reading about jealousy, picking nettles, making cheese, fetching swill and dabbling about in hogwash." On the twelfth anniversary of their first meeting, he wrote, "And in all those years and months dear Diana, I have not seen one fault in you. No my darling Diana, not one fault have I seen. It is the truth."

How different from her friendship with Waugh, punctuated by friction, disagreement, asperity! (Diana referred to it as "that jagged stone.") Their correspondence (edited by her granddaughter Artemis Cooper), beginning in 1932 and lasting until his death, in 1966, makes it clear that they enjoyed snapping at each other almost as much as they enjoyed being together. Diana's need for unrelenting activity drove him crazy: "If only you could treat friends as something to be enjoyed in themselves not as companions in adventure we should be so much happier together."

They also disagreed about religion, he writing to her on Christmas Eve 1951 that he has been praying "that you may one day find kneeling space in the straw at Bethlehem." She takes him seriously enough to answer:

> One cannot embrace something so serious as the church, for a whim, a love for another—(not God) or as an experimental medicine. I must wait for the hounds of heaven—or some force—some instance—that is irresistible—no reasoning is any good (a) I'm incapable of the process (b) I don't believe reasoning counts any more than it does when explaining music to the tone deaf or rainbows to the blind.

He tells her,

> I can't see you as the pathetic waif. I have always seen you as a ruthless go-getter, enormously accomplished, dauntless, devoid of conscience or delicacy, Renaissance or Italian, a beautiful and sweet tempered Venetian but more frivolous. . . . I always see you as having everything you want.

She to him, after Duff's death:

> I'm not sure you know human love in the way I do. You have faith and mysticism, intense inner interests, a diverting, virile mind, gusto for vengeance and destruction if necessary, a fancy, a gospel. What you can't imagine is a creature with a certain incandescent aura and nothing within but a beating, frightened heart built round and for Duff.

He addresses her as Baby (so did Duff), Pug, Sweet Baby-Doll; he is Darling Wu, Dearest Bo. Once he calls her Darling Stitch Pug Baby, Stitch being the name he gave her in *Scoop* (she sets the plot in motion, indulging in her genius for interfering with her friends' lives) and again when she turns up in the *Sword of Honor* trilogy. As John Julius was to write, "My Mother had only to see a string to be compelled to pull it, with almost invariably disastrous results." She was just too good a character for Darling Wu to use only once.

HER LETTERS ARE FILLED with vivid snapshots of the great and famous. About "my darling President" (FDR to us), she reports to ten-year-old John Julius that at tea at the White House just after the repeal of the Neutrality Act, "if his legs had not been paralyzed he'd have danced a war-dance." After a luncheon party at the palace alone with the king and queen and the two princesses, she reports, "They don't listen to him much; it's *her* family and household. 'All right, Daddy,' then a quick turn away and 'What did you say, Mommy darling?'" About Truman Capote: "A sturdy little pink girl of fourteen, with her blonde straight hair plastered neatly down all round, short for her age in rather light grey trousers and turtle-necked sweater with feminine curves suggesting through." Hemingway? "The greatest bore to end bores we've ever struck: gigantic, ugly, spectacles with fairy glasses."

As for the Windsors (from an account in a letter to Conrad Russell of a royal cruise before the Abdication): "It's impossible to enjoy antiquities with people who won't land for them and who call Delphi Delhi. Wallis is wearing very very badly. Her commonness and Becky Sharpishness irritate. . . . The truth is she's bored stiff by him." From Duff in his diaries: "It is sad to think that he gave up the position of king-emperor not to live in an island of the Hesperides with the Queen of Beauty but to share an apartment on the third floor of the Ritz with this harsh-voiced ageing woman who was never even very pretty."

And then there was Hitler, whom she and Duff encountered at a Nuremberg rally in 1933:

> I watched him closely as he approached, as he passed, as he retreated, compelling my eyes and memory to register and retain. I found him unusually repellent and should have done so, I am quite sure, had he

been a harmless little man. He was in khaki uniform with a leather belt buckled tightly over a quite protuberant paunch, and his figure generally was unknit and flabby. His dank complexion had a fungoid quality, and the famous hypnotic eyes that met mine seemed glazed and without life—dead colourless eyes.

That many of these descriptions appear in Diana's letters to John Julius suggests the openness with which she always treated him—as the reliable, intelligent boy he seems always to have been. Diana had never been drawn to children yet very much wanted one, and when he was born, in 1929, it was by Caesarian, hence Julius. (Among his godparents, the Aga Khan, J. M. Barrie, and Lord Beaverbrook.) When in 1940 the bombing intensified, she panicked and sent him off to Canada, where he was installed in a good boarding school, spending vacations with Bill and Babe Paley. But then he was missed too badly, and the Coopers wangled his way home on a Royal Navy cruiser.

Diana's letters to him are filled with good counsel. When, for instance, he's abroad perfecting his French after quitting Eton:

> Don't get engaged or married in Strasbourg. You must see a world of women before you pick one and *don't get picked yourself*, especially not in the street or bar. They'll contaminate and deceive you and most probably give you diseases of all kinds and so . . . keep yourself and your love for something or somebody almost exactly like me, with a happier disposition.

She reproaches him for not writing more frequently (he's twenty-two):

> Whenever you are in pain of heart or body, or in despair of jams, dishonour, disillusion, nervous apprehension, drink or blackmail, you may rely on your mother trudging thro' snow, thro' bars, to perjure, to betray, to murder, or—most difficult of all—behave courageously to help you—but in your own smooth days, I must be courted and petted and needed or I can't react. I was ever so, with lovers too, neglect never roused me; only true love and cosseting got good exchange.

She was equally candid with him about her own emotional condition. John Julius writes in his commentary to *Darling Monster,* "But now, as the letters make all too clear, depression has struck my mother—as bad as I think she had ever suffered. 'Melancholia,' as she called it, had always been the bane of her life. She worked hard to conceal it from the outside world but never made any secret of it to my father or to me."

Melancholia, and anxiety. "When I was six," she wrote to her mother, "and you were late, I used to be sure of your murder and lie awake all night." In London, Ziegler tells us, "she would rush from her bed to the window when he left in the morning to make sure he [Duff] survived the crossing of the road." Once, in Monaco, she became hysterical when Duff was an hour late coming back from the casino, certain that he had been assassinated, and was relieved to learn that he had merely been visiting a lady friend. Her tenacious morbidity led her to imagine that she was dying of everything from heart failure to leprosy. She understood that she succumbed to her black moods when she was without occupation, excitement. "It's not in my nature to be quiet. I have no wealth within me. All stimulus has to come through my eyes and ears and movement. Once still, I'm listless and blank and tortured by dread thought."

CRUSHED AS SHE WAS BY DUFF'S DEATH, in 1954, in the thirty-two years that followed she kept going . . . and going. There were balls, parties, dinners; there was incessant travel—to Noël Coward in Switzerland; to Kenya, Portugal, Moscow, Washington, where she wowed the Kennedys. ("What a woman!" the president exclaimed.) She wrote and published her memoirs, spent time with John Julius and his family. And she was always driving—her favorite occupation. (At eighty-six she drove herself in her Mini to the north of Scotland and back.) But her driving, always erratic, got worse as her sight failed. Nor did she pay much attention to the rules, parking illegally and leaving notes for the traffic wardens. ("Dear Warden. Please try and be forgiving. I am 81 years old, *very* lame and in total despair.") Then, John Julius reports, when she was eighty-nine, "she hit a traffic island in Wigmore Street. She drove straight home, locked the car, went up to bed and never drove again. 'I never saw it,' she told me later, 'it might have been a child.'" And, he goes on, "She never left her bed again; there was no point." She died in 1986, a few weeks before her ninety-fourth birthday.

In the final words of her memoirs she says:

> Age wins and one must learn to grow old . . . so now I must learn to walk this long unlovely wintry way, looking for spectacles, shunning the cruel looking-glass, laughing at my clumsiness before others mistakenly condole, not expecting gallantry yet disappointed to receive none, apprehending every ache or shaft of pain, alive to blinding flashes of mortality, unarmed, totally vulnerable.

Yet, she concludes, "The long custom of living disinclines one to dying. . . . Besides, before the end, what light may shine?"

Showing Off

JOHN WILKES BOOTH AND HIS BROTHER EDWIN

W AS SIBLING RIVALRY RESPONSIBLE for the assassination of
Abraham Lincoln? So you would conclude if you took seriously the phrase "The Bitter Rivalry Between Edwin
and John Wilkes Booth That Led to an American Tragedy," which is
blazoned across the dust jacket and the title page of *My Thoughts Be
Bloody*, a new book by Nora Titone, with a hyperbolic foreword by her
"teacher and mentor," Doris Kearns Goodwin.

Titone (this is her first book) has done her homework and digested
it. If she had restrained herself from attempting to fit the Booth story
into a soap-opera construct "filled with ambition, rivalry, betrayal, and
tragedy . . . as gripping as a fine work of fiction," as Goodwin puts it,
she would have performed an even more valuable service than she has.
Although there have been many books about John Wilkes Booth and
the assassination, few have focused to this extent on his place in the
theater dynasty of which he was a less distinguished member than his
biographers—and he himself—would have liked us to believe. He
started acting late, he was untrained, and his exceptional looks and
natural charm and athleticism could carry him only so far.

He certainly, however, had his share of the family ambition. The
father, Junius Brutus Booth, was the grandson of a Jewish silversmith
whose origins lay in Portugal. Having failed to unseat Edmund Kean
as London's leading tragedian, Junius emigrated to America in 1821
and quickly established himself as one of the nation's most famous
actors, despite his chronic alcoholism and his periodic bouts of insanity.
Junius Brutus Booth II, the oldest of his ten children born here, was
only modestly talented as an actor, knew it, and wisely established

John Wilkes Booth

himself as a theatrical manager. (He had an even temperament, but the Booth streak of madness emerged much later on in one of his children, who in middle age shot and killed himself and his wife.)

The second son, Edwin, born in 1833, grew up in the theater and began acting in his late teens, determined to rise to the very top, and by the time he was in his mid-twenties, this ambition, combined with his great talent and relentless work ethic, had propelled him there. The third son—variously known as Wilkes, John, Johnny, and Jack— was driven by fantasies of stardom, but circumstances, together with his lack of discipline and judgment, stood in his way.

There was no rivalry between the two older brothers. Junius II opened up his San Francisco company to Edwin, and kept him busy learning stagecraft from the ground up, playing, as Titone puts it, "every part handed to him. He obediently donned blackface, thumped his banjo, sang minstrel tunes, and hoofed it in clogs. He acted comedies, melodramas, burlesques, variety shows, and farces." (Later he would

Edwin Booth (as Hamlet)

grasp how important this broad experience had been for his art, even if it had been humiliating at the time. He called it "a lesson for crushed tragedians.") In time, he graduated to more significant parts, then to sudden and sustained success in his father's most famous role, Richard III, and Hamlet, which would become his own most famous role.

Edwin was also leading a wild life in the highly permissive atmosphere of the San Francisco of the 1850s. His drinking was out of control—perhaps even more serious than his father's. (His grandfather and great-grandfather had been alcoholics, too.) His womanizing was notorious. "At twenty I was a libertine. . . . All the vices seemed to have full sway over me and I yielded to their bestializing voices." (He paid the usual price—venereal disease.) But although he was seen as a happy-go-lucky, friendly young man, already the deep melancholy that was to characterize his life was upon him. At the age of twelve, he had been chosen to accompany Junius on his endless tours—to endure the horrific travel conditions of the day; to dog his father's footsteps after every performance in order to keep him from drinking the night's earnings away, sometimes shadowing him through the dark streets until morning; to act as Junius's dresser and general dogsbody; to trick him into getting to the theater on time for performances; to tend him through his outbursts of lunacy. "I had no childhood," Edwin was to say.

There are endless examples of Junius's erratic behavior. Once, playing in Boston, he burst into tears and "turning to the audience . . . screamed, 'take me to the Lunatic Hospital!' and ran sobbing toward the exit." ("The stage manager stepped forward to announce, 'Ladies and gentlemen, Mr. Booth cannot appear this evening. His reason has left him.'") Even more serious, one morning in a hotel lobby he announced, "I must cut somebody's throat today, and whom shall I take?" then whipped out a dagger and attempted to stab a prominent member of the company.

As Junius deteriorated, the theater world grew wary of him—of "Crazy Booth, the mad tragedian"—but audiences still responded to his thrilling performances. We can imagine how his behavior affected the boy Edwin, who, apart from everything else, loved his father. These painful years, however, were the foundation of Edwin's knowledge of the theater, of acting, and of the repertory. They lasted until he was nineteen—seven years.

WHENEVER POSSIBLE, father and son repaired to the large family farm in Bel Air, Maryland, where Junius was always happy being with his adored "wife," Mary Ann. (He had married very young and very badly in England, fathered a son, and then, abandoning wife and child, eloped to America with Mary Ann, a beautiful teenage flower seller. It was only well after she and Junius had produced their ten children that they were able to regularize their union.)

Of the children, four were to die of dysentery or cholera—Booth's grief was inconsolable. Still living at home with Mary Ann were their reclusive daughter Rosalie, who would spend her entire life with her mother; their younger daughter, Asia, handsome, intelligent, and strong-willed; John Wilkes; and a final son, Joseph, who would lead a bewilderingly feckless life until at the age of forty-nine he became a doctor. When the family was together, usually during the summers, Junius enjoyed running the farm, steadfastly refusing to own slaves while hiring the help he needed, both black and white, from around the neighborhood.

But if Bel Air was an idyll for Junius, for Johnny Wilkes it was a cage. To him, Edwin's harrowing years with his father represented freedom, excitement, glamour; why was *he* trapped on a Maryland farm with his mother and siblings while Edwin was living a great adventure? Doris Kearns Goodwin tells us that "when Junius chooses the older son, Edwin, to accompany him on the road, a fierce jealousy begins to fester in John Wilkes." Yes, young children can be violently jealous, but even in a family as far from conventional as the Booths, no one would seriously have considered sending an eight-year-old on such a mission.

In 1852 Junius suddenly died of cholera while returning alone from a tour in California, Edwin having decided to stay behind to chart his own course. It was now that he took his first steps toward ascendancy in his profession. And he needed only four years—after rough early times in California and an unfortunate detour to Australia and Hawaii, followed by his successes in San Francisco—before he was back in the East, with a purse filled with gold and a copy of a proclamation from the California state legislature referring to him as "a treasure, a gift of great value that the people of California were bestowing on the rest of the United States."

IN 1856, when Edwin arrived home, John Wilkes was eighteen and on fire with energy and zeal. He was building, Asia would write, "fantastic temples of fame. . . . For my brother, no visions or dreams were too extravagantly great." His mother had sent him to a series of reputable boarding schools, in which he failed to shine. (At school he was thought of as a pugnacious bully who appeared to enjoy treating "the smaller boys cruelly.") On the farm, though, with the older Booths on the road and young Joseph off at school, the teenage John "became the only male in his mother's home, sole recipient of all female attentions. . . . His older sisters . . . tiptoed past his bedroom as if it were a shrine."

Indeed, throughout his brief life John's effect on women was electrifying. Taller than his (short) father and brother, with his jet-black hair and piercing eyes, his superb mustache and magnificent marble-white neck and shoulders and arms, he was often referred to as the handsomest man in America. And when things were going well for him, he had extraordinary charm and a real kindness. "There was something so strong and sweet in his nature," a fellow actor wrote, "that it won the love of those who knew him."

Early on he had decided that his way to glory lay in outshining both his father and his brother in the family trade, but since there was no one to teach him, no available apprenticeship, he would go out into the woods of Bel Air and spout Shakespeare under the eye of his sister Asia. "How shall I ever have a chance on stage?" he burst out one day, Asia reported. "Buried here, what chance have I of ever studying elocution or declamation?" When he was just seventeen, he sneaked away to make his stage debut in a small role in *Richard III* at an insignificant theater in Baltimore. (His looks and the Booth name would always guarantee him a job.) But at his debut his acting was so poor that he was hissed, and it would be two years before he acted again.

By late 1859 he was playing minor roles, often as an extra, at the Marshall Theatre in Richmond. By this time his pronounced sympathies for the South in the charged atmosphere leading up to secession were well-known—in fact, he broadcast them everywhere. The romance of the Southern "cause" appealed to him, not least because of its defense of slavery, which he regarded as "one of the greatest blessings . . . that God ever bestowed on a favored nation"—a position one is tempted to ascribe to some kind of Oedipal reaction to his father's.

And then one day, during a rehearsal, he rushed from the theater and bluffed and bribed his way into an elite militia known as the Richmond Grays who were grouping in Washington on their way to help guard John Brown, on his way to his execution, from possible rescue attempts. On December 2, 1859, dressed up in a gray military uniform, he was within easy viewing distance of the hanging. (It shook him badly.) Later, he would boast to Asia that he had been "one of the party going to search for and capture John Brown," and that he had been "exposed to dangers and hardships." His need to dramatize himself, to appear a hero, was already fully developed. This unauthorized two-week absence from the theater branded him with a reputation for unreliability. "The stunt seemed [to the family] the height of immaturity," writes Titone, "a sign that John Wilkes Booth was unfit for stage work."

IN THE SUMMER OF 1860 the family was living in Philadelphia, supported by Edwin, who was already, still short of twenty-seven, the most highly acclaimed, and probably the most highly paid, actor in America. John, dependent on his brother, mortified that at twenty-three he had accomplished nothing, frantic to shine, was determined to carve out his own career as a star by touring nationally in the roles in which Junius and then Edwin had triumphed. But to Edwin it seemed preposterous—and potentially bad for business—that his less talented, less experienced, and less reliable younger brother might be competing with him in the major Eastern cities, which he more or less ruled. Laying down the law, he divided the country in half—he would perform in New York, Boston, Philadelphia, Baltimore, Washington; John Wilkes would be free to make his way in New Orleans, Chicago, St. Louis, Charleston, and the many other cities of the South and West.

Edwin felt he was being generous; John Wilkes—not surprisingly, given his sense of himself as being undervalued and patronized—was enraged by what he saw as a heavy-handed move to suppress him. It is this incident upon which Titone most heavily depends to support her theory that the "rivalry" between the brothers was central to John's later actions—"The one thing Edwin was determined to prevent was his brother's acting in New York; that city was Edwin's domain, and no other Booth would be allowed to knock him from his pedestal there. The star wanted no competition from a younger, handsomer copy"— all this while acknowledging that Edwin "knew he could beat John in the realm of talent—his brother lacked a natural gift." She doesn't see that Edwin's precautions made sense, and not only for himself: John badly needed more stage experience before facing East Coast audiences and critics.

Despite what Titone sees as this insidious plot to stifle his brother, Edwin—starring at the Marshall Theatre, where John was still performing as an extra—invited him to play Horatio to his own Hamlet and Othello to his Iago. Assuming as usual that Edwin's motives were questionable, Titone suggests that "it was almost a cruel trick on Edwin's part, to force a comparison between his own ability and his brother's inexperience." (Edwin can do nothing right.) But Edwin didn't need to resort to trickery to underline John's lack of ability.

Occasionally critics would recognize in the younger man sparks of Junius's genius—like his father, he would explode into thrilling melodramatic moments, particularly in scenes involving swordplay. "He would have flashes, passages, I thought of real genius," wrote Walt Whitman. And the supposedly unsympathetic Edwin, seeing John in a popular melodrama, would exclaim to a friend, "He is full of true grit. I am delighted with him." And "when time and study rounded his rough edges, he'll bid them all 'stand apart.'" But John's overwrought and limited approach, as opposed to Edwin's revolutionary realism and profound response to poetry, doomed his future as an actor. The theater was evolving rapidly away from the old-fashioned declamation of his father's day.

When in 1862 John defied Edwin's proscription and, taking advantage of his brother's absence in England, presented himself as a star in Boston and New York, the results were predictable: The critics were almost universally severe. "We have no place," the *Boston Daily Advertiser* pronounced, "for a professed vocalist who should be false in intonation, wrong in accent and in rhythm, inaccurate in phrasing, imperfect in vocal method and deficient in quality of tone, though his person and action might be pleasing to the eye." By December, he was back in Chicago, where he "was catering less to critics than to the boot-stomping hordes who enjoyed [his] swordplay." For two years or so he was able at times to command enthusiastic audiences and large fees.

He was also indulging more and more publicly in his anti-Lincoln, anti-Union rhetoric. "What a glorious opportunity there is for a man to immortalize himself by killing Lincoln!" he was overheard saying, suggesting that his strongest impulse was less political than a desire to gain the fame and prestige that by this time he must have realized would not come to him through his art.

His moods, Titone writes, "became darker and more intense," as did his displays of belligerence. On a train in August 1864, John Sleeper Clarke, Asia's husband and a close associate of Edwin's, made a disparaging remark about Jefferson Davis, and John instantly grabbed him by the neck and began choking him, his face "twisted with rage," and then cried, "Never, if you value your life . . . speak in that way to me again of a man and a cause I hold sacred." It does not come as a surprise that John T. Ford, proprietor of the theater where Lincoln would be shot, remarked of John that he "was animated by a pride that contained elements of insanity."

IT WAS AT THIS TIME, when he was allowing his acting career to peter out, that John was approached and co-opted by Confederate agents plotting against Lincoln and his administration. Fervently flinging himself into their plans, he took charge of their idea of kidnapping the president and holding him hostage. Gathering a small cadre of conspirators around himself, and clearly enjoying the cloak-and-dagger aspects of what he was planning, he came close to pulling it off, but by the time Lee surrendered at Appomattox and Richmond was captured by the Union army, kidnapping would have come too late. Swiftly, John determined on assassination, his justification being that Lincoln was planning to install himself as an American monarch, not only destroying the South but destroying American democracy itself. On April 14, 1865, he acted.

After the fatal shooting in Ford's theater, the dramatic leap to the stage clutching a dagger to the cry of *"Sic semper tyrannis"* ("Ever thus to tyrants"), and throughout the agonizing twelve-day manhunt that culminated in his being shot to death by soldiers in a flaming barn on a farm in northern Virginia, John clung to the belief that he had committed an act of heroism and self-sacrifice. Almost his final words as he lay gasping his life out were "Tell my mother I die for my country."

The world's verdict, however, even in the defeated Confederacy, was that he was neither a hero nor a patriot but a madman and a villain. Colonel Adam Badeau, General Grant's aide-de-camp and for decades Edwin's closest friend, saw things from a different perspective. John, he felt, was first and foremost an actor, and this murder was first and foremost a piece of acting. "It was all so theatrical in plan and performance," he was to write. "The conspiracy, the dagger, the selection of a theater, the cry *'Sic semper tyrannis'*—all was exactly what a madman brought up in a theater might have been expected to conceive."

John Wilkes Booth's most thorough and persuasive biographer, Michael W. Kauffman, in his *American Brutus* (2004), summed him up succinctly:

> By April 14, all he could do was sacrifice himself for the Cause, or accept the fact that his Unionist friends had been right about him all along—that he was a hotheaded loser who only talked while others gave their lives. Booth could not bear the thought of life as a former actor . . . or a pale shadow of his brother Edwin. His choice was made.

THE BOOTH FAMILY WAS SHATTERED BY JOHN'S ACT. Edwin was in Boston when he was awakened with the news and, disguising himself to avoid the rage of the populace, he rushed to New York in order to comfort his mother, who was in an anguish of grief—Johnny had always been her favorite. Now she could only pray that he would be killed on the run, to avoid the horror and disgrace of being hanged. Junius Jr. only barely escaped being lynched by a mob in Cincinnati, and was soon imprisoned for two months on suspicion of conspiring to kill the president. Asia Clarke, in the late stages of a dangerous pregnancy, was under house arrest, with a soldier assigned to follow her from room to room. Her husband, too, was held for months in prison.

These indignities were minor compared to the way scores, perhaps hundreds, of suspects were treated in the immediate wake of the assassination. Secretary of War Edwin Stanton took charge of the pursuit of the murderer and determined the methods used to obtain convictions of the conspirators; to begin with, the trial was to proceed as a court-martial, not under civil law. Kauffman describes conditions aboard the warships in which many prisoners were secured, most of them held without specific charges: "The Sec'y of War requests that the prisoners on board the iron clads . . . shall have for better security against conversation a canvas bag put over the head of each and tied around the neck with a hole for proper breathing and eating but not seeing." The prisoners were also constrained by wrist irons, bolted in place, so that they couldn't use their hands. Not since 1696, Kauffman points out—and not again until 2001—would prisoners in America be treated this way.

Thanks to Edwin's reputation and his friends in high places—he had succeeded, uniquely among actors, in gaining acceptance by America's social elite—he was never arrested, but he was certain that he could never appear on a stage again. (The entire acting profession felt itself endangered.) Titone blames Edwin for being concerned about this: "He interpreted Lincoln's murder as a direct attack on the celebrity he worked so hard to win." Immediately he issued a public statement: "My detestation and abhorrence of the act in all its attributes, are inexpressible; my grief is unutterable. . . . I shall struggle on in my retirement, bearing a heavy heart, an oppressed memory and wounded name—heavy burdens—to my too welcome grave."

In the event, he was back on the stage in well under a year, accorded an idolatrous reception from admirers both inside and outside the Broadway theater in which he was opening as Hamlet, the role in which he had recently enjoyed an unprecedented run of one hundred consecutive performances, a record he retained until John Barrymore pointedly kept his 1922 production going for one hundred and one. Titone quotes a journalist who wrote that the enthusiasm for Booth was "so strange and unique it amounts to a positive psychological phenomenon—the niche in which his country's heart has enshrined him was never filled before by mortal man."

What was his quality as an actor? Never rant or fustian, but a calm intensity, a manifest identification with the characters he portrayed. He triumphed not only as Hamlet, whose melancholy temperament somewhat mirrored his own, but as Iago—baleful, conniving—and, grand and commanding, in the title role of Edward Bulwer-Lytton's

Richelieu. His standard repertory included *Macbeth, King Lear, The Merchant of Venice*; and not only *Richard III* but *Richard II*, a play practically unknown in America. And despite his slight physical presence, he frequently played Othello, most famously in London, when he and England's leading actor, Henry Irving, alternated Othello and Iago, with Ellen Terry as their Desdemona. At a time when theater was the nation's dominant form of entertainment, he was the star of stars—treated everywhere as royalty.

YET HIS LIFE HAD BEEN A SERIES OF TERRIBLE BLOWS, beginning with his painful childhood and the death of his father. He married a young woman, Mary Devlin, whom he worshipped—John Wilkes was the only family member at the wedding, and Adam Badeau remembered that "after it was over, Wilkes threw his arms about Edwin's neck and kissed him"—but Mary died after only a few years of what seems to have been an exceptionally happy marriage. "I was as calm outwardly," Edwin told a friend, "as though a wedding had taken place instead of a death—but, oh, the hell within me is intense! . . . My grief *eats* me." His second wife, also a Mary, gradually succumbed to a debilitating disease tinged with severe paranoia.

There were other disasters. In 1867, a fire at his theater, the Winter Garden, destroyed all his costumes and effects and forty thousand dollars' worth of property. The luxurious theater he later built, the Booth, he lost through mismanagement and duplicitous colleagues. (Although he had earned fortunes, he was aware that he lacked business skills.) He had many friends devoted to him, and he cherished his daughter, Edwina, but there seems to have been an essential coldness to his nature; he warded off intimacy.

Edwin had often spoken of death as a release, and he didn't seem to lament his rapidly diminishing forces as he entered into a premature old age—one writer pronounced, "Booth at 58 is older than many a man of 70." He stopped acting in 1888, five years before he faded out of life, not yet sixty. He had founded the opulent Players club (it cost him two hundred thousand dollars, a vast sum for the day), which numbered among its members Mark Twain, Grover Cleveland, William Tecumseh Sherman, J. Pierpont Morgan, John Singer Sargent, and Frederic Remington, and it was in his apartment there that he spent his final years.

In his bedroom overlooking Gramercy Park and available for viewing today in its close-to-original state, the walls and tables are covered with portraits and photographs, prominent among them his mother and Mary Devlin. To the right of his bed hangs a photograph of John Wilkes Booth, conspicuously displayed, so that all his many visitors would be forced to take note of it. The story of the brothers may be compounded, as Titone and Goodwin would have it, of "ambition, rivalry, betrayal, and tragedy." But in this close-knit family, it was also shaped by love. And by irony. As more than one biographer has observed, John Wilkes had not ruined his brother's career; he had just made him more famous.

The New York Review of Books
APRIL 28, 2011

The Lyricist

LORENZ HART

It's smooth! It's smart!
It's Rodgers! It's Hart!

IT'S COLE PORTER in *Du Barry Was a Lady*—the song, "Well, Did You Evah!"; the singers, Betty Grable and Charles Walters; the year, 1939. When the song was recycled for Bing Crosby and Frank Sinatra in the 1956 movie *High Society*, this snatch of Porter's lyric was gone, but smooth, smart Rodgers and Hart weren't, and more than half a century later they're still with us, on scores of CDs and on iTunes, their most famous songs the meat and potatoes (or maybe the caviar) of countless jazz and cabaret artists. The year before Porter's *Du Barry*, R&H had triumphed with both *I Married an Angel* and *The Boys from Syracuse*. A slew of other hit shows lay in the past, and *Pal Joey* was coming up, with *By Jupiter* on its heels.

The quality of their work was at its peak, their fame and fortune at their height. Yet just a few years later, the partnership was over, and Larry Hart—at forty-eight—was dead, while Dick Rodgers, only forty-one, was launched on his even more triumphant partnership with Oscar Hammerstein. The story of the irresistible and tragic Lorenz Hart, of his collaboration with the more grounded and less exuberant Richard Rodgers, and of the Broadway musical comedy from the twenties to the forties is the subject of Gary Marmorstein's new soup-to-nuts biography of Hart, *A Ship Without a Sail*.

The book begins at the end of the story—with Larry's death, and the complicated and ugly fight over his will, and the way Teddy Hart, his beloved younger brother, and Teddy's wife, Dorothy, were (or weren't?) done out of their fair share of his money. There was a ruthless,

Lorenz Hart with cigar, Richard Rodgers at piano

perhaps dishonest manager, but to Marmorstein there was a more subtle villain: Richard Rodgers. Not that he grabbed money for himself—he was scrupulous in his business dealings—but, we're told, "countering Teddy Hart's accusation of undue influence on his brother, Rodgers tiptoed along the precipice of perjury." In the lawsuits that followed, Marmorstein writes, "Teddy Hart lost one appeal after another. Rodgers secured what he'd wanted: control of the copyrights to those extraordinary songs." So ended the exhilarating and rewarding collaboration of twenty-five years—in rage, in grief, and in court.

LARRY HART AND DICK RODGERS were both bright Jewish boys from Manhattan who at one point or another went to Columbia, but there the similarity in their backgrounds ends. The Rodgerses were well-to-do, Dr. Rodgers a prominent physician who enjoyed an haute-bourgeois life—elegant apartment, good connections, conventional environment. Max Hart, Larry's father, wasn't prominent, elegant, or conventional. Known as the Old Man, he was short, coarse, with a thick accent, and his manners were less than genteel. (No one ever forgot that at least once, in a moment of impatience, he urinated out a window.) Max claimed he was in real estate, among other respectable things, but essentially he was a con man with strong Tammany associations, convicted once for grand larceny and another time for fraudulent use of the mails, but both times freed on appeal. He never appeared abashed, and Larry had fun telling people that his father was "a crook." Fortunately for the family, Max was usually in funds, and he spent his money lavishly—mostly on them.

Nothing was too good for Frieda Hart—Momma—a tiny, open-minded, open-hearted woman everyone adored. And nothing was stinted when it came to Larry and Teddy: the best food, the best clothes, the best schools in town.

Throughout Larry's high school and college years, the Harts' house was an almost abnormally hospitable gathering place for all the pals the two boys brought home: an endless flow of food, drink, laughter, warmth, and talk that was both serious and provocative. Max, who liked a good laugh, a good meal, a good drink, and a good dirty story, would often join in and be the life of the party, while Frieda smiled and provided. As Frederick Nolan wrote in his excellent 1994 biography of Hart, Frieda "didn't seem to mind [the gang's] stripping her front parlor of furniture and turning the room into a sort of debating hall where politics, literature, poetry, and girls were hotly discussed until dawn." No one else had a family like Larry's. Yes, the Harts were disreputable, but they were generous and lively and fun. Dick Rodgers, years later, would call them "unstable, sweet, lovely people."

Even as a young adolescent, Larry was writing lyrics and sketches, and Max, who had theatrical friends like Lillian Russell, took his older son's precocious talent seriously. He had started taking Larry to theater and vaudeville when he was six, and the kid soaked it all up. He was also reading voraciously, mastering languages, writing for the school paper, going to a series of summer camps that specialized in putting on plays, skits, and revues. By the time he was in his twenties, he was in charge of the entertainment, staging such musicals as *Leave It to Jane*, one of the most popular of the famous Jerome Kern–P. G. Wodehouse–Guy Bolton Princess Theatre shows that he revered.

All of this was an invaluable training ground and apprenticeship as Larry started moving into semiprofessional areas of the theater, most significantly the annual Columbia University Varsity Shows, which would run for a week in places like the Hotel Astor. He got the job of adapting the songs for an English-language version of a German musical that played in Yorkville, its star named Mizi Gizi, its hit song "Meyer, Your Tights Are Tight." Soon he was translating German plays for the Shubert brothers, at fifty dollars a week. Not that he needed to earn a lot of money—Max had more than enough, and Larry lived at home, sharing a bedroom with Teddy (which he went on doing until Teddy married, in 1938).

While Hart's career was inching forward, Rodgers was growing up. By the time he was nine he was composing melodies at the family piano—they just poured out of him. As a teenager, Dick was good-looking, athletic, sociable, interested in girls, and as conventional as the rest of his family. He provided tunes for a few amateur shows—fundraisers for *The Sun* Tobacco Fund and the Infants Relief Society—and people were knocked out by his gifts. But he badly needed a writing partner, and in the spring of 1919 a friend had an inspiration: Larry Hart! He led Dick to the Hart ménage, and after a few awkward moments, Dick started to play some of his melodies, at which point, as Marmorstein (unfortunately) puts it, "Larry's ears pricked up like a startled deer's."

Then Larry began to talk. As Dick remembered it years later, "He knew a great deal about rhyming, about versification, and I thought he was wonderful. He felt that lyric writers didn't go far enough, that what they were doing was fairly stupid and had no point, didn't have enough wit, they were too cautious, and he felt that the boundaries could be pushed out a good deal." From the first moment, there was no doubt that the two of them would work together: It was love at first sight. Larry was twenty-three, Dick not yet seventeen. "I left Hart's house," wrote Rodgers a lifetime later, "having acquired in one afternoon a career, a partner, a best friend, and a source of permanent irritation."

THE BOYS GOT AN EARLY BREAK. Through a pal from summer camp, Herb Fields, they came to know the Fields family—Herb's sister, Dorothy, who would herself become a brilliant lyricist, and their father, Lew Fields, a onetime great vaudeville star who was now a major force on Broadway. By hook or by crook—or just family pressure—Fields picked up a very early R&H number called "Any Old Place with You" and stuck it in a current show of his. The show ran for only another half-dozen weeks, and the song went nowhere, but there they were, Dick just turned seventeen, on Broadway!

It would be a long time before they were back. After six years of turning out (or churning out) songs and librettos for various amateur venues like the Park Avenue Synagogue—that one was called *Temple Belles*—they were in despair. Dick, despite unwavering support from his family, knew he had to start earning a living, and was seriously considering going into the children's-underwear business. Larry was heading for thirty, apparently going nowhere.

And then lightning struck. In 1925, New York's most prestigious production company, the Theatre Guild, decided to put on a low-cost revue to cover the price of a set of tapestries for its new theater. Through the Guild's lawyer, who happened to be a patient of Dr. Rodgers's, Dick and Larry were granted an audition with Theresa Helburn, one of its founders and directors. "When they came to the song 'Manhattan,'" she would one day recall, "I sat up in delight. These lads had ability, wit, and a flair for a light sophisticated kind of song." She gave the boys a five-thousand-dollar budget and a month to get *The Garrick Gaieties* on—for two performances only, on Sunday, May 17, 1925. Audiences and critics were so enthusiastic that the Guild scheduled half a dozen special matinee performances and, when its current Lunt-Fontanne show, *The Guardsman*, closed, turned the theater over full-time to the *Gaieties*. It ran for half a year, "Manhattan" was a smash, and Rodgers and Hart were on their way.

The next decade, despite the usual crises and disappointments that punctuate the life of the theater, was a fulfilling time of shows, movies, hit songs, and international recognition. Their first Broadway "book" show, *Dearest Enemy*, was a romantic comedy set during the American Revolution. A dozen or more shows in New York and London followed, plus some Hollywood musicals starring such performers as Maurice Chevalier, Jeanette MacDonald, Al Jolson, and Bing Crosby. Life was easy on the Coast, and the money all too seductive, but their hearts belonged to Broadway. The roster of classic songs from this period includes "My Heart Stood Still," "Blue Moon," "With a Song in My Heart," "Thou Swell," "Dancing on the Ceiling," "Ten Cents a Dance," and "Lover."

The turning point came in 1935 with *Jumbo*, a colossal circus musical that was the idea of the egomaniacal showman Billy Rose, who took over the famous and failing Hippodrome, touted as the largest theater in the world. (It took so long to get the theater ready and the show up and running that *The New Yorker* observed, "Well, they finally got *Jumbo* into the Hippodrome. Now all that remains is to complete the Triborough Bridge and enforce the sanctions against Italy.") It had trapeze artists, tightrope walkers, clowns, Paul Whiteman, Jimmy Durante, and Rosie the elephant. Marmorstein remarks that numerous little boys were taken to *Jumbo*, one of them "the adopted son of vaudeville impresario E. F. Albee, a six-year-old named Edward" (actually, he was seven). Another of them was me—the first time I was ever in a theater. I can't have been five, and all I remember is a vast space and, just maybe, an elephant.

Jumbo was a spectacle. *On Your Toes*, the boys' next show (starring hoofer Ray Bolger, three years before his Oz Scarecrow), was a revelation, and a landmark in the history of the modern musical: the first to center on a ballet—the marvelous "Slaughter on Tenth Avenue," the creation of George Balanchine. It was through Larry that Balanchine was added to the mix—and he stayed in the mix: *Babes in Arms*, *I Married an Angel*, *The Boys from Syracuse* were to follow. Although the *On Your Toes* score included the usual hits, the music that made the biggest impact was Dick Rodgers's score for "Slaughter," which is still performed around the world as a stand-alone ballet.

Balanchine and Hart chummed around together, and Balanchine

reported that Larry "always appeared happy and laughing. He was so full of fun and energy, throwing his money around. From every pocket would come money and he paid everyone's bills wherever he went." He didn't mention Larry's heavier and heavier drinking, preferring to remember that it was Larry who taught him how to speak proper English.

AFTER *JUMBO*, EVERYTHING CHANGED. From then on it was Larry and Dick who came up with the concepts for their musicals and were in control of them; they were no longer journeymen for hire. It was they who decided that next up after *On Your Toes* would be something completely different: a bunch of kids putting on a show—no stars, no sophistication. The score of *Babes in Arms*, another major hit, may be their greatest: "The Lady Is a Tramp," "My Funny Valentine," "Where or When," and the title song (most of which, in the great Hollywood tradition, were dropped from the Judy Garland–Mickey Rooney MGM musical).

On they went: *I'd Rather Be Right*, with the great George M. Cohan playing FDR (whom he despised); *I Married an Angel*, with Vera Zorina as an angel who descends from heaven to Budapest to marry a banker; *The Boys from Syracuse*—Shakespeare's *Comedy of Errors*, with one of the Dromios played by Teddy Hart; *Too Many Girls*, a football musical that launched the career of Desi Arnaz, whom Larry had come upon in a Miami nightclub called La Conga.

By now, every Rodgers and Hart show was an event, and they themselves were celebrated figures—on the cover of *Time*, subjects of a two-part profile in *The New Yorker*. They were overdue for a flop, and they got one: something called *Higher and Higher*, which bombed, leaving nothing behind except the plangent "It Never Entered My Mind."

But around the corner was *Pal Joey*, the most controversial, and influential, of all their shows. The book came from a series of stories John O'Hara had written for *The New Yorker*, about a seedy nightclub singer/emcee (Gene Kelly) and the women he seduces and abuses. It wasn't a pretty story, and some critics, including the most important, Brooks Atkinson of *The New York Times*, found that its obvious virtues were undercut by its sordid story: "Although *Pal Joey* is expertly done, can you draw sweet water from a foul well?" When it was revived a dozen years later, it would be an even bigger success than it had been in 1940, and Atkinson took it all back, but by then, Larry, who had been devastated by that first review, was long since dead. *Pal Joey*'s songs retain their power and charm: "I Could Write a Book," a first-rate romantic ballad; "Bewitched, Bothered and Bewildered," a mordant masterpiece and a triumph for Larry's favorite, Vivienne Segal (she sang it in the revival too); and "Zip," a singularly witty take on the "intellectual" stripper Gypsy Rose Lee:

> Zip! Walter Lippmann wasn't brilliant today.
> Zip! Will Saroyan ever write a great play?
> Zip! I was reading Schopenhauer last night.
> Zip! And I think that Schopenhauer was right.

There would be one more big hit—back to the ancients with *By Jupiter*, reuniting the boys with Bolger, in their third show to be directed by Joshua Logan. But by now Larry was essentially gone, succumbing to acute alcoholism. He couldn't or wouldn't take on a whole new show, but when Dick decided to revive their 1927 hit, *A Connecticut Yankee*, he managed to come up with some new lyrics, including one of his very wittiest, "To Keep My Love Alive" (for Vivienne, of course). When he was sober, his mind was as quick and clever as ever.

But he wasn't sober often. On opening night of *A Connecticut Yankee* he turned up at the theater drunk, ill, and noisy. Teddy's wife managed to get him home to their place, but by morning he had vanished into the ugly November weather and couldn't be found. That night, a pal, searching for him, came upon him sitting shivering in the gutter outside a bar on Eighth Avenue. Nothing they could do at the hospital helped—neither the oxygen tent nor penicillin, the new wonder drug that Eleanor Roosevelt interceded with the War Production Board to procure. It was over. Lorenz Hart was dead of pneumonia, and "Rodgers and Hart" was dead as well. The fun-loving, generous, ebullient guy everybody loved—"the most lovable, cuddly, honey bear," Josh Logan called him—had self-destructed in the most painful and public way, a desperate, irresponsible drunk no one could help, whose death seemed a relief if not a blessing.

How did Rodgers and Hart write their songs? This is how Larry characterized their work method to a reporter:

> We map out the plot. Then Dick may have a catchy tune idea. He picks it out on the piano—I listen and suddenly an idea for a lyric comes. This happens often. On the other hand, I may think of a couple of verses that will fit into the show. I write them out and say them over to Dick. He sits down at the piano and improvises. I stick my oar in sometimes and before we know it, we have the tune to hang the verses on. It's like that—simple!

Did they ever quarrel? In his introduction to *The Rodgers and Hart Song Book*, Dick wrote that Larry

> loathed changing any word once it was written down. When the immovable object of his unwillingness to change came up against the irresistible force of my own drive for perfection, the noise could be heard all over the city. Our fights over words were furious, blasphemous, and frequent, but even in their hottest moments we both knew that we were arguing academically and not personally. I think I am quite safe in saying that Larry and I never had a single personal argument with each other.

They had differences, though. At first, Larry was the mentor, the semipro; Dick was a schoolboy. The age difference didn't affect their work, but as time passed, their opposite approaches to life affected their relationship. Marmorstein writes:

> Larry Hart never had much use for Café Society, High Society, or the so-called Four Hundred, except as a dartboard, its members largely figures of fun. But the teenage Dick Rodgers was fascinated by that world, which remained exclusive, open only to the wealthiest Ameri-

cans of the "highest" (i.e., invariably Caucasian, usually with English derivation) pedigree.

Dick's obsession with being classy never diminished. Max Hart described his apartment on West End Avenue as "like Frank Campbell's Funeral Parlor, beautiful but dead!" In contrast, Larry, for all his erudition, reveled in the nightlife of Harlem and Damon Runyon's Broadway— the "characters," the bars, the seamy side. And he had no interest in money—it came and went, only important so that it could be quickly spent, usually on others.

From the start, Dick was focused on finances and business arrangements; in his later, post-Larry, years, he not only controlled those R&H copyrights but owned and ran, with Hammerstein, major production and music companies. Josh Logan's theory was that Dick was "a bit embarrassed about the ease of writing music, as though it were too easy, too soft a thing for a man to do," and was "only really happy making contracts, haggling about royalties, salaries or theatre leases." It also seemed to Logan that Larry "envied and therefore hated Dick's rugged self-discipline, his ability to be punctual, efficient and to bring a show in on time. It was agony for Larry to sit down to work. Perhaps it was his fear of being less than perfect or just the painful fact of being Larry."

One of Richard Rodgers's strongest characteristics was his lifelong need to control, and unfortunately Larry Hart, from first to last, was uncontrollable, as chaotic in his work habits as his partner was disciplined. He was out drinking and partying late every night and never out of bed till midday, inevitably hungover; Dick was ready and eager to work hours earlier, frustrated by Larry's no-shows. And then there were Larry's broken promises about delivery of lyrics or dialogue. He was always remorseful, but what good did that do? Dick, so earnest and methodical in his work habits, grew into an angry taskmaster, the bad cop, and he more and more resented having to be one. Larry bitterly referred to Dick as "the principal" with "a sour-apple face"; Dick referred to Larry as "my favorite blight and partner." The partnership made in heaven was turning into a working hell. Yet the two men had loved each other. (Some people believed Larry had been in love with Dick from the start. The unambiguously heterosexual Dick, however, both before and after his marriage to the beautiful, elegant, and difficult Dorothy Feiner, was widely known for his devotion to the girls.)

Although by the early 1940s Larry was disappearing for days at a time, his drunken binges more and more appalling, Dick proposed that they get to work on an offer from the Theatre Guild: turning the play *Green Grow the Lilacs* into a musical. "I want you to have yourself admitted to a sanitarium," he said to Larry. "I'll get myself admitted, too. We'll be there together and work together. But you've got to get off the street." As Marmorstein relates, paraphrasing Rodgers's autobiography, Larry

> made it clear that he was not checking himself into any sanitarium—that he was on his way to Mexico.
>
> "Larry, if you walk out now, someone else will do the show with me."
>
> "Anyone in mind?"
>
> "Oscar will write the lyrics."
>
> "There's no better man for the job," Larry said. "I don't know how you put up with me all these years. The best thing would be for you to forget about me."

He walked out of their meeting, leaving Dick—and the show that became *Oklahoma!*—behind. "Alone in the boardroom Dick sighed, the burden of tolerating an increasingly truant, irresponsible partner over the course of twenty-four years having been lifted in an instant. And then he wept." This, at any rate, was Dick's conveniently touching version of their parting.

YEARS LATER, Rodgers would describe what Hart looked like to him at their first meeting. "His appearance was so incredible that I remember every single detail. The total man was hardly more than five feet tall." He was unshaven, unkempt. "But that first look was misleading, for it missed the soft brown eyes, the straight nose, the good mouth, the even teeth and the strong chin. Feature for feature he had a handsome face, but it was set in a head that was a bit too large for his body and gave him a slightly gnome-like appearance." He also had a vigorously receding hairline, and he usually had a cigar stuck in his mouth.

Gnome, pixie, troll, dwarf—that's how Larry was seen by his world (Dick's "shrimp" was affectionately mild). In public he was dignified about what he clearly saw as his deformity. Balanchine remembered, "There was never any mention of his height, though he called the built-up heels in his shoes 'the two-inch liars.'" "The cost of his brave face, though," writes Marmorstein, "would emerge over ... twenty-five years in dozens of lyrics that were less about being small than about what it's like to *feel* small—to be dismissed, excluded, denied admission, and left standing out in the cold."

Certainly he believed that no one, especially no woman, could love him. Frederick Nolan tells us that Larry was asked by a reporter about his love life. "'Love life?' Larry replied. 'I haven't any.' Then he was a confirmed bachelor? 'Of course,' he said. 'Nobody would want *me.*'" Yet there were women in his life to whom he was seriously attached and to whom he proposed. Frances Manson was a story editor at Columbia Pictures who would later say, "I adored Larry. . . . He was so dynamic and energetic, his presence was so magnetic, that I honestly never gave a thought to his being shorter than I was, though I am not at all tall." Her reluctance to marry him came from her fear that she might end up drinking as much as he did. The popular young opera singer Nanette Guilford said, "He was absolutely adorable, and to know him was to love him. I loved him. But he never believed me. He didn't believe any woman could fall in love with him."

Undoubtedly the woman he cared for most was Vivienne Segal, who was clever, funny, sexy, with a fiery temperament. (Larry once said, "I would rather be caught dead wearing a suit I wouldn't be caught dead wearing than weather one of Viv Segal's storms.") One account concludes, "Although everyone who cared for Larry believed him to be seriously in love with Vivienne Segal, it is our view that his admiration for her was an emotion that bordered on love but stopped short of sexual desire." Still, he proposed more than once, and more than once she turned him down. Poor Frieda Hart—all she wanted was for her boy to settle down with Mrs. Right. One friend remembers sitting next to her listening to Larry singing "Have you heard, I married an angel" and Frieda whispering, "How I wish my Larry would marry an angel!" Instead, he shared a huge apartment with his angel mother until she died, only seven months before he did.

It's taken for granted now that to the extent Larry Hart had a consistently active sex life, it was homosexual. But discreet. Marmorstein speculates about the where and when of Larry's encounters with other men. Turkish baths? A hideaway hotel room? He seems to have preferred rough trade, going off to Miami or Mexico and enjoying himself with beach boys. (Balanchine reported to his assistant that on a trip the two men took together to London, he "got him out of brawls, when Larry would pick up sailors and get beat up.") The homophobic Maurice Chevalier, for whom R&H were writing that unique movie *Love Me Tonight*, warned his young male assistant to stay away from Larry "or he'll try to get into your pants." According to Meryle Secrest, Rodgers's most assiduous biographer, Hart brought an actor named Peter Garey home to the Hart apartment one night. Mrs. Hart "stood on the couch by the window and said, 'If you go out with my son I am going to jump.'" (He did, and she didn't.) A frequent guest at another louche Hart party reported, "Larry was more of a voyeur. I can remember going to parties and seeing his eyes glittering, watching this orgy going on. When it came to sex, Larry left an awful lot to be desired. I was one of his boys, and I know."

It's easy to hear sly echoes of homosexuality in Hart's lyrics (there would certainly be none in Oscar Hammerstein's), but although his great subject was love, he didn't write much about sex. The following, from *On Your Toes*, is just about as explicit as he gets:

Mother warned me my instincts to deny.
Yet I fail.
The male is frail.
The heart is quicker than the eye!
She said, "Love one time, Junior,

Look at the Lunts!"
I've fallen twice—with two at once.
Passion's plaything—that's me, oh me, oh my!
But at least
I'm quite a beast.
The heart is quicker than the eye!

This was remarkably confessional for the Broadway of 1936.

There were rumors about Larry while he was alive, but nothing about his sexuality ever appeared in print. One night in Los Angeles, in 1933, someone from a Hollywood trade magazine approached Dick at a party and said, "I've got to ask you something about Larry. . . . Is it true Larry's a fairy?" Dick grabbed him by the collar, Marmorstein recounts, and said, "I never heard that. And if you print it, I'll kill you." Time marches on. According to the memoirs of Diahann Carroll— who in 1962 starred in Dick's *No Strings*—one night he sighed to her, "You can't imagine how wonderful it feels to have written this score and not have to search all over the globe for the little fag."

WITH HIS UNFAILING GENEROSITY, Larry embraced Dick at the opening-night party for *Oklahoma!* after its jubilant premiere and said, "This is one of the greatest shows I've ever seen, and it'll be playing twenty years from now!"

It seems likely that he understood how everything was changing— that a new era of musical plays rather than musical comedies had begun, and that the heartfelt moralistic values of wartime America, and of Oscar Hammerstein, were the future. It's as inconceivable that Larry Hart could have written "Oh, What a Beautiful Mornin'" as it is that Hammerstein could have written "Zip." "Hart," said the director George Abbott, "was a much more sophisticated writer than the mature, assured, poised Hammerstein. Hart saw everything fancifully. His tongue was in his cheek, his poetry was light and airy. He saw love dancing on the ceiling. Oscar saw it across a crowded room."

The Rodgers and Hart shows have vanished (only *On Your Toes* and

Pal Joey seem to be revivable; maybe *A Connecticut Yankee*), while the main Rodgers and Hammerstein shows are always with us. Hart would be a footnote to Broadway history if not for the songs. And they don't die; they're as viable today as they ever were, perfect conjunctions of words and music. (*Words and Music*, by the way, is the title of the ludicrous Hollywood biopic, with Mickey Rooney as Larry—well, they were both short—and Tom Drake and Janet Leigh as the Rodgerses.) They're not as jazzy as the Gershwin songs, not as cannily grassroots as Berlin's. They're closest, perhaps, to Cole Porter's in their combination of sophistication and melodic originality, but, as the songwriter Hugh Martin said, "Cole Porter was all about sex. Larry was about love." The musical-comedy expert Ethan Mordden put it another way:

> At bottom, the difference between Hart, the cleverest of the [era's] lyricists, and Porter, the funniest, is that Hart saw the love plot in the shows as something worthy, almost unattainable, while Porter didn't see love at all. . . . The odd fact is that for all Hart's jesting and all Porter's lyricism, Hart was a romantic and Porter a satirist.

He was also sad. And as time passed he grew sadder, and more cynical. Remember: His career takes off in 1925 with a paean of praise for "Manhattan," and only fourteen years later he's telling the world:

> Broadway's turning into Coney,
> Champagne Charlie's drinking gin,
> Old New York is new and phoney—
> Give it back to the Indians.

His words reveal his self-doubt, his loneliness ("All alone, all at sea! / Why does nobody care for me?"), but he's never angry, only rueful and disconsolate. As he sums it up in "Bewitched, Bothered and Bewildered": "The laugh's on me." It's not for nothing that the playwright Jerome Lawrence named him "the poet laureate of masochism."

And yet . . . the joy in invention, the sheer energy of a song like "The Lady Is a Tramp"! Who else could have topped himself again and again, frisking from

> I like the free, fresh wind in my hair.
> Life without care.
> I'm broke—it's oke

to

> I like the green grass under my shoes.
> What can I lose?
> I'm flat! That's that!

to

> I like to hang my hat where I please.
> Sail with the breeze.
> No dough—heigh-ho!

and landing up on

> I like the sweet, fresh rain in my face.
> Diamonds and lace,
> No got—so what?

And who has written more tenderly of a beloved one than Hart does of his "funny valentine," with his figure less than Greek and his mouth a little weak?

Then a sudden naughty strike, as in these throwaway lines from a throwaway song called "Harlemania":

> With the best of intentions,
> Folks who used to be nice

Shake what nobody mentions,
Not once, but twice.

He could be everything but corny.

And he knew how good he was. "I've got a lot of talent, kid," he told the lyricist Alan Jay Lerner. "I probably could have been a genius. But I just don't care." Lerner concluded, "Somewhere along the line, there obviously did come a time when the joy of his professional success became drowned in the lost misery of his handicapped life."

Gary Marmorstein has written a direct and ample—perhaps *too* ample—chronicle of that life, containing more professional detail and history than the average reader may want to absorb. Frederick Nolan's book, now almost twenty years old, is less comprehensive, more fluent. Both biographers clearly have reservations about Richard Rodgers as a man; they both warmly celebrate Hart's remarkable achievement; and they both express tremendous sympathy for Hart himself. And how could they not, given the combination of his generous and lovable nature with the tragic arc of his life? Max Hart, Larry's rambunctious father, died saying, "I haven't missed a thing." How sad that the last words of Larry himself—this man who gave so much pleasure to so many— were "What have I lived for?"

The Atlantic
APRIL 2013

The Belter

ETHEL MERMAN

TWO NEW BIOGRAPHIES OF ETHEL MERMAN in the same month? You may think that's overkill, but you may also think that *one* new biography of Ethel Merman is overkill, considering that there already are two, one of them very recent, plus a pair of autobiographies. The real problem isn't the duplication; it's that although she had one of the greatest careers in Broadway history, she was just an uninteresting woman. Even the story of her success is uninteresting: She had no struggle getting to the top and no struggle staying there. Miserable childhood? The opposite. Bad marriages? Only four—but she rode them out with something approaching equanimity. Trouble with her children? Yes, but did she notice?

Her life began as it was meant to go on—easily. No one ever had more loving and supportive parents, and no one ever cared more for parents in return. Even once she became a star, she would go home after her show every night to where they all still lived, in Astoria, Queens. And when she married, she had Mom and Pop Zimmermann ("Merman" was a contraction) living a few floors away from her in a fancy building on Central Park West.

Merman was in fourteen Broadway shows over thirty-five years, including a sensational stretch in *Hello, Dolly!*, and they were fourteen hits. Her voice never gave out. Her fans never abandoned her. Her only professional disappointment was that her movie career never really flourished. (Worst was being screwed—she thought—out of the film version of her greatest role, *Gypsy*'s Mama Rose.) She was a star from the beginning. She was rich. She had dozens of pals—the Duke and Duchess of Windsor among them. She had a lot of "escorts" (including Walter Annenberg), and a big public romance with the highly conspicuous Sherman Billingsley, millionaire owner of the Stork Club. But did she have real friends?

According to the wonderful lyricist Dorothy Fields, who was fond of her, "She knows all the small talk, but you can't sit down and talk to her, you just can't." Arthur Laurents, who wrote the book for *Gypsy*, found her dumb: "She doesn't calculate. She doesn't weigh things. She just blunders ahead." (Apparently, she never picked up a newspaper, let alone a book.) Pete Martin, the ghostwriter of autobiography number one, said, "Ethel seemed to have little perspective, or insight, into her spectacular career." The reviews said worse: "It is difficult to believe that Ethel Merman, as dynamic a stage personality as Broadway has ever produced, could possibly be the dull-witted, tiresome egoist off-stage that this book makes her appear to be." Not, perhaps, a good omen for the biographer.

SO WHAT do Caryl Flinn, author of *Brass Diva*, and Brian Kellow, author of *Ethel Merman*, have to contribute to the Merman saga? Very different things, it turns out. Professor Flinn is an academic, at the University of Arizona, and author of *The New German Cinema: Music, History, and the Matter of Style.* This perhaps accounts for the flaws in her otherwise careful and intelligent book. One of them stems from the negative side of her admirably zealous research: too much detail. Do you want to know, for instance, exactly where young Ethel lived in Astoria? "In her first autobiography, she gives 2903 1st Avenue as the place where she grew up; in her second, 31st Avenue. Her biographer Bob Thomas claimed it was 359 Fourth Avenue. Saved mail to the family postmarked in November 1931 was received at both 2908 31st Avenue and 3056 30th Street." Thank you, Professor.

In the same spirit, Flinn provides extended plot summaries of a series of insignificant and forgotten one- and two-reelers that Merman made for Paramount in the early 1930s. This is material previously untouched by critical hands, and for the sake of grasping Merman's early performance style I'd love to sample throwaways like *Her Future*, *Ireno*,

SUNDAY NEWS
NEW YORK'S PICTURE NEWSPAPER

July 17, 1938

ETHEL MERMAN

and *Song Shopping*. But reading seven tight pages about them is just too much of a good thing.

And then there's Flinn's insistence on placing Merman sociologically. Issues of feminism, class, and culture are constantly put forward: "Ethel was always a lightning rod that reflected changes in the social landscape, and in her (and responses *to* her), we see evolving attitudes toward family, sex, celebrity, class, and age." Sorry, but that's not what I saw. It's not that the professor plays down Merman the phenomenal performer, it's that she plays up the idea of finding significance where only achievement matters.

Brian Kellow's background lies in music and performance (he's the features editor of *Opera News*), and therefore he's more focused on

Merman's actual singing and stage smarts. His fluent book, then, is more useful on the musician, less perceptive about the life.

AND WHAT *WAS* THE LIFE? Ethel Agnes Zimmermann was born on January 16, 1906, 1908, 1910, 1911, or 1912 (the last of which, if true, would have seen her graduating from high school at twelve). Her parents—Pop's background was German, Mom's Scottish—were hardworking, frugal, serious, churchgoing, and musical. Baby Ethel's voice was huge from the start, and by the time she was five she was making public appearances, not only in church choirs but in Pop's Masonic lodge, pageants, the Women's Republican Club. (One of her boasts was that she never took a singing lesson in her life.) Cautious and pragmatic like her parents, she chose to take commercial courses in high school in case singing didn't pan out, which is how she came to be working as a stenographer, first at Boyce-ite (antifreeze), then at BK Vacuum Booster Brake Company (power brakes). Meanwhile, she was doing nighttime radio shows. By 1927 she has her photo on sheet-music covers; by 1928 she's singing at the Democratic convention that nominated FDR for governor and performing in tony nightclubs. By 1930 she's playing the Palace.

It was at the Brooklyn Paramount that she was approached by a top Broadway producer, Vinton Freedley, who was looking for the second female lead for the new Gershwin show, *Girl Crazy*. (Ginger Rogers was the ingénue.) He was knocked out by her, and hurried her to George and Ira's apartment for an audition. They were knocked out, too, and in a famous exchange recounted over and over again (usually by her), George said, "Miss Merman, if there's anything about these songs you'd like to change, I'd be happy to do so." "They'll do very nicely," she replied.

"These songs" included "Sam and Delilah," "Boy! What Love Has Done to Me!" and, of course, "I Got Rhythm," which, when she blasted it out at the end of act one, made Broadway history. No one had ever heard a sound like hers, or seen such confidence in someone so young.

But then Merman never suffered from stage fright. "What's there to worry about? I know my lines."

From then on it was triumph after triumph, including five shows written for her by Cole Porter—most famously, *Anything Goes* (1934). Then there was Irving Berlin's *Annie Get Your Gun* (1946), for 1,147 performances, and eventually *Gypsy* (1959), maybe the greatest of all musicals and the greatest of all star performances. And consider the list of American standards written with Ethel's voice in mind: "Eadie Was a Lady," "I Get a Kick Out of You," "You're the Top," "Blow, Gabriel, Blow," "It's De-Lovely," "Ridin' High," "Hey, Good Lookin'," "There's No Business Like Show Business" (and all her other numbers from *Annie*), "Everything's Coming Up Roses." Only Fred Astaire was as much in demand by the great American songwriters.

How did she sing? The word usually applied to her is "belter," but it was more complicated than that—more than just a huge voice trumpeting every syllable to the back of the house. Kellow refers to her vocal production being extraordinarily even throughout her range; to her "naturally forward placement, superb command of breath support," and the solid physique that "helped her to sing like an operatic tenor; the sound moved up through her chest and resonated in her head, with true tenorlike ping on the high notes." Indeed, the only artist she ever reminded me of *was* an opera singer—but not a tenor. In 1952 the greatest of Wagnerian sopranos, Kirsten Flagstad, gave her final performances at the Met, in Gluck's *Alceste*. Portly, in simple powder-blue robes, she planted herself downstage center, opened her mouth, and out came an immense and beautiful column of sound. No acting, no effort— just splendor. That was Merman, given the differences between *Alceste* and, say, *Panama Hattie*.

Merman always knew exactly what worked for her, and although she listened carefully to directors, she made the important decisions for herself—in particular, about what songs suited her. She didn't go in for motivation or analysis. What was there to analyze? When Jule Styne and Stephen Sondheim added "Rose's Turn" to *Gypsy*, Sondheim tried explaining it to her. She listened politely, then interrupted him.

"There was just one thing she wanted to know," Kellow reports. "Did 'Mmmmmm-mmm-Mama' come in on an upbeat or a downbeat?"

She was a consummate professional—always on time, never missing a show, never allowing her boozing to impinge on her work, never compromising the level of her performance—and she expected the same professionalism from her colleagues and lowered the boom if they disappointed: "This is a job like any other job you go to. It's like being a plumber or carpenter or anything else. You come to the theater and you come to work."

She was also efficient and methodical in private life. Proud of her stenographic experience, she typed her own letters and did her own accounts. And nobody took advantage of her. The morning after *Annie* opened, says Kellow, "Ethel didn't have time to look over the notices carefully, for she was on the telephone with the manager of their local grocery store, demanding to know why she'd been charged so much for a can of peaches that hadn't been delivered the day before."

THE ONE AREA in which she was vulnerable was her romantic life. Not a very pretty girl, she was robustly sexy onstage rather than erotic or seductive; she was the quintessential good egg, someone you rooted for rather than rooted after. Her first marriage lasted only a few weeks. Her second, to Bob Levitt, was more serious. He was the promotion director for the *New York Journal-American*, well-read and sophisticated. They had two children and for a while got along well, but eventually proved incompatible. As Ethel, with her innate delicacy, put it, "Levitt would fuck a snake!" Yet decades after their divorce, long after he'd died, she had his body exhumed and cremated and kept his ashes in an urn in her bedroom.

Number three was Robert Six, founder and head of Continental Airways, headquartered in Denver. Retiring (for the moment) from the stage, Ethel moved to Colorado and set herself up as a traditional wife and mother—gardening, cooking, working for the Boy Scouts. Unfortunately, Six was another womanizer, and violently abusive to Ethel's kids and to her parents. Goodbye, Denver.

Number four was the notorious and momentary mismatch with Ernest Borgnine.

Not a very happy record. And, given her fraught relationship with her son, Bob Jr. (her daughter, Ethel Jr., had died a drug-related death), there was not much left in life for Ethel. She went on making appearances—in concerts, on TV—but her kind of Broadway vehicle was a thing of the past. She lived alone in hotel suites, finally at the Surrey on East Seventy-Sixth Street, where she had the stove removed, using only a small toaster oven in which, Caryl Flinn reports, she would reheat Chinese takeout or cook chicken hot dogs. All over the apartment she displayed her needlepoint work "alongside her beloved Raggedy Anns and Muppet friends." In early 1984 she succumbed to an inoperable brain tumor. Before her death, her mental powers had deteriorated, and her fabulous energy and drive were gone.

Twenty-odd years have now passed and there's still no one like her. But what could today's theater do with her if she were to be reborn? Ethel Merman in *Phantom of the Opera* or *Mamma Mia*? Yet she remains an icon. Her too-few records are still in demand and often thrilling, and from the movie of one of her stage hits, *Call Me Madam*, plus a 1954 telecast of *Anything Goes*, co-starring Bert Lahr and Frank Sinatra, we get a sense of her extraordinary talent as a performer. Alas, from these two biographies what we get is a sense of the otherwise mostly empty life she apparently lived.

The New York Observer
NOVEMBER 27, 2007

The Wit

DOROTHY PARKER

W HAT ARE WE TO MAKE TODAY of this famous woman who, beginning almost a century ago, has fascinated genera- tions with her wit, flair, talent, and near-genius for self- destruction? For some, what registers most strongly is her central role in the legend of the Algonquin Round Table, with its campiness of wisecracks, quips, and put-downs—a part of her life she would come to repudiate. For others, it's the descent into alcoholism, and the sad final years holed up in Manhattan's Volney hotel. Pick your myth.

As for her writing, it has evoked ridiculous exaggeration from her votaries, both her contemporaries and her biographers. Vincent Sheean: "Among contemporary artists, I would put her next to Hemingway and Bill Faulkner. She wasn't Shakespeare, but what she was, was true." John Keats in his biography of her, *You Might as Well Live* (1970): "She wrote poetry that was at least as good as the best of Millay and Hous- man. She wrote some stories that are easily as good as some of O'Hara and Hemingway." This is praise that manages to be inflated and quali- fied at the same time.

And here is Regina Barreca, a professor of English literature and feminist theory at the University of Connecticut, in her introduction to the Penguin edition of the *Complete Stories*: "If Parker's work can be dismissed as narrow and easy, then so can the work of Austen, Eliot, and Woolf." Well, no. Exaggerated claims don't strengthen the case for Parker's literary accomplishments. As is inevitably the case with criti- cism grounded in agenda, they diminish it. But this doesn't mean that her work is without value or interest.

Certainly she struck a chord with the public. From the start, her voice spoke to a wide range of readers. Her generally sardonic, often

Dorothy Parker, photographed by Edward Steichen

angry, occasionally brutal view of men and women—of love and marriage, of cauterized despair—triggered recognition and perhaps even strengthened resolve. She told the truth as she perceived it, while using her wit and humor to hold at arm's length the feelings that her personal experiences had unleashed in her. An uncanny modern descendant is Nora Ephron in her novel *Heartburn*, which re-imagines her ugly and painful breakup with Carl Bernstein as a barbed comedy.

In 1915, Parker, aged twenty-two, went to work at *Vogue* (for ten dollars a week), writing captions, proofreading, fact-checking, et cetera, and after a while moved over to the very young *Vanity Fair*; her first poem to be published had recently appeared there. She happily functioned as a kind of scribe-of-all-work until three years later when she was chosen to replace the departing P. G. Wodehouse as the magazine's drama critic. She was not only the youngest by far of New York's theater critics, she was the only female one.

It was at the magazine that she met the lovable and sympathetic Robert Benchley, who would become the closest friend of her life, as well as Robert Sherwood, long before his four Pulitzer Prizes (three for drama, one for biography). They became a threesome, and started eating lunch together at the nearby Algonquin Hotel because it was affordable and the food was okay. At about the same time, another threesome drifted in, graduates of *Stars and Stripes*, the overseas Army's weekly newspaper. They were Alexander Woollcott, Harold Ross, and Franklin Pierce Adams, who as "F.P.A." was the most influential newspaper columnist of the day. Soon Adams was quoting Parker's *Vanity Fair* verses and, even more effectively, her bon mots. Quickly "Dorothy Parker" was a celebrity.

It didn't hurt that she was very pretty, very sexy, and had a somewhat checkered personal life. She had married a good-looking, not very interesting (to others) young WASP businessman named Edwin Parker—she liked to say she did it in order to legitimately shed her maiden name of Rothschild (no, not *the* Rothschilds). He went into the Army in 1917, and she followed him around Army bases in the States, but when he came back from overseas, it was over; apart from anything else, he had become seriously addicted to morphine.

Many amours followed, all of them disastrous and all of them feeding her eternal presentation of herself in her prose and poetry as wounded, heartsick, embittered, soul-weary. Along the way, she had a legal but frightening abortion (she had put it off too long), the father being the charming, womanizing Charles MacArthur, who would go on to co-write *The Front Page* and marry Helen Hayes. Parker was crazy about him; his interest waned. The gossip was that when he contributed thirty dollars toward the abortion, she remarked that it was like Judas making a refund.

———

IN 1920 *Vanity Fair* fired her at the insistence of several important Broadway producers whom her caustic reviews had managed to offend. (Benchley immediately resigned in solidarity with her; Sherwood had already been fired.) Another literary magazine, *Ainslee's,* with a far larger readership, took her up and gave her a free hand, and she went on laying waste to the tidal wave of meretricious plays and musicals and revues that opened every year, sometimes ten a week; one Christmas night there were eight premieres. Yet—always just, if not always kind—she recognized and saluted real achievement when she actually came upon it.

Meanwhile, her verses and stories were appearing profusely and everywhere: not only in upscale places like *Vanity Fair* (which was happier to publish her than employ her), *The Smart Set,* and *The American Mercury,* but also in the popular *Ladies' Home Journal, The Saturday Evening Post, Life* (when it was still a comic magazine), and—starting with its second issue, early in February 1925—her old pal Harold Ross's new venture, *The New Yorker,* with which she would have an extended on-again, off-again love affair.

At first, the stories were essentially sketches fed by her perfect ear for foolish, self-absorbed conversation and her scorn for middle-class hypocrisies. They appealed to the same cast of mind that was responding so clamorously to Sinclair Lewis's puncturings, in *Main Street* (1920) and *Babbitt* (1922), of what H. L. Mencken called the "booboisie." As time passed, though, her intentions grew more serious, culminating in her longest and best-known story, "Big Blonde," which won the 1929 O. Henry Award (Faulkner, Cheever, Updike, Carver, Oates, and Munro were among later winners).

"Big Blonde" reveals the desperate life of a fading party girl who's run out of steam and tries, and fails, to kill herself. It's convincing in its verisimilitude and deployment of pathos, but finally it comes across as a masterly performance rather than a reverberant vision of life. (Compare it to Edith Wharton's *The House of Mirth.*) It's also Parker dealing with her own failed suicide attempts—slashed wrists, Veronal (Big Blonde's drug of choice). Suicide was a constant reality for her. The novel she began was to be called *Sonnets in Suicide.* One of her most famous poems, "Résumé," summed things up:

Razors pain you;
Rivers are damp;
Acids stain you;
And drugs cause cramp.
Guns aren't lawful;
Nooses give;
Gas smells awful;
You might as well live.

Death and suicide were never far from her thoughts—she titled her collections *Enough Rope, Sunset Gun, Death and Taxes,* and *Not So Deep as a Well,* the first of them a major best seller in 1926, confirming her fame.

Was her poetry just rhyming badinage dressed up as trenchant, plaintive ruminations on love, loss, and death? Her subjects are serious, but her cleverness undercuts them: There's almost always a last line, a sardonic zinger, to signal that even if she *does* care, the more fool she. Even her most famous couplet—"Men seldom make passes / At girls who wear glasses"—bandages a wound, although plenty of men made passes.

She was clear about her versifying. "There is poetry and there is not," she once wrote in *The New Yorker,* and she knew hers was not. She thought her stories were superior to her poems (she was right), but that wasn't good enough for her. She never managed to write The Novel (as at that time every writer dreamed of doing). Did Hemingway like her work? Did he like *her*? (He didn't, but she didn't know it. As she was dying, Lillian Hellman had to assure her that he did.) Nor did she have much respect for what she and her second husband, the handsome, possibly gay actor and writer Alan Campbell, whom she married twice, did in Hollywood. (She liked referring to him publicly as "the wickedest woman in Paris.") They worked hard at their assignments and raked in the chips, and she was twice nominated for an Oscar (*A Star Is Born,* 1937; *Smash-Up: The Story of a Woman,* 1947), but her view of film writing never changed from her verdict about it when she was first venturing out to California: "Why, I could do that with one hand tied behind me and the other on Irving Thalberg's pulse."

A TURNING POINT IN PARKER'S LIFE came in 1927 when she went to Boston to protest the executions of Sacco and Vanzetti. It was her first political action, but it came from deep inside her, and she persisted—infiltrating the prison, getting arrested, marching with other writers like John Dos Passos, Edna St. Vincent Millay, and Katherine Anne Porter. They didn't prevail at this low point in the history of justice in America, but she hadn't backed down. And as time would show, her actions were not just some outburst of what, decades later, would come to be labeled radical chic.

From then on she was committed to liberal or radical causes. She vigorously supported the Loyalists in Spain, even spending ten days with Alan under the bombs in Madrid and Valencia. She helped found the Hollywood Anti-Nazi League. Whether she actually joined the Communist Party for a short time remains an unanswered question. Although Hellman claimed she had been subpoenaed by HUAC and appeared before the committee, this (like so much else in Hellman's memoirs) is simply untrue. She was, though, visited by two FBI agents in 1951. When they asked her whether she had ever conspired to overthrow the government, she answered, "Listen, I can't even get my dog to stay down. Do I look to you like someone who could overthrow the government?" The FBI gave her a pass.

In the 1930s she had raised money for the defense of the Scottsboro Boys, and she never relaxed her efforts in the field of civil rights: When she died, in 1967, her literary estate was left to Martin Luther King, and then to the NAACP, and her ashes are buried in a memorial garden at the organization's headquarters in Baltimore.

Her emotional life was less consistent. Men had always been in and out of her life, and she inevitably ended up feeling rejected, betrayed, unwanted. She and Campbell loved each other in their way, but their way seems to have been that of a convenient partnership—he could construct stories, she could come up with convincing dialogue; he flattered and cajoled her out of her anxieties and despairs, she legitimized him in the big world. It might have been different if they had had the child she desperately wanted, but in her forties she miscarried more than once, had a hysterectomy, and that was that.

The Campbells tried the rustic life, acquiring an ambitious property near Sid and Laura Perelman in Pennsylvania, but, predictably, that didn't last. In the early 1940s she went back to Hollywood with modest success—some minor work on *The Pride of the Yankees*, dialogue for Hitchcock's *Saboteur*—but it was a far cry from the high-flying (and high-paying) days of the previous decade. Her stories now appeared only sporadically, and no longer were automatically accepted by *The New Yorker*—some were simply too stridently political. One magazine editor, she wrote in 1939 in the far-left magazine *New Masses*, tactfully not naming him, "told me that if I changed my piece to make it in favor of Franco, he would publish it. 'God damn it,' he said, 'why can't you be funny again?'" That editor was Harold Ross.

Worst of all, as time went by everybody was dying, and far too young, from her idol Ring Lardner at forty-eight and Benchley at fifty-six to Scott Fitzgerald at forty-four. ("The poor son-of-a-bitch," she murmured over his coffin at his sparsely attended Hollywood funeral.) Helen, her sister, was gone. Who was left? Edmund Wilson was still around—they had almost had a fling way back in 1919; now he paid occasional painful visits to her at the Volney. ("She lives with a small and nervous bad-smelling poodle bitch, drinks a lot, and does not care to go out.")

She was still devoted to the Golden Couple, Gerald and Sara Murphy. ("There aren't any people, Mr. Benchley, except you and the Murphys. I know that now," she had written to him in 1929.) She had lived with the Murphys in their famous spread on the Riviera, and had spent a good part of a year with them in the Swiss sanitarium to which they moved when their son Patrick contracted tuberculosis. Their lives, however, rarely converged now. Difficult friends like Hellman and recent ones like Gloria Vanderbilt and her husband, Wyatt Cooper, couldn't take up the slack.

She was still revered, a legend, but she had also become a pathetic relic. Yes, "you might as well live," but for what? And *on* what? Not only was she running out of old friends, she was running out of money, though uncashed checks, some quite large, were strewn around her apartment (along with the empty bottles), not helping with unpaid bills.

BY THE MID-1950s she was finished with fiction and verse and screenplays, but now she returned to the field in which she had first made a splash and which she had never entirely abandoned: criticism. We mostly don't think about this work because it hasn't been available—until very recently, only her *New Yorker* book reviews, written between 1927 and 1933, had been collected, and that was in 1970. Her column was called "Constant Reader," a name immortalized in her review of A. A. Milne's *The House at Pooh Corner*. Pooh, she tells us, is reciting a song to Piglet which begins "The more it snows, tiddely-pom—"

> "'Tiddely what?' said Piglet." (He took, as you might say, the very words out of your correspondent's mouth.)
> "'Pom,' said Pooh. 'I put that in to make it more hummy.'"
> And it is that word "hummy," my darlings, that marks the first place in *The House at Pooh Corner* at which Tonstant Weader Fwowed up.

The thirty-one reprinted reviews range in subject from the ludicrous to the sublime. Predictably, Parker is deadly when dealing with nonsense or pretension. Her targets include Nan Britton, who wrote a tell-all book about her love affair (and illegitimate baby) with President Warren Harding; the notorious evangelist Aimee Semple McPherson; and Emily Post and her *Etiquette*. (She did not react positively to Post's suggestion that to get a conversation going with a stranger, you might try, "I'm thinking of buying a radio. Which make do you think is best?")

So she's funny. More impressive is her uncannily astute judgment. She admires Katherine Mansfield, Dashiell Hammett (she loved thrillers almost as much as she loved dogs), Ford Madox Ford's *The Good Soldier*, Hemingway's short stories (more than his novels), of course Ring Lardner, Gide's *The Counterfeiters*—"too tremendous a thing for praises.

To say of it 'Here is a magnificent novel' is rather like gazing into the Grand Canyon and remarking, 'Well, well, well; quite a slice.'"

Her most impassioned praise is reserved for Isadora Duncan. Despite calling it "abominably written," she characterized Duncan's posthumous autobiography, *My Life*, as "an enormously interesting and a profoundly moving book. Here was a great woman; a magnificent, generous, gallant, reckless, fated fool of a woman. There was never a place for her in the ranks of the terrible, slow army of the cautious. She ran ahead, where there were no paths." Parker would always rise to the challenges of greatness and of garbage; it was what fell in between that drove her crazy.

LAST YEAR THERE APPEARED a five-hundred-page collection of Parker's early drama criticism, edited by Kevin Fitzpatrick and titled *Complete Broadway, 1918–1923*. Except for half a dozen of these pieces that appear in an updated edition of the essential *Portable Dorothy Parker*, none to my knowledge has ever been reprinted, and yet not only are they wickedly funny and to the point, they unearth for us what Broadway was actually up to in that hyperactive period in the history of the American theater.

Her first piece, from April 1918, sets the tone. It covers the latest musicals and it begins in raptures about the new Wodehouse-Bolton-Kern show, *Oh, Lady! Lady!!* "Not even the presence in the first-night audience of Mr. William Randolph Hearst, wearing an American flag on his conventional black lapel, could spoil my evening."

Then things go downhill. *Girl O' Mine* was "one of those shows at which you can get a lot of knitting done." And on to *The Love Mill* and its "two hundred and fifty pounds of comedienne throwing herself into a man's arms, felling him to the earth." And finally there's *Sinbad*, the latest Al Jolson extravaganza: "Of course, I take a certain civic pride in the fact that there is probably more nudity in our own Winter Garden than there is in any other place in the world, nevertheless, there are times during an evening's entertainment when I pine for 11:15, so that I can go out in the street and see a lot of women with clothes on."

Yet even when she yields to her funny bone at the expense of some monstrosity, she finds time to praise. She may poke fun at a vast and gorgeous spectacle called *Mecca*—"It is comfortable to reflect that it gives congenial and remunerative employment to hundreds, including two exceedingly shabby camels, who, I am willing to wager, although my memory for faces is not infallible, made their debut in the world premiere of *Ben Hur* . . ."—but she goes on to say "the most important announcement is that Michel Fokine directed the dances, for they are startlingly beautiful." Who knew that the renowned choreographer of *The Firebird*, *Scheherazade*, *Petrushka*, and *Les Sylphides* had once worked side by side with camels?

It's all here right at the start of her career—the wit, the fun, the creation of "Dorothy Parker" as a character: She was determined to make a name for herself, and she did. But not at the expense of the worthy. She might deride the endless longueurs of Shaw's *Back to Methuselah*, but she's enthusiastic about his *Candida*. She's in awe at *The Hairy Ape*: "One is ashamed to place neat little bouquets of praise on this mighty conception of O'Neill's." About Karel Čapek's *R.U.R.*: "Here is a play stamped all over with the poisonous marks of the lofty-browed . . . yet it will give you just the same sort of good, homemade thrills that *The Bat* did."

After apologizing at length for her inability to enjoy Shakespeare on the stage, she notes,

> I am willing to go down to my plot in Woodlawn secure in the conviction that never has there been so fine a Hamlet as John Barrymore's. He makes the Prince of Elsinore a young and engaging man, gives him flashes of quiet, skillful humor, grips you suddenly with a glimpse of his desperate loneliness. . . . As to his sanity, you are never in a moment's doubt. You leave the theatre ready to take the thing to court, if necessary.

And in that same column of February 1923, she gives an equally ardent and convincing account of Jeanne Eagels's famous performance in the dramatization of Somerset Maugham's *Rain*: "Her voice, her intonations, her bursts of hard laughter and flaming fury—great is the least that you can call them."

Parker loves Ethel Barrymore, she loves Laurette Taylor, she loves, sometimes, Sir J. M. ("Never-Grow-Up") Barrie, she loves George M. Cohan, she's nuts about scary melodramas. For theater-history buffs, all this is catnip. For Parker-lovers, it's revelation. Yes, she gets repetitious, repeats some gags, stumbles, but in the face of Broadway 1918 to 1923, wouldn't you?

THEATER CRITICS ARE TRAPPED by opening-night schedules. Book critics can be more elastic—if they're lucky, they can pick and choose. In December 1957 Parker began writing a monthly book column for *Esquire*—monthly in name only, since getting copy out of her was anguish for the editors. (According to her biographer Marion Meade, the magazine's formidable publisher, Arnold Gingrich, viewed his job with her as "obstetrics, and often referred to the monthly operation as a 'high-forceps delivery.'")

For almost five years her column was an ornament to *Esquire*. She announced her standards in her first article, a roundup of the year's best fiction: William Faulkner is "the greatest writer we have," and she characterizes 1957 as "the year in which *The Town* appeared." She then obliterates James Gould Cozzens's *By Love Possessed*—"cold, distant, and exasperatingly patronizing"—anticipating by several weeks Dwight Macdonald's famously savage assault in *Commentary*. She highly recommends Cheever's *The Wapshot Chronicle*, Sybille Bedford's "almost terrifyingly brilliant" *A Legacy*, Nabokov's *Pnin*, and Brian Moore's *The Feast of Lupercal*. (Among the books she nixes is Waugh's *The Ordeal of Gilbert Pinfold*, which "must have been written while he was waiting for the lift to reach his floor.") And she doles out Yeses and Nos and Maybes to a host of others. She had done her work, and then some.

Some of the columns are workaday, but many are stellar—not only for the acuity of her judgments ("*Lolita* is a fine book, a distinguished book—all right, then—a great book") but for the pleasure of her writing. Because these *Esquire* pieces have never been reprinted, I will indulge myself with some extensive quotation.

About Sheilah Graham's tell-all *Beloved Infidel*, Graham lets it be known

> that of course she felt something awful after [her lover Scott Fitzgerald] died, but of course she had to go on living, and so she married and had two children—quite big children it seems, for they were old enough to hear about Scott Fitzgerald, and they asked Mommie if they weren't related to Mr. Fitzgerald, and Mommie said yes, darlings, in a way you are.
>
> I present this as the possible all-time low in American letters.

About the divine Zsa Zsa:

> It will be a black day in these grubby diggings when some stony-eyed precisionist shall enter, uninvited, and explain to me that there really *is* a Zsa Zsa Gabor. To me, the lady is a figment of mythology. In my mind, she is one with the unicorn, all shining white and gold, forever swift and lovely, immortal because fabulous. It is a simple belief, and harms no one.
>
> So it is a pleasure to me to set down here that even after a careful reading of *Zsa Zsa Gabor: My Story Written for Me by Gerold Frank* my faith is still unshattered, and Miss Gabor keeps her place in the land of faerie.

And in a review of James Thurber's *The Years with Ross*, she draws a heartfelt portrait of her old colleague and friend Harold Ross, their political differences long behind her:

> His improbabilities started with his looks. His long body seemed to be only basted together, his hair was quills upon the fretful porcupine, his teeth were Stonehenge, his clothes looked as if they had been brought up by somebody else. Poker-faced he was not. Expressions,

sometimes several at a time, would race across his countenance, and always, especially when he thought no one was looking, not the brow alone but the whole expanse would be corrugated by his worries over his bitch-mistress, his magazine.

This is Parker prose at its absolute finest—and another example of how her take on things is almost inevitably personal rather than analytical.

The saddest and most telling moment in her five-year run at *Esquire* comes at the very end of a discussion of a book about James McNeill Whistler and his circle. She is writing this in 1960, and she is sixty-six. She talks of Whistler, Rossetti, Swinburne, Wilde. "There were giants in those days," she remarks. "And fools talk about the round table at the Algonquin!"

Dorothy Parker was too smart to buy the legend and too clear-headed to slide into nostalgia. That left her having to acknowledge some bitter realities. If only she hadn't won celebrity so early and so easily. If only she had been blessed with Hemingway's talent, had written her novel (and it had been any good), hadn't succumbed to the easy life and money of Hollywood. If only she had married Mr. Right instead of lumbering herself with all those Mr. Wrongs. If she had had that baby . . .

She was too sensible to live in regret, but she certainly understood how much of her life she had spent carousing and just fooling around. The tragedy of Dorothy Parker, it seems to me, isn't that she succumbed to alcoholism or died essentially alone. It was that she was too intelligent to believe that she had made the most of herself.

The New York Review of Books
APRIL 7, 2016

The Genius

THOMAS WOLFE

T HE MOVIE *Genius*, which recently came and went with predictable celerity, is an earnest attempt to track the relationship between Thomas Wolfe and his famous editor, Maxwell Perkins, by turning it into a high-flown literary bromance: boy meets man, soul meets soul, deeply needy young writer bonds with melancholic son-less editor (he has five daughters), boy rejects man as the Oedipal dynamic inexorably has its way, boy dies, yet love and trust prevail even unto—and beyond—death. "It's a true story," the movie announces right at the start, and most of the "facts" are close enough to accurate, give or take a little exaggeration. Nor do we expect biopics to cling neurotically to mere data—the crucial thing for a commercial movie is "story," not "true."

But true or false, this story could never have stood much chance at the box office. Who could have believed that the relationship between Wolfe and Perkins would find an audience today? I saw *Genius* twice, at two different Manhattan theaters, and if there were any people in the house under sixty-five, I didn't spot them. And there weren't many *over* sixty-five, either.

The reality is that Thomas Wolfe has gone over the cultural cliff. From the 1930s through the 1950s—maybe a little longer—his *Look Homeward, Angel* was a rite of passage for sensitive literary adolescents (mostly boys, though some girls, too). In 1957, a play based on it and starring Anthony Perkins as young Eugene Gant played on Broadway for well over a year and won the Pulitzer Prize. But by the 1960s, the sardonic *Catcher in the Rye* had become the go-to novel for sensitive adolescents: a very different kettle of angst from the overwrought prose of

Colin Firth as Max Perkins and Jude Law as Thomas Wolfe in *Genius*

Wolfe's famous book, and a lot shorter. Yet the myth of Wolfe's short, dramatic life, and of his relationship with the exemplary Perkins, hung on, reinvigorated when in 1978 the young A. Scott Berg published his highly regarded biography of Perkins. Berg, as it happens, is one of the six "Executive Producers" of *Genius*, and the script is officially based on his book. Don't you ever wonder what executive producers execute?

I myself came upon *Look Homeward, Angel* at the appropriate moment in my life—I was fourteen or fifteen—and it stunned me. No matter that Wolfe's Eugene Gant grew up as part of a cluttered family in North Carolina, his father (like Wolfe's) a stonecutter, and I grew up an only child in New York, my father a lawyer: We both had suffered! What's more—and this is the embarrassing part—I was deeply affected by Wolfe's rhapsodizing style. Can I really have thrilled to such writing as "life unscales its rusty weathered pelt, and earth wells out in tender exhaustless strength, and the cup of a man's heart runs over with dateless expectancy, tongueless promise, indefinable desire"? What could I have made of "the earth was spermy for him like a big woman"? I take comfort in reminding myself that the nonpareil Perkins had thrilled to it as well, and Perkins was not only a great editor but an adult. Fortunately for me, within a year I had encountered and absorbed the antidote to Wolfe: Jane Austen's *Emma*.

AND YET, this is not totally fair to *Look Homeward, Angel*. Rereading it, I see real virtues—a voice that, however out of control, is sincere, rich, and, sometimes, moving; a considerable gift for descriptive prose; and a mind driven by fervent intellectual curiosity. The unendurable verbal torrent, the unbearable self-dramatizing—these are distorted reflections of the serious intentions and ardent convictions of a talented if wholly unsophisticated adolescent mentality. No wonder so many adolescents rose to the occasion. When Max Perkins first read Wolfe's manuscript, he had no doubts about the largeness of his new writer's talent. And as he got to know Wolfe personally (and intensely: There was no other way to know him), he grew more and more taken by the young man himself.

Wolfe was twenty-nine when *Look Homeward, Angel* was published after an exhausting editorial process throughout which the editor proceeded with his habitual modesty and tact and the writer (at least at first) responded with intoxicated eagerness. Describing it all to Margaret Roberts in a letter so long it might have tried the patience even of this doting former teacher, he told her that at the first meeting of editor and author, Max "began cautiously on the book" but then went on to say that the book was "new and original" and that "these people . . . were 'magnificent'—as real as any people he had ever read of." This from the celebrated editor of Fitzgerald and Hemingway! Naturally, young Tom had been "wild with excitement."

In the event, some ninety thousand words were stripped from the book, which nevertheless weighed in at well over five hundred pages when it was published in the fall of 1929, instantly elevating Wolfe to the higher ranks of contemporary American writers. Yes, there were blemishes on this sprawling bildungsroman, but the general view was that the talent was prodigious, the ambition immense, the future limitless. And Wolfe himself was so *different*—not only an unlicked provincial despite his three years spent under George Pierce Baker, the famous professor of drama at Harvard, but physically so extraordinary: unkempt, clumsy, six feet four inches tall—a mountain of a young man, a phenomenon. The notion of genius was in the air.

Actually, it had been in the air for some time. David Herbert Donald, Wolfe's biographer, tells us that in college he was talked about as "an eccentric genius," and Professor Baker referred to him as "a genius somewhat out of control." Madeleine Boyd, the neophyte literary agent who steered him to Scribner's, reading the manuscript of *Look Homeward, Angel* for the first time, "looked up to find that it was three in the morning. Thrilled, she began to run up and down the hall of the apartment, shouting at the top of her voice: 'A genius! I have discovered a genius!'" Even the restrained Perkins would write to him in a moment of crisis, "You are one of the few men of genius writing in English today." As for the genius himself, he wrote to his mother from Harvard, "I don't know yet what I am capable of doing but, by God, I have genius . . . and I shall yet force the inescapable fact down the throats of the rats and vermin who wait the proof."

Did Wolfe ever doubt himself? Toward the end of *Look Homeward, Angel*: "But what, said Eugene very slowly into the darkness, if I'm not a Genius? He did not ask himself the question often." And at least once he ups the stakes: In a 1928 letter to his lover, Aline Bernstein, he tells her, "I must find work that I believe in, and then I must believe in my own excellence and importance as a kind of modern Christ."

LOOK HOMEWARD, ANGEL sold well, if not spectacularly, and Wolfe was now a famous writer and a figure. The expectations for his next novel were feverish, but it would be six years before the world would see *Of Time and the River*. The problem wasn't that the author was blocked— no writer was ever less blocked than Thomas Wolfe. Tsunamis of words poured from him, all scrawled into large notebooks—perhaps five thousand words a day, day in, day out. The manuscript grew and grew, but it was formless. *Look Homeward, Angel* had been given shape by eliminating digressions that got in the way of its relatively direct if flowery account of a young man leaving home and beginning to find himself. *Of Time and the River* was writing by accretion, not trajectory—Wolfe just set down everything that occurred to him, with profuse detail and unabashed repetition. When, under Perkins's prodding, he would go off to reduce and tame the profusion, he would come back with thousands and thousands of new words, equally unstructured. If something happened, he wrote it down: genius by blogging.

Eventually Perkins insisted that Wolfe hand over the manuscript, and a few days later Tom delivered a crateful of pages, totaling five hundred thousand words—and a few days after this, brought in another five hundred thousand. Perkins dug in. Night after night, for many months, Wolfe would arrive at the Perkins apartment, Max having already put in an eight-hour day at the Scribner's offices, and the two men would toil over the manuscript, at first pleasantly enough, eventually combatively, the editor deleting, the author furnishing new material. "For instance," David Donald tells us in *Look Homeward*,

> in order to illustrate the tensions in the Gant family while Eugene was waiting to learn whether a New York producer had accepted his play, Wolfe composed an account that ran to 240 pages—about eighty thousand words, or the size of an average novel—that, covering a period of only about five minutes, recaptured every move, gesture, and word uttered in a long, and largely pointless, conversation designed to get Eliza Gant [Eugene's mother] from the kitchen of her house into a car waiting in front.

Whereas the editor knew that the book was still a hopelessly unwieldy morass, the author was certain that if only he were allowed six *more* months (and Lord knows how many more words), he would have the book he had always intended. The struggle continued until at last Perkins decided that he could start readying at least the first third of the manuscript for publication. Dispirited, Wolfe lost interest, the depleted Perkins could do no more, and *Of Time and the River*, in all its lack of structure and focus and with an inconclusive ending, went on sale in 1935, a mere 912 pages in length.

Critics again heralded Wolfe's large talents, comparing him to Dickens, Rabelais, Melville, Whitman, Joyce, Proust, and more, yet coming down hard on his all too obvious flaws. Clifton Fadiman in *The New Yorker* found his style "wondrous, Elizabethan" at its best, but at its worst "hyperthyroid and afflicted with elephantiasis." Malcolm Cowley in *The New Republic* found that despite the novel's tremendous virtues, all too much of it was "possibly worse than anything that any other reputable American novelist has permitted himself to publish."

Wolfe had got out of town before the book was published—off on one of his seven sojourns in Europe. He was startled and relieved by the generally admiring attention *Of Time and the River* was receiving back home, and the fact that it was turning into a considerable commercial success (number-three fiction seller for the year). When on his return he was met by Perkins at the dock, he swept up his usually decorous editor and they rampaged through the night, actually climbing up a fire escape to break into the scruffy loft apartment in which he had written most of *Angel*. It was, he was to say, the happiest day of his life. And no doubt one of Max's happiest, too. The bromance was in full bloom.

Of course this escapade features prominently in *Genius*, and why not? Not many dramatic incidents capable of being exploited on film punctuate the relationship between a writer and an editor. In place of drama, the movie gives us a good deal of weather. Apparently it was always raining in New York in the 1920s and 1930s, beginning with the rain that's pouring down on young Tom as he squelches up and down Fifth Avenue, bracing himself to enter the Scribner's building for the first time. And even when it isn't raining, it's dark, indoors and out—how Perkins could read in his gloomy office is a mystery.

ODDLY, *GENIUS* IS A BRITISH PRODUCTION, not one of its stars American. Tom is played by Jude Law, who despite being short and slight rather than hulking gives the film's finest performance, unerringly capturing Wolfe's intensity and passion and charm. Max is efficiently impersonated by Colin Firth, but Perkins was the opposite of a dramatic personality, and his inner conflicts don't provide Firth with much to do except sport the fedora that Max was famous for wearing even at the dinner table. Finally, and most bizarrely, Aline Bernstein—well into her forties when she first meets Tom, a warmhearted, plumpish Jewish New York success story—is played by the Australian Nicole Kidman at her frostiest. What were they dreaming of?

When Max meets Tom's boat on that day in 1935 he's forced to report that Aline, whom he'd barely encountered before, had recently turned up in the Scribner's offices and made a scene, threatening to create trouble if Tom writes about their affair to the distress of her family. During their confrontation, Aline may or may not have mentioned a gun—Max, hard of hearing, thought she may have, but went on to qualify that he wasn't sure whether she intended to use it on him, Tom, or herself. Needless to say, in *Genius* the unverified gun is front and center. The bromance has become a noir triangle.

Maxwell Perkins was not a man prepared by temperament or inclination to participate in high drama. He had his idiosyncrasies, but the surface of his days was essentially unruffled: work, work, work—in the office, on the commuter train, at home. Even so, his emotional life was not unruffled. His wife, Louise, was a difficulty—he had damaged their marriage at the start by forbidding her the career in the theater that she longed for, and now she was both dabbling in the outskirts of the theater world and, to his rock-ribbed Yankee-Episcopal vexation, turning to Catholicism for comfort, while to *her* vexation, she was watching her husband more or less adopt Tom as a sixth Perkins child.

There were Max's other "children," too: fragile Scott Fitzgerald, whom Max loved and struggled to support and protect, and Hemingway, wayward and ornery, perhaps, but at first supportive of Wolfe. (Later, he would refer to him as "a glandular giant with the brains and the guts of three mice" and "the over-bloated Lil Abner of literature.") Both Scott (Zelda in tow) and "Hem" are given embarrassing cameos in *Genius*. On the other hand, the happy relationship between Max and his five girls is charmingly represented in the movie, even if there's a touch of *Life with Father* to their encounters. If you want to love Max Perkins as well as admire him, dip into *Father to Daughter*, a collection of his letters to his little girls. One letter perhaps can stand for all, this one to six-year-old Elizabeth from a trip abroad in 1920:

> E, a daddy can't have any fun without his children. There is no use his trying. Everywhere he goes he thinks, "Yes, this would be fun if only my little girls were here; but what good is it without them."—He can't get them out of his head. He may go to see statues of something, but they are not what he really sees:—he sees his little girls, playing, far away.—But when he gets their letter, then he is happy.
>
> Daddy

The relationship between the mutually devoted Max and Tom began to fray seriously in the wake of *Of Time and the River*, Tom driven to break free of the mentor/father who was also the closest friend he'd ever had. A catalytic agent was a brutal attack in 1936 by the esteemed Bernard DeVoto in *The Saturday Review of Literature*. Wolfe, DeVoto wrote, was an "astonishingly immature" writer who had "mastered neither the psychic material out of which a novel is made nor the technique of writing fiction. . . . However useful genius may be in the writing of novels, it is not enough in itself." Most shattering to Tom was the explicit allegation that it was Perkins who was really responsible for his success. Max came to think that this charge, gnawing at Tom's precarious ego, was what ultimately led him "to believe he must prove that I was not necessary to him."

To leave Scribner's or not to leave—for well over a year the question hung in the air, Tom torturing both Max and himself with agonized discussions about his publishing future. The ultra-patient Perkins finally snapped: "If you *must* leave Scribner's, go ahead and leave, but for heaven's sake, *don't talk about it anymore!*" In November 1937, Tom formally left—signing a contract with a young editor, Edward Aswell, at Harper and Brothers, but not before sending Max a twelve-thousand-word letter explaining and defending himself—a letter that devastated Perkins, but to which he replied with his customary understanding and sympathy. And the writer and his former editor went on spending time together, each of them repeatedly expressing the loving admiration he felt for the other. Awkwardly, in his will Tom made Max the executor and trustee of his estate, so that when he died the grieving and conflicted Perkins was left in the unhappy position of overseeing Aswell as he dealt with the mountain of material Wolfe had left behind.

NO ONE WAS LESS SURPRISED by Tom abandoning Max than Aline Bernstein, who in 1930 had presciently written to Tom, "Some day your friend Mr. Perkins when he suffers at your hand the way I do now, will find you out. If you can hurt a dear friend once, you will do it again." But then Aline, even at the height of her passion for Tom, had always seen him clearly. The two of them had met on a ship returning from Europe in 1925, were instantly smitten with each other, and soon fell into the most passionate relationship either would ever experience. Yet Aline was, and remained, contentedly married to a successful and wealthy stockbroker by whom she had a son and a daughter only a few years younger than Tom.

She was also a leading figure in the New York theater world, one of the two or three most admired set and costume designers of her time, working through the decades for New York's most distinguished directors and stars, from Eva Le Gallienne's Civic Repertory Company to Tallulah Bankhead in *The Little Foxes*, even Balanchine's 1946 production of Ravel's *The Spellbound Child*. She was a byword for distinction—as well as the first woman to be accepted into the tough Brotherhood of Painters, Decorators, and Paperhangers.

She was also elegant, a perfect hostess, a virtuoso cook, and devoted to her family, whereas Tom was an indigent, unpublished, rough-mannered twenty-four-year-old, twenty years her junior. It didn't matter: The sexual pull between them was overwhelming. Her love for him was total, open, and distressingly self-abnegating, while he adored her—and abused her. During the years in which he was becoming a novelist, she helped him stay financially afloat, slept with him, made his meals, and revealed herself to him completely, fully aware that he would one day use her life (and her) as "material." When *Look*

Homeward, Angel was published, the dedication read "For A.B.," but in the copy he presented to her, Tom wrote beneath the dedication:

> To Aline Bernstein[:]
>
> On my 29th birthday, I present her with this, the first copy of my first book. This book was written because of her and was dedicated to her. At a time when my life seemed desolate, and when I had little faith in myself, I met her. She brought me friendship, material and spiritual relief, and love such as I never had before. I hope therefore that readers of my book will find at least part of it worthy of such a woman.

But by then he was already withdrawing. The next years were terrible for her, as she yearned for him physically and then for his mere presence in her life. He avoided her, wrote ugly letters to her, yet couldn't make a conclusive break—the emotional dependency was as strong as the original sexual impulse had been. In 1931 he wrote to her, "I shall love you all the days of my life, and when I die, if they cut me open they will find one name written on my brain and on my heart. It will be yours. I have spoken the living truth here, and I sign my name for anyone to see. Tom Wolfe." He wouldn't return to her, though. In the three works of fiction Aline wrote during the 1930s, she gives three versions of their relationship, one of them—the first-rate *The Journey Down*—a powerful and moving account of her slow and painful recovery from a failed suicide attempt.

THE UGLIEST, SICKEST ASPECT of the relationship was Tom's obsessive vision of Aline as "my Jew." He both found it sexy that she was Jewish and hated and feared her Jewishness. From *The Web and the Rock*, about the Aline character, Esther Jack:

> Fixed in an arrogant power, her face as he saw it then flamed like a strange and opulent jewel. . . . He saw a dark regiment of Jewish women in their lavish beauty, their faces melting into honey, their eyes glowing, their breasts like melons. . . . They were the living rack on which

the trembling backs of all their Christian lovers had been broken, the living cross on which the flesh and marrow of Christian men had been crucified.

Aline was not the only Jew he struck out at. His New York is filled with Jews—it's Jew-ridden. In the short story "Death the Proud Brother" we find "a little gray-faced Jew, with a big nose, screwy and greasy-looking hair, that roached backward from his painful and reptilian brow"; "an assertive and knowing-looking Jew, with a large nose, an aggressive voice, and a vulturesque smile"; and more. Yet not all Jews are caricatured or derided; indeed, one of his most effective stories is "I Have a Thing to Tell You," a barely fictionalized account, published in *The New Republic*, of a horrifying incident he had witnessed in Nazi Germany when a middle-aged Jewish man was torn from a railway car while trying to leave the country.

Although as the 1930s progressed Tom's social consciousness was expanding, his personal behavior was deteriorating. We learn from Carole Klein's revealing biography of Aline (1979) that one night in 1937 she was summoned to the lobby of the Gotham Hotel where Tom, wildly drunk, was demanding to see her. "He started the most awful row about the Jews," she wrote to her great friend the playwright Bella Spewack (*Boy Meets Girl, Kiss Me, Kate*), denouncing the entire race who "should be wiped off the face of the earth" and shouting "Three cheers for Hitler! Three cheers for Hitler!" "Bella . . . do you know what I did? I landed out [*sic*] and punched Tom in the nose!" He was so drunk he fell to the floor, and Aline had him thrown out of the building. "It was the most sickening experience of my life." His rabid anti-Semitism, you won't be surprised to hear, is not featured in *Genius*.

Tom's deep confusion about Aline was exacerbated by his identification of her with the sophisticated New York literary and theater worlds that enraged him and that he clearly also envied: His later work is permeated with tantrums about

the fine horse-manure with which we have allowed ourselves to be bored, maddened, whiff-sniffed, hound-and-hornered, nationed, new-republicked, dialed, spectatored, mercuried, storied, anviled, new-massed, new-yorkered, vogued, vanity-faired, timed, broomed, transitioned, and generally shat upon by the elegant, refined, and snob-ified Concentrated Blotters of the Arts. . . . He was none of your little franky-panky, seldesey-weldesey, cowley-wowley, . . . steiny-weiny, goldy-woldly, sneer-puss fellows. . . .

But the heart of his anguish about her lies in his conflicted psyche. He is insanely in love, sexually besotted, and in Oedipal terror. She is Helen of Troy, she is Penelope, but she is also, he tells her, "my grey haired wide hipped timeless mother." In his draft for *The Web and the Rock*, the Tom character asks the Aline character, "Am I your child?" "Yes," she answers, "yes." "Are these my breasts?" "Yes," she replies. "Have you any milk there for me?" When she tells him no, he snorts, "Hah, . . . if you really loved me, you would have milk for me." "My heart is smothering in its love for you," he writes to her. "You are the most precious thing in my life, but you are imprisoned in a jungle of thorns, and I cannot come near you without bleeding." Here is vagina dentata tooth and claw—surely a textbook lesson in psychopathology.

David Herbert Donald in his biography comments:

In some ways he always remained an infant—as an adult, a gigantic infant, to be sure—unwilling to give up its mother's breast. He desired to devour everything in sight, whether it was mountains of food or libraries of books. He had grandiose fantasies of unlimited success, power, brilliance, and endless love. In other ways he was always a small boy—unable to drive a car or to use a typewriter, unwilling to bathe regularly, uninterested in keeping his clothes clean.

Self-absorbed, he took a childish pleasure in the functioning of his own body. Even as a man he felt great satisfaction when he had a bowel movement. . . . Even as an adult he continued to play with his genitals. . . .

Feeling unloved by both of his parents, Wolfe grew up with an insatiable need for recognition and praise and with an extraordinary sensitivity to criticism of any kind. At the same time his sense that his mother and his father had failed him produced in Wolfe, as it does in other narcissistic personalities, an urgent "need to reunite with a powerful and nourishing figure" who could take their place.

And so he adopted Max and Aline as alternative parents to his larger-than-life but distant father and his tenacious, grasping mother, only in the long run to reject them, too.

AFTER DISMISSING MAX and depositing at least a million words with Aswell, Tom started traveling—south to home, west to explore. By the time he was roaming around the Northwest, his health had utterly collapsed: He had pneumonia on top of a dangerous tubercular condition. Brought east by train, he was admitted to Johns Hopkins, where it quickly became clear that he was dying, although in a final (futile) gesture, the doctors trepanned his skull. He died shortly before his thirty-eighth birthday, in September 1938. At the hospital were his mother, two of his siblings, Aswell, his agent Elizabeth Nowell, and Max. Aline had been told that her presence would outrage the family, who loathed her. Afterward, Aswell tried to assuage her grief by reporting that Tom's last words were of her. His eyes searching the room, he had whispered, "Where's Aline . . . I want Aline . . . I want my Jew." "I told him you were coming," Aswell said, "and he smiled, and lay down again."

Tom's farewell to Max was in a letter—the last he ever wrote. "No matter what happens or has happened," he wrote, "I shall always think of you and feel about you the way it was that Fourth of July day three years ago when you met me at the boat, and we went out on the café on the river and had a drink and later went on top of the tall building, and all the strangeness and the glory and the power of life and of the city was below. Yours always, Tom."

This letter was written from a hospital in Seattle some five weeks before he died in Baltimore. The *Genius* people improve on this scenario: Tom is in a final coma from which he's not expected to emerge, yet to the astonishment of the nurse attending him, his eyes flutter open and he signals her to bring him paper and pencil. Slowly, laboriously, he strives to scrawl the final loving words . . .

WHAT ARE WE LEFT WITH of Thomas Wolfe, other than the vanishing legend and the vanishing books? The sense of a monstrous prodigy, on the one hand possessed of immense energy and kindness (the Perkins girls, for instance, adored him), generous to his family, brilliantly read, but on the other hand tormented by demons, alcoholic, vainglorious, both self-destructive and destructive of others. Everything about him was huge, from his physical frame to his appetites to his emotions, and—yes—to his talent. That was real. There are splendid stories, novellas, stretches of the novels—but only when he escapes from his narcissism and looks outward rather than inward. The portrait of his mother that constitutes the somewhat Joycean novella "The Web of Earth," the portion of *Look Homeward, Angel* dealing with the death of Eugene's brother Ben, the historical sections of the unfinished *The Hills Beyond*—these justify or at least explain the fuss that was made about him, and the high expectations.

As Wolfe grew older, his writing grew less ornate and rhapsodic, more focused and disciplined. If he had lived, he might, someday, have warranted the praise heaped on him by Sinclair Lewis, who when interviewed on winning the Nobel Prize singled him out as having "a chance to be the greatest American writer," and indeed, "one of the greatest world writers."

Even, perhaps, a genius?

The New York Review of Books
DECEMBER 8, 2016

The Sensationalist

WILKIE COLLINS

THERE ARE NOVELS THAT GRIP YOU despite inconsistencies of plot, failures of tone or characterization, lack of depth—you may not even like them, but you have to go on reading: Their sheer force and urgency are irresistible. *The Three Musketeers* and *Uncle Tom's Cabin* are not *Middlemarch* or Proust, but they've thrilled generations of readers. And regardless of its distressing historical attitudes and mundane prose, *Gone with the Wind* goes on selling in the tens of thousands because Margaret Mitchell just sweeps you along.

One of the most enthralling of all popular novels is Wilkie Collins's *The Woman in White*, which began serial publication in 1859—to almost frenzied success—in *All the Year Round*, the new magazine founded and edited by his close collaborator and friend Charles Dickens. *A Tale of Two Cities* had been the cornerstone of the opening issues; *The Woman in White*, which followed it, did even better—"Queues of eager readers formed outside the offices on press days," Collins's finest biographer, Catherine Peters, reports in *The King of Inventors*. It was like the good old days of *The Old Curiosity Shop* almost twenty years earlier, when the whole world waited desperately to learn whether Dickens would really allow Little Nell to die.

There was a "Woman in White Waltz" and a "Fosco Galop" (named for the spellbinding villain, Count Fosco). There was merchandise—"Woman in White" bonnets, shawls, perfumes. And when the novel was published in book form, new readers were captivated: Gladstone canceled an evening at the theater to keep reading it; Thackeray stayed up all night to finish it. At least one of Collins's other novels rivaled it in popularity—*The Moonstone*, written a decade later—but the epitaph he devised for his tombstone reads: "Wilkie Collins—Author of *The Woman in White* and other works of fiction." He knew.

Collins was thirty-five when he began writing *The Woman in White*, with four novels, an estimable biography, a great deal of excellent journalism, and two successful collections of short stories behind him; his reputation was rapidly growing. But the new book instantly placed him among the leading novelists of the day.

His first novel, *Antonina; or, The Fall of Rome*, was a mishmash—an "impossibly melodramatic and impossibly dull" rip-off of Bulwer-Lytton's *The Last Days of Pompeii*, as Dorothy Sayers called it.

His next, *Basil*, was so much better than *Antonina*—and so different—that it's hard to believe they're by the same writer. *Basil* is markedly personal in tone—the story of an upper-class young man who disastrously falls in love at first sight with a young woman, from a lower class, whom he encounters on a bus, and who deceives him and blights his life. It's a stab at realism, and it was much admired: Dickens, for instance, foreseeing a major career for its author, praised its "admirable writing" and "delicate discrimination of character." In *Wilkie Collins*, Collins's latest biographer, the prodigious Peter Ackroyd, with his bent for hyperbole, calls it "a novel of fatality and obsession that might almost earn a place beside the great Russian novels of love and madness." Sorry, Mr. Ackroyd, but not even "almost." Yet it remains readable both for its realistic surface account of London life, anticipating George Gissing, and for its highly charged melodrama. It's very, very far from Dostoevsky, but it's a respectable precursor of Somerset Maugham's *Of Human Bondage*.

THESE AND COLLINS'S OTHER EARLY VENTURES into fiction reveal a hardworking, highly capable craftsman, but one still in search of his true métier. With the first installment of *The Woman in White*, his essential style and power broke through. Dickens (himself no slouch in the hyperbole department) hailed it as one of the two most dramatic scenes in literature, the other being the march of the women to Versailles in Carlyle's *The French Revolution*.

Walter Hartright, Collins's hero, is walking alone through London, late at night,

> when, in one moment, every drop of blood in my body was brought to a stop by the touch of a hand laid lightly and suddenly on my shoulder from behind me.
>
> I turned on the instant, with my fingers tightening round the handle of my stick.
>
> There, in the middle of the broad, bright high-road—there, as if it had that moment sprung out of the earth or dropped from the heaven— stood the figure of a solitary Woman, dressed from head to foot in white garments; her face bent in grave inquiry on mine, her hand pointing to the dark cloud over London, as I faced her.

From here the novel rushes forward, inexorably unspooling its riveting story of mistaken identity, faked death, kidnapping, conspiracy, and lunatic asylums, all revealed in a series of interlocking narratives by the characters themselves, and all convincing because the voices are so natural; so *normal*. Nothing here of the high Gothic nonsense of Ann Radcliffe, Horace Walpole, and "Monk" Lewis, but a patina of domesticity laid over a cruel and vicious story. Henry James gave credit to Collins for "introducing into fiction those most mysterious of mysteries, the mysteries that are at our own doors. . . . Instead of the terrors of Udolpho we were treated to the terrors of the cheerful country house, or the London lodgings. And there is no doubt that these were infinitely the more terrible."

Collins is generally regarded as the inventor of what came to be known as the "sensation novel"—a contemporary story crammed with lurid incidents and constantly building in suspense. (His principle in writing fiction, he liked to say, was "Make 'em cry, make 'em laugh, make 'em wait.") At its most extreme, the melodrama is out of control, as in one of his later—and worst—novels, *The Two Destinies*, about which *The Saturday Review* said: "This is an amazingly silly book. . . . It records, if we have counted rightly, three attempts at suicide, two plots to murder, one case of bigamy, two bankruptcies, one sanguinary attack by Indians, three visions, numberless dreams, and one shipwreck."

But his four most considerable works compel belief because they're anchored in credible characters and consummately crafted plots. And in *The Moonstone* there is practically no "sensation" at all. Instead, we identify it as the grandfather of all detective novels, featuring, as it does, a baffling crime, a handful of plausible suspects, a startling yet logical solution, and a perfectly conceived venue: an isolated English country house, complete with loyal old family retainer and ex-convict maid. Again, you accept the complicated story because you believe the voices of the narrators, from the mercurial hero to the elderly Gabriel Betteredge (with his conviction that everything worth knowing can be found in the pages of *Robinson Crusoe*), to the maddening religious crank Miss Clack. Finally, in Sergeant Cuff (with his passion for roses), based on a famous Scotland Yard investigator, Collins created the template for the thorough, unflappable detective who would dominate the genre for decades.

The Moonstone, though less febrile and turbulent than *The Woman in White*, continues to hold the reader. T. S. Eliot, who twice wrote extensively about Collins, called it "the first and greatest of English detective novels." And Dorothy Sayers (who should know) called it "probably the very finest detective novel ever written."

COLLINS—WHO BEFORE HE STARTED WRITING A NEW BOOK spent months working out, detail by detail, the intricacies of the story—has generally been seen as stronger on plot than on characterization. But what most forcefully grips the reader of *The Woman in White* are its two central and mesmerizing characters—who also mesmerize each other. Count Fosco, the villain, is corpulent, sensual, a tyrant to his wife, ruthless in pursuit of his goals, grotesquely attached to the pet canaries and white mice who run freely over his body, and with an insinuating feminine charm. The heroine is not the passive, pretty Laura Fairlie, victim of Fosco's intrigues, but her older half-sister, Marian Halcombe. When Walter Hartright first sees Marian across a room he is "struck by the rare beauty of her form, and by the unaffected grace of her attitude." When she turns toward him and begins to advance,

> the easy elegance of every movement of her limbs and body . . . set me in a flutter of expectation to see her face clearly. She left the window— and I said to myself, "The lady is dark." She moved forward a few steps—and I said to myself, "The lady is young." She approached nearer—and I said to myself (with a sense of surprise which words fail me to express), "The lady is ugly!"

But Marian—as Walter, and Fosco, and the reader will discover—is resilient and courageous, with a strong mind and a loving heart. Indeed, Fosco himself is powerfully drawn to her, while Marian is both repelled and fascinated by *him*. "Something transsexual," Catherine Peters suggests, "is hinted at" between the "feminine" count and the "masculine" Marian (with her famous trace of a mustache), whose appearance, it has been proposed, was modeled in part on George Eliot's.

Marian Halcombe is Collins's first commanding female character, but her heroism is essentially reactive, prompted by her concern for her endangered sister.

THE CENTRAL CHARACTER of *No Name*, the book that followed *The Woman in White*, is totally *pro*active. In the face of disaster, a young and cosseted gentlewoman, Magdalen Vanstone, assumes control of her life, lying, cheating, assuming a false identity—even taking to the stage!— and marrying a man she loathes (who conveniently dies), all in order to regain her situation in society. Her beloved parents, it transpires, had not been able to marry legally until shortly before her father was killed in a train crash and her mother died in childbirth. Whereupon Magdalen and her sister were, under the current laws, labeled illegitimate and brutally thrown upon the world.

Magdalen's behavior is both heroic and dismaying; we admire her boldness and audacity while nervously acknowledging that her actions border on the criminal, and are certainly far from ladylike. That she prevails—eventually marrying an admirable man who cherishes her strength of mind and purpose—is the first sign we have that Wilkie Collins's view of morality is radically different from that of his Victorian contemporaries. There is no woman in Dickens remotely like Magdalen Vanstone, and Thackeray's Becky Sharp is a conniver, not a triumphant woman warrior who can finally gloat: "I am a respectable married woman, accountable to nobody under heaven but my husband. I have got a place in the world, and a name in the world, at last. . . . [My wickedness] has made Nobody's Child, Somebody's Wife."

No Name is not only an unsettling drama centered on a powerful woman, it's also the first of Collins's agenda novels, in which he challenges Victorian legal and cultural injustices, almost always from a strongly feminist viewpoint—although he firmly resisted being labeled a feminist. ("He is the most genuinely feminist of all the 19th-century novelists," wrote Sayers, "because he is the only one capable of seeing women without sexual bias and of respecting them as human individuals in their own right, and not as 'the ladies, God bless them!'")

The Law and the Lady features a resolute and brave young woman successfully defying convention—and risking her skin—in her determination to remove the stigma of the deplorable Scottish verdict of "not proven" after her husband's trial for murdering his first wife (who—spoiler!—had actually committed suicide). *Heart and Science* is a fierce crusade against vivisection. *Man and Wife* has *two* agendas. It's an attack both on the confusing and unfair marriage laws and on the "muscular Christianity" of Charles Kingsley and his followers: The heroine, at bay, has been betrayed by the handsome young athletic luminary the world worships. (He's found out. She's saved.) *The Evil Genius* takes on divorce and the custody of children. *The Black Robe* is anti-Jesuit. *The New Magdalen* and *The Fallen Leaves* deal with redeemed, or redeemable, prostitutes. It was novels like these that prompted Swinburne's much-invoked couplet "What brought good Wilkie's genius nigh perdition? / Some demon whispered—'Wilkie! have a mission.'"

Not only did Collins's novels grow less convincing as they grew more missionary, but their melodrama grew coarser as he more and more frequently conceived them in relation to potential stage adaptations—his passion for the theater was lifelong. But he could be unconvincing even without an agenda on his mind, or a dramatization in view. *Poor Miss Finch*, written soon after *The Moonstone*, has a crackpot plot involving a rich blind girl who despite her blindness has an unconquerable aversion to the color blue; her doting suitor, Oscar, who *turns* blue from a medical procedure; and his identical-twin brother, Nugent, who also falls in love with Miss Finch. (He intrigues to marry her in place of his blue brother but—defeated and remorseful—dies on a polar expedition, "found dead," as Ruskin put it, "with his hands dropped off, in the Arctic regions.")

I can confirm that *The Woman in White* and *The Moonstone* remain irresistible, and that the other two Collins novels that can still be read with considerable pleasure are those that came between them: *No Name* and *Armadale*, his longest and most extravagantly plotted book. (T. S. Eliot wrote that *Armadale* "has no merit beyond melodrama, and it has every merit that melodrama can have.")

Peter Ackroyd, however, repudiates the idea that the great majority of Collins's novels are without real value. "All of his work remains powerful and ingenious, striking and persuasive," he sums up. "It is true that his later novels are no longer widely read, but modern taste is not impeccable." Can he and I have read the same thirty novels? This is Ackroyd at his most provocative and least plausible, comparable to the near-fanatic insistence—which mars his magisterial biography of Dickens—that, despite both the evidence and common sense, Dickens never consummated his years-long liaison with Ellen Ternan.

The hard truth is that if Collins had not written his four major novels, no one today, with or without impeccable taste, would have heard of him. His minor books are far inferior not only to the Big Four but to a number of other sensation novels of the day: Mary Elizabeth Braddon's wildly successful *Lady Audley's Secret* and *Aurora Floyd*, for instance; even Mrs. Henry Wood's *East Lynne*. Whereas within the ten-year span of his finest work, he was a major force in British fiction, remaining highly popular until the end of his life. That is enough to justify a biographer of Ackroyd's stature devoting a book to him.

WRITING ABOUT COLLINS in the late 1920s, Eliot complained that there was no "adequate biography" of him. Since then, as *The Moonstone* and *The Woman in White* have stubbornly refused to go away, the literature on him has swelled, and today there are at least a dozen substantial books, apart from Peters's and Ackroyd's, ranging from general biographies (*The Secret Life of Wilkie Collins*; *Wilkie Collins: A Life of Sensation*) to specialist academic literature (*Wilkie Collins: Women, Property and Propriety*; *Wilkie Collins's American Tour*). But it's not only Collins's achievement that has fascinated so many writers. It's also the complicated, almost brazenly unconventional life he chose to lead—and that he got away with.

His father, William Collins, through heroic diligence rather than extraordinary talent, became one of England's most successful painters. He was a benign and loving parent, though somewhat strict and relentlessly narrow-minded in religious matters. (He "would not shake hands with a Unitarian"!) And he adored his wife, Harriet, a clever, fun-loving, sociable woman of relatively good birth who had once worked as a governess. After her husband's death she remained the central figure in the lives of her two sons, who made their official home with her well into their adulthood.

But Wilkie was also out on the town. After a desultory dip into the legal profession—disappointing his father, who had hoped he would go into the church—he flirted with painting but soon realized that what he wanted to do was write. Soon enough, when he was only twenty-four, he published a very well received two-volume biography of his father that launched him into the London literary world. At the same time, he was launching himself into the life of a young voluptuary, having (he boasted to Dickens) enjoyed his first sexual adventure with a much older woman when he was thirteen or so while the family was living temporarily in Italy. Was it true?

Certainly Wilkie admired women, pursued women, and succeeded with women, despite the fact that he was physically unprepossessing—quite short and (writes Catherine Peters) "oddly disproportioned, with a bulging forehead, head too large for his body, short arms and legs and 'pretty little hands and feet, very like a woman's.'" It was his charm and vivacity that attracted women to him, plus their appreciation of how much he appreciated *them*.

His unembarrassed sexual activity—to one correspondent he wrote, "I have had between 40 and 50 years Experience of women of all sorts and sizes"—was one of the many things about him that appealed to Dickens, who was not only twelve years older than he was but, pub-licly, far more straitlaced. The aggressively domestic Dickens relished adventuring with Wilkie both on their long nighttime traipses through the slums of London and on their stays together in Paris, where lads could be lads, even though Dickens was a lad with ten children. The relationship between the two men was crucial for Wilkie—Dickens would become mentor, intimate friend, collaborator (they wrote plays and fiction together), boss (when Wilkie worked as well as wrote for *All the Year Round*), and publisher. They also became related by marriage, when Wilkie's artist brother, Charley, whom he loved deeply, married Kate Dickens, her father's favorite child.

The marriage was a disaster: Charley was physically fragile and sexually ambivalent, if not asexual, and Dickens came to despise him. This did not help the Dickens–Collins friendship—Wilkie, always fiercely protective of his younger brother, began distancing himself from The Inimitable, and when Dickens died suddenly in 1870, at the age of fifty-eight, Wilkie took the death coolly. (He was certainly cool in his description of the unfinished *Edwin Drood* as "Dickens's last laboured effort, the melancholy work of a worn-out brain.")

The death he had not taken coolly was that of his mother, which had occurred two years earlier while he was struggling to finish *The Moonstone* and suffering agonies from the rheumatic gout that tormented him throughout his adult life. He was in his mid-forties when Harriet died, and again and again through the following years he would refer to her death as "the greatest sorrow" of his life. She had moved out of London sometime before dying, but by this time he had a home of his own—two homes, in fact, and two "wives."

ALMOST ALL THE MAJOR VICTORIAN NOVELISTS had irregular private lives. (Trollope was the great exception: He lived, apparently happily, with his wife until he died, and we know almost nothing about her.) Bulwer-Lytton so hated his wife that he once had her confined to a lunatic asylum. Thackeray's wife, depressed and suicidal, spent most of her life in an institution. George Eliot lived in solemn sin with the married George Henry Lewes, whom, due to the complicated divorce laws, she couldn't marry. About Dickens's double life and wreck of a marriage we now know a great deal.

But Wilkie Collins was violently opposed to marriage, so that his double life was both more and less scandalous than the others. He simply practiced what amounted to legal bigamy, setting up two women in separate establishments, each knowing about the other and knowing about (and known to) his friends. To his male friends, that is: Neither Caroline Graves, who lived with him on and off for more than thirty years, nor Martha Rudd, who came along later and bore him three children, could be acknowledged by the ladies of his acquaintance, beginning with his mother. Harriet Collins had simply refused to acknowledge the existence of Caroline, a respectable and intelligent lower-class woman who acted as Wilkie's hostess, dined out and traveled with him, and was a recognized and constant part of his life—more a common-law wife than a disreputable mistress, as Catherine Peters puts it.

When they met, Caroline was a widow with a young child whom Wilkie raised, educated, and loved. In later years, this girl, Carrie, functioned as his secretary—he even dictated parts of his later novels to her—and he gave her in marriage to a young attorney whom he then (disastrously) employed. Wilkie spoke of Carrie as his adopted daughter, and she and her children remained central to his life.

The most dramatic story told about Wilkie has to do with his first encounter with Caroline Graves. Supposedly, he, Charley, and their great friend the artist John Everett Millais were walking through the streets late one night when a woman—dressed, of course, in white—darted out of a house in terror and fled into the dark. Wilkie, consumed with curiosity, followed her and claimed her.

This story, so conveniently reflecting the opening of *The Woman in White*, seems to have no basis in fact—it was spun by Millais's son years after all the players in the drama were dead. More prosaically, it appears that when she and Wilkie met, Caroline was running a small marine shop near where the Collins family lived.

The origins of Martha Rudd are equally obscure. The daughter of a shepherd, she came from a small fishing village in Norfolk where Wilkie often spent time sailing, and where he discovered her and attached her to himself, again for life. (It's also been suggested that he came upon her when she was working as a housemaid in his mother's home—to me, a more plausible story.) Martha was an attractive young woman, modest, capable, and practical, who seems not to have minded her irregular situation—no doubt she saw it as a big step up in the world: a good man, a famous man, security, affection. Certainly Wilkie treated her generously, lived with her—often under an assumed name—when he wasn't living with Caroline, and loved their children.

Although the two "wives" probably never met, Martha's children mingled happily with Caroline and with Carrie's children, and they were all treated equally and fairly in Wilkie's will. After Wilkie died, Ackroyd tells us, Caroline "took care of the grave at Kensal Green until her own death in 1895 placed her in the same earth. Martha Rudd then tended the grave until her death in 1919." So who are we to bridle at these unusual arrangements?

WILKIE'S OPENLY UNORTHODOX DOMESTIC LIFE, his peculiar appearance ("flamboyant . . . eccentric rather than dandyish"), and his championship of unpopular causes in his novels all went to sustain what Peters calls his "more or less conscious decision to be not quite a gentleman." But none of this had a negative effect on those who knew him. He had to an abundant degree the gift of being loved—by colleagues and friends, by men and women, by young and old. Nina Lehmann, a first-rate pianist and for decades with her husband at the center of London artistic life, said of him and the twenty years of what she called their "steady friendship": "always the same, always kind, always earnest, always interested, always true, always loving and faithful . . . I value my Wilkie and I love him dearly." Her son, Rudy, reminisced about "our dear old Wilkie Collins, the kindest and best friend that boy or man ever had." Even George Eliot was conquered, remarking on "a sturdy uprightness about him that makes all opinion and all occupation respectable."

When Wilkie died, in 1889, at the age of sixty-five, his health had entirely given way from the combination of his agonizing arthritic gout and the immense amount of laudanum (a liquid tincture of opium) that he had taken through the years to combat the pain. He was unable to finish his final novel (his friend Walter Besant did it for him), and one feels he was surprised that he had survived as long as he had. He had no reason, however, to regret his life: He had successfully flouted convention, was fulfilled sexually and emotionally, and had enjoyed an immensely successful and well-rewarded career from start to finish.

Of course we recognize the limits of his accomplishment—Dickens, wrote T. S. Eliot, is "separated from Collins by the difference between pure unaccountable genius and pure consummate talent." But to be mentioned in the same breath with Dickens is a remarkable tribute. As Dorothy Sayers put it, "When we have said that he cannot equal the giants of his age, the fact remains that it is with giants that we compare him."

The New York Review of Books
JUNE 8, 2017

A Russian Classic Revisited

ONE OF THE ADVANTAGES of getting old—and, believe it or not, there are others—is that you get to reread (and sometimes re-reread) books that you first knew sixty or more years earlier. Some writers are always with us—Jane Austen, for instance, for people like me; some books we may go back to every decade or two: *War and Peace, Anna Karenina, The Idiot*—an admired new translation may spur us on; *Middlemarch, Moby-Dick,* Proust. But other remarkable works drop out of sight, if not out of mind.

Very recently, after playing with the idea for half a dozen years, I went back to one of the most famous of all Russian novels, Ivan Goncharov's *Oblomov,* a book that all too many Western readers, if they know about it at all, think of as the novel about a man who never gets out of bed. They're right in one sense: It's the central figure of Ilya Ilyich Oblomov who for more than one hundred fifty years has supplied Russia with a word for an apparently fundamental quality of the Russian identity: *oblomovshchina.* Which is the state of being like Oblomov—a man, a member of the landed gentry, who is so without strength of will or purpose that he simply does nothing.

Though he *does* get out of bed—sort of. His serf-servant Zakhar, one of the major comic characters of literature, helps him put on his stockings and boots and attends to his basic needs, but he's as lazy as his master. Yet Zakhar is shrewd in his peasant way, whereas Oblomov is the opposite of shrewd: He's a sublime innocent, completely without guile and without protection from the predatory people who surround him. He's far from stupid, he's educated, his looks are appealing, his estate (which he never visits) provides him with enough to live on, although he's being robbed blind. He just lacks all energy, and his placid good nature protects him from suspicions, resentments, or ambitions. In other words, he's a hopeless case—and a beautiful soul.

His great friend Stolz is his exact opposite—dynamic, tireless, indefatigable. (Well, of course: He's half German.) While Oblomov hardly ever strays from his bed, his sofa, and his dressing gown, Stolz is rushing around the country, around Europe, in a whirlwind of productive activity, every once in a while coming home to St. Petersburg to prod and poke his friend into doing . . . something. Anything. *Go to your estate and fix it up; come to Europe with me; get back into society.* Oblomov would obey if he only could, but he can't: *Yes, of course you're right, Stolz—but not now.* And then, through his friend, he encounters a woman who rouses his ardor: the beautiful, intelligent, soulful Olga. Can she really love him back? Can it be true that she will marry him? It *is* true, and he is incandescent with happiness. Except that he ponders, hesitates, procrastinates, postpones. And Olga is a young woman in love with life, with a passion for seeing, doing, seeking. Before it's too late she steps back, anguished but clear-minded, and eventually finds in Stolz himself the man she can spend her life with. Though even in her happiness with him she is questioning her purpose, almost abandoning herself to an insidious (Russian?) melancholy, from which he determinedly succeeds in rescuing her.

Whereas the nineteenth-century European novel is almost dominated by women toying with, or surrendering to, adultery, Olga is a woman toying with despair. What is life about? What is it for? How to live it? She isn't political—she isn't going to become a bomb-throwing anarchist. She isn't driven intellectually or artistically—a George Sand, say. She's the opposite of socially ambitious. She may be the first woman in fiction to find herself in the grip of what we would call an existential crisis. The second major strand of *Oblomov* is the desperate, painful evolution she forces herself to experience, in contrast to the hero's resistance to *all* evolution—indeed, to all action.

In their marital happiness, Stolz and Olga go about their busy, productive life together, almost forgetting their great friend. Stolz has rescued Oblomov from the predatory crooks who have been robbing him, but years go by with no contact between them—Stolz is so busy, Oblomov is so lazy. But eventually husband and wife go to St. Petersburg to bring Oblomov back into their lives. And find him exactly where they left him, comfortably established in his old apartment, and more or less married to the loving and worshipful landlady whose sexy bare elbows and exquisite cooking provide him with all he wants and needs in life. He has rediscovered the secure and undemanding world of his childhood, in which he takes for granted everything that is unstintingly done for him; he's re-created the world of *oblomovshchina*. At least, though, he's managed to father a little boy, named for Stolz, whom Stolz carries away to be raised by him and Olga and presumably infused with their own life-force. Yet much as they deplore Oblomov's failure of vitality and stamina, the Stolzes never cease honoring his "pure, pure heart." His, says Stolz, "is a transparent, incorruptible soul." A Russian soul.

I must be Russian. There's a side of me that could happily never get out of bed, given a stack of books and a good reading lamp: I'm Oblomov. But then there's the side that can't bear to be without a job to do, without something to accomplish: I'm Stolz. How did Goncharov, back in 1859, know me so well?

From the start, *Oblomov* was recognized as a masterpiece. "Goncharov is ten heads above me in talent," said Chekhov. "I am in rapture over *Oblomov* and keep rereading it," said Tolstoy. And Dostoevsky came to rank it with *Dead Souls* and *War and Peace*. Who are we to disagree?

Departures
SEPTEMBER 8, 2016

Just for the Fun of It

FIFTY BOOKS OF THE TWENTIETH CENTURY

WHAT A PECULIAR LITTLE BOOK! John Carey, Merton Professor of English Literature at Oxford and lead book critic of the *Sunday Times* of London, picks the fifty books of the twentieth century that have given him the greatest reading pleasure. These are definitely *not*, he reassures us, books reflecting anything so pretentious as "literary 'greatness,' the testimony they bear to the human spirit or anything of that kind." No, pleasure is the only guiding principle.

Who wouldn't enjoy playing this kind of game? And in *Pure Pleasure* Professor Carey, with his academic certainties and his deft journalist's touch, plays it cleverly and at times instructively. *The Great Gatsby*'s "tight little plot, simple as a Greek tragedy, radiates doubts like artificial rainbows around a fountain." *The Secret Agent* is "packed round with the ice of Conrad's irony." "If a cat could write novels, they would be like Muriel Spark's." But occasional felicities and a generally sound response to text can't disguise the superficial nature of most of these short takes—you only have to compare them to what V. S. Pritchett achieved in the same vein to realize how far literary journalism in England has lowered its sights.

And then there's the almost bizarre parochialism of Carey's choices. Is England really this narrowly self-regarding, or is he an isolated case? Of the fifty books on offer as pleasure-providers, thirty are English and several others are from the Commonwealth. France scores twice (Gide and Sartre), Russia twice (both memoirs), and Germany twice (Mann and Grass). No doubt America should be flattered with its five nominations, but what a weird selection: *Gatsby*, Eliot's Prufrock poems, Updike's *Rabbit* trilogy (word of the fourth volume has apparently not reached

Oxford), Steinbeck's *Of Mice and Men* (!), and S. J. Perelman's *The Road to Miltown* (by no means Perelman's best work, as it happens).

As it also happens, only five women have given the professor pure pleasure, all English or Commonwealth: Spark, Elizabeth Bowen, Stevie Smith, Sylvia Townsend Warner, Katherine Mansfield. No Colette, say, or—keeping to the safe side of the Channel—no Woolf (it will become clear later why). Forget Edith Wharton (American), forget Marguerite Yourcenar's *Memoirs of Hadrian* (French), for that matter forget *Gone with the Wind*.

But then *Gone with the Wind* fails another significant test: length. Apart from the *Rabbit* trilogy, *The Old Wives' Tale*, Vikram Seth's *A Suitable Boy*, and one or two others, the chosen fifty are conspicuously short. Size apparently *does* matter, but not in the usual way. Joyce is represented by the *Portrait*, not *Ulysses*; V. S. Naipaul by *The Mystic Masseur*, not *A House for Mr. Biswas*. Does Carey's reading pleasure really diminish the longer a book gets, or is this a nod to the presumed impatience of the *Sunday Times* readership? He does tell us that he's avoided "the thumping masterpieces" and "books which I do not like, or have never been able to finish"—Faulkner and Proust. (I assume that it's Faulkner he doesn't like and Proust who's just too goshdarn long.) "If you cry up unreadable books, just because they have been highly thought of in the past, you may deceive the young and innocent into trying them—and put them off reading for life." And here I've been snobbishly boosting Proust all these years, without realizing that I was endangering the future of reading!

The repetition of certain words or locutions reveals the professor's strongest feelings. *Pure Pleasure* is a not-very-covert attack on the highbrow, the literati, the intellectual. No, it's not Faulkner or Proust (or Nabokov or James or Svevo) who truly delights us, but such staunch storytellers as Arnold Bennett and Conan Doyle and G. K. Chesterton. "If one of his highbrow contemporaries had written [*The Hound of the Baskervilles*], the Grimpen Mire would have been stuffed with symbolism.... In Doyle it is ... just a marsh, not an excuse for pretentious abstractions." "From the view point of the highbrows of his day [Arnold Bennett] committed two unforgivable sins. He came from the north of England and he made money by his writing." "The literati used to scorn Kipling for his imperialism." (What literati? Kipling has been passionately championed by T. S. Eliot, Randall Jarrell, Lincoln Kirstein, Angus Wilson, Craig Raine, et al.) "There is no denying that [Edward Thomas] is a poet of Englishness, and this has earned him the contempt of intellectuals." Katherine Mansfield "knew what it was to be cold-shouldered by the literati." Carey's anti-intellectualism masquerading as anti-snobbism is so acute, so personal, that one can only wonder whether he himself comes from the north of England and has been attacked for making money by writing.

This posture is partially justified by Carey's brilliant earlier book *The Intellectuals and the Masses: Pride and Prejudice Among the Literary Intelligentsia, 1880–1939*. It's true that once again we encounter a parochialism surprising in so educated a commentator: "The leading poets writing in English in the second half of the twentieth century, Larkin, Hughes, and Heaney"—so much for all American poetry. An allusion in Virginia Woolf to the servant problem is "quite in keeping with . . . Bloomsbury and modernism as a whole." I don't remember those notorious modernists Picasso, Balanchine, Joyce, and Stravinsky being caught up in the servant problem, but for Carey only what's English is truly real. And his need to pursue an argument to extremes backs him into treacherous corners. After praising *Ulysses* for showing "that mass man matters, that he has an inner life as complex as an intellectual's," he goes on to complain that mass man Leopold Bloom himself "would never and could never have read *Ulysses* or a book like *Ulysses*. . . . This means that there is a duplicity in Joyce's masterpiece." By this standard, we would condemn *Lassie Come-Home* because Lassie couldn't appreciate it.

But *The Intellectuals and the Masses* advances a convincing argument that prevails over all such polemical excess by identifying a line of thinking that runs from Nietzsche through the eugenicists and early fascists of Europe and the upper-class intellectuals and writers of England—Woolf, Forster, Huxley, Waugh, Greene, Clive Bell, the Irish

Yeats—to the extreme reactionary ideas of Wyndham Lewis and from there, by a short step, to *Mein Kampf.* For Carey, modernism—which he equates with obscurity—was the visceral recoil of intellectuals from the threatening growth of a literate lower-middle class that represented all those things the "elite" found disgusting: suburbanism, the popular press, the "clerks," even tinned food. By inventing a literature (and a music and an art) that these poor sods couldn't decipher, the "natural aristocrats" could ward off the invasion of their culture by the masses. That this is a reductive argument is clear, and the author acknowledges that it can be carried too far (though that doesn't prevent him from doing so), but the evidence he compiles through analysis and the deadly use of quotation supports his thesis and forces one to reconsider the English writers of the past century. One example will do, an excerpt from a 1941 entry in Virginia Woolf's journal: She has observed, in a restaurant, "a fat, smart woman, in red hunting cap, pearls, check skirt, consuming rich cakes. Her shabby dependent also stuffing. They ate and ate. Something scented, shoddy, parasitic about them. Where does the money come to feed these fat white slugs?" This is the violence of snobbery that lies beneath the surface of a *Mrs. Dalloway.*

Of course, England being Carey's arena, the America of *Sister Carrie*, *McTeague*, and *Main Street* doesn't occur to him as a counterbalance to the attitudes he deplores. Which is why he's left with Arnold Bennett and Conan Doyle as his heroes. Well, they're admirable, if less exalted than he makes them out to be, and his close readings of Bennett, George Gissing, and (another hero) H. G. Wells are a valuable contribution to our grasp of who they were and what they accomplished. Here the depth of attention makes up for the narrowness of vision. When, however, the focused argument of *The Intellectual and the Masses* is reduced to the self-indulgent potshots of *Pure Pleasure*, one loses confidence in the author's objectivity and judgment.

Even so, the enthusiasms of the latter book urge you back to many works you already know and forward into new territory—in my case, Bulgakov's *A Country Doctor's Notebook*, Sartre's *The Words*, and Edward Thomas's poems. In return, let me tip Carey off to such novels as

Junichirō Tanizaki's *The Makioka Sisters*, Salman Rushdie's *Midnight's Children*, and Vargas Llosa's *Aunt Julia and the Scriptwriter.* True, one of them is Japanese, one is Indian, and the third is Latin American, and they're definitely long. But all of them—take it from me, Professor—provide pure pleasure.

The New York Observer
2001

In the Mood for Love

ROMANCE NOVELS TODAY

He: SIMON ARTHUR HENRY FITZRANULPH BASSET, Earl Clyvedon, Duke of Hastings, whose face "put all of Michelangelo's statues to shame"—"the perfect specimen of English manhood," whose "opinion on any number of topics" is sought after by men and at whose feet "women swooned," yet whose tragic childhood has left him determined never to marry and, above all, never to father a child who might suffer as he had.

She: Lady Daphne Bridgerton, daughter of a viscount, beautiful, witty, sympathetic, bored by her conventional suitors, and yearning to have children—she's one of a happy brood of eight.

They: Meet at a ball, banter, begin to fall in love. Yet so many things keep them apart! Will he be able to conquer his demons? Will she be able to help him to? You'll have to read Julia Quinn's *The Duke and I* to find out. I can reveal this much, however: The sex is great, he "squirming with desire," she "writhing with delight."

He: Carver is a top FBI agent, determined to protect the woman he loves from a killer who's stalking her.

She: Zoe is an ex–New York cop, fed up with the corruption of the police force and now a successful private eye, not at all happy at being protected. "I don't need you to take care of me."

They: Are caught up in a spiraling thriller, danger from a psychopathic killer looming everywhere. Will she survive? More important: Will she let Carver back into her life? Go straight to Cheris Hodges's *Deadly Rumors* to find out. But, once again, the sex is great: "He licked, sucked and nibbled at her throbbing bud until she screamed his name as she came over and over again," and her "knees quivered and shook as if she were on the San Andreas Fault in the middle of an earthquake." Zoe and Carver are African Americans—you can tell from the cover. They: Are young Cameron, a single father, and young Kirstin, who works like a dog on the family ranch. We're in Montana, where we often are in books like these, unless we're in Wyoming or Colorado. Clearly, Cam and Kirstin are made for each other, and we're not kept in suspense over their fate. The *real* romance is between Cam's mother, Maddie, a famous detective-story writer who's just come through a successful bout with chemo, and Kirstin's cantankerous, aggressive, and overprotective father, Sam. She's sixty-seven, he's sixty-eight, but who's counting? Not much suspense here either, but lots of comfortable detail about food. Rugged Cam "loved to create different dishes from scratch and had an uncanny sense of what flavors complemented others." In fact, the first time Kirstin tastes his cucumber salsa she exclaims: "Recipe, please.... It would be great as a veggie dip." Everyone's problems are resolved at the big holiday dinners they all share. This cozy romance is called *The Christmas Room* and is by the popular Catherine Anderson. Her pleasingly written books have sweetly pretty covers, and this one has an extra added attraction: the author's recipe for Russian tea cookies.

THE SCORES OF ROMANCE NOVELS—perhaps hundreds, if you include the self-published ones that constitute their own phenomenon—just published or due to appear in the next few months essentially fall into two categories. There are the Regency romances (descended from the captivating Georgette Heyer, whose first one, *Regency Buck*, appeared in 1935). And there are the contemporary young-woman-finding-her-way stories that are the successors to the working-girl novels that for decades provided comfort and (mild) titillation to millions of young women who dreamed of marrying the boss. This formula reached its apogee in 1958 with Rona Jaffe's *The Best of Everything*, whose publishing-house heroines find either (a) business success at the price of stunted love, (b) true love and wifey bliss, or (c) death. But sixty years have gone by since the virgins of *The Best of Everything* hit the Big Apple, and real life has had its impact not only on modern romance but—as we shall see—on modern Romance.

The Regencys, however, have barely altered *their* formula. You may be Georgette Darrington—of Bridget Barton's *A Governess for the Brooding Duke*—who's left penniless by her improvident father and perforce becomes governess to the adorable wards of the taciturn, unfeeling Duke of Draycott, suffering such humiliations as being served burnt toast by the antagonistic upper servants. . . .

Or Lady Honora Parker, who's struggled for years to wrest autonomy from her father ("the eighth Earl of Stratton and a bunch of lesser titles not worth repeating at the moment") and is the heroine of Joanna Shupe's *A Daring Arrangement*, set in the late nineteenth century, though Regency in all but chronology. Honora takes New York by storm, entering into an agreement with the notorious rakish financier Julius Hatcher to pretend to be engaged—his entrée into top society, her strategy in her war with the earl. . . .

Or Emma Gladstone, a vicar's penniless daughter in *The Duchess Deal*, by Tessa Dare, author of *Romancing the Duke, Any Duchess Will Do, One Dance with a Duke*, and *Say Yes to the Marquess*. (Not everyone can be a duke.) The young Duke of Ashbury is traumatized by the terrible scarring that one side of his face has suffered in battle. He doesn't want love, he doesn't want a real wife, he wants an heir. Emma is working as a seamstress (though every inch a gentlewoman), and when the duke proposes at their very first meeting, what choice does she have? "She would be a fool to refuse any duke, even if he were a bedridden septuagenarian with poor hygiene. This particular duke was none of those things. Despite his many, *many* faults, Ashbury was strong, in the prime of life, and he smelled divine." And—a bonus—it turns out that "bringing a woman to orgasm had always been a particular pleasure for him." . . .

Or Wilhelmina Ffynche, the most beautiful girl in London, who has rejected fourteen proposals of marriage and has no intention of being "won." But when she encounters Lord Alaric Wilde, second son of a duke, who's just back in England after becoming a Byronic legend through his fabulously successful books about his adventures around the world, she agrees to rescue him from the crazed attentions of female fans. She's funny, she's sexy, and as the funny and sexy (at least on the page, and for all I know in real life) Eloisa James, author of *Wilde in Love*, puts it, "In the last half decade, he'd seen an enormous white whale, the Great Wall of China and the aurora borealis. And now he'd seen Miss Willa Ffynche." Robust sex and amusing plotting follow, as we would expect from a writer who in her other life is the daughter of the poet Robert Bly and a professor of English literature at Fordham.

Whichever of these heroines you may be, you are guaranteed to end up in marital (often ducal) heaven, after dealing with one or another of the ingenious obstacles that create whatever suspense the genre can generate. As has often been noted, the Regency romance is a cross between *Pride and Prejudice* and *Jane Eyre*: Either the lovers discover their true affinity through their intelligence and humor or, as mousy Jane does with fierce Mr. Rochester, the heroine tames her man by helping cure him of his anger, depression, self-loathing, trauma. Or both. The only new element in the genre these post-Heyer days is the relentless application of highly specific sex scenes featuring his "hardened rod" and her orgasm that "went on for what felt like hours but was probably only a minute or two." Bodices no longer need to be ripped—your bosom happily meets his abs halfway. Twenty years ago, a Regency would not have ended, as *The Duchess Deal* does, on this rapturous note: "They reached a toothache-sweet climax together, as if simultaneous bliss wasn't a rarity but the most natural thing in the world. The sun rises; the wind blows; orgasms arrive in tandem." Now *that's* Romance.

NO ORGASM, SOLO OR IN TANDEM, we should note, graces the pages of the most prolific and successful romance queen of all time, Barbara Cartland, step-grandmother of Princess Diana and author of 723 novels, 160 of them unpublished at her death (just before her ninety-ninth birthday) in 2000. Her son is still doling these out, one a month, as *The Pink Collection*, and they are without benefit of sex. The formidable Barbara knew where *her* readers wanted the line drawn: No Cartland heroine ever came into contact with a hardened rod.

Cartland's successor as Queen of Romance is America's Nora Roberts. And she deserves to be. Roberts is not only extraordinarily industrious—215 or so novels, including close to fifty futuristic police procedurals under the pseudonym J. D. Robb, also big best sellers—but her books are sensibly written and on the whole as plausible as genre novels can be. I remember being struck some years ago by her common sense about what women want, need, and deserve. Unlike her leading competitors' heroines, for whom the ultimate goal remained scoring the ideal mate, a Nora Roberts heroine was encouraged not only to score him but also to score a satisfying career: It wasn't either/or, it was both—and he'd better adjust to it!

Today, indeed, a plot limited to catching a man would seem an anomaly. Not only do young heroines work hard and well, they may even be the boss. Consider Maggie and Owen—*both* bosses—who grew up together in adjoining mansions on the Jersey shore in Caridad Pineiro's *One Summer Night*. The famous retail chain that Maggie and her father run together is faltering, and real estate tycoon Owen has reappeared in her life—they've drifted apart since that one magical summer night on the beach when they were kids. (Standing in the way of their mutual attraction was the mortal enmity between their fathers, New Jersey's Lords Montague and Capulet.) Owen has all the standard appurtenances—he's "the epitome of male perfection—raven-black hair, a sexy gleam in his charcoal-gray eyes, broad shoulders and not an ounce of fat on him"—plus the sensitivity today's heroines demand in their men: He wants to *help* Maggie, not dominate her. Even so, it's not Owen but his equally sexy and macho brother, Jonathan, who's taken some cooking lessons in Italy and makes them all dinner, the pasta "deliciously al dente while creamy at the same time." The sex between Maggie and Owen is equally delicious: "When he danced his tongue across perfect white teeth, she playfully chased it and then lightly bit his lower lip, jerking a groan from him," shortly before he's caressing "the swollen nub." Maggie also has the support of today's de rigueur group of women friends, wise in the ways of romance. (I'm absolutely certain that lawyer Connie is going to end up with Jonathan of the Bolognese.)

A gang of girlfriends also rushes to the support of *their* friend, Pallas Saunders, who loves her work running Weddings in a Box, a "theme wedding" venue. Sparks fly between Pallas and Nick Mitchell ("he was a world-renowned artist who had won awards" and has been in *People* magazine), but he's finding it hard To Commit. The real conflict, however, is between Pallas and her domineering mother, who is determined to have Pallas join her in running the family bank. What's a girl to do? Luckily, the sex in Susan Mallery's *You Say It First* is just fine.

And then there's Catherine Bybee's Lori, in *Fool Me Once*, a flourishing attorney who works with a small elite marriage-for-hire service for the rich and famous, marriages designed to be temporary that include an uncontested and lucrative divorce. Lori takes three of her recent divorcées off on a European jaunt to help them re-enter a husbandless existence, and they bond: "First Wives Club or bust." "Girl power." But what about gorgeous Reed, some mysterious kind of private investigator? Whom is he working for? Can he be trusted? No matter: "His kiss was an inferno in under a second," so no surprise that "a lick, a nibble and a suck, and Lori was lost." But Reed still must earn her trust. The lesson: A lick and a nibble are all to the good, but complete honesty is essential. All truths must be told, especially by the man.

THE EMPOWERMENT OF WOMEN, abundant sexuality steamily reported, and female bonding rule the current roost, yet the biggest phenomenon in recent romance is atypical. Originally published privately in Australia, the E. L. James *Fifty Shades* trilogy, with its saga of a nice college girl giving herself over to the S & M predilections of a tormented (but gorgeous) zillionaire, has sold over 125 million copies in half a dozen years. James has been derided for her less-than-sterling prose, but mostly by readers—Salman Rushdie is one—who I doubt are familiar with the standard romance literature: E. L. James is no better or worse a writer than most of her compeers. What's made her so astoundingly successful is the trope of spanking, give or take the odd whip and manacle.

Does this mean that what vast numbers of women are really looking

138

for is bondage, not bonding? Or is this just a daring momentary flirtation with one extreme possibility of romantic relationship? If this season's crop of romances is anything to go by, there's no general rush to the whip: E. L. James and a few other spankers may have both stirred up a vast market and satisfied it. We shall see. Not unexpectedly, her books, while breaking the rules in some areas, hew slavishly to others. Yet again we have the girl of modest circumstances winning today's equivalent of the duke, the multimillionaire—the Lizzie Bennet syndrome. And yet again we have the girl of empathy and generosity curing the tormented man: Jane Eyre redux. Spanking apart, it's the same old song.

You can't get farther away from quirky E. L. James than adorable Debbie Macomber (200 million copies sold). In her recent *If Not for You*, not only does piano teacher Beth defy her controlling mother to mate with superior garage mechanic Sam, but she reunites her beloved Aunt Sunshine (yes), a highly acclaimed artist, with the man she loved when they were young, pulling off this miracle through a canny ruse featuring fish tacos. In Macomber's current *Any Dream Will Do*, she brings together the tragically widowed Pastor Drew Douglas with the just-out-of-prison Shay (she embezzled only to save her brother's life). Best line of dialogue, spoken by Sadie, Shay's co-waitress at the café where they work: "You got the hots for a man of God?" And in Macomber's just-off-the-press annual Christmas book, *Merry and Bright*—she's MERRY Smith, he's Jayson BRIGHT, get it?—handsome, rich, but deeply despondent boss and pretty, warm, life-loving temp fall in love through the Mix & Mingle dating website, unaware that they've crossed swords (and looks) in the office. (Yes—it's *You've Got Mail*, fully acknowledged—to say nothing of Lubitsch's sublime *The Shop Around the Corner*, unacknowledged.) Crucial to the story is Patrick, the light of Merry's life: her enchanting eighteen-year-old brother, who has Down syndrome.

And finally there's the redoubtable Danielle Steel, who according to Wikipedia is the fourth-best-selling writer of fiction in history, right behind Agatha Christie, Shakespeare, and Barbara Cartland. Recently Steel abandoned her predictable contemporary world of the rich and famous overcoming adversity, and ventured back into the Regency. Yes, Danielle Steel has given us the bestselling *The Duchess*! A Regency with a twist.

Exquisite Angélique is the eighteen-year-old daughter of the Duke of Westerfield (cousin of George IV) and Marie-Isabelle, "a Bourbon on one side of her family and Orléans on the other, with royals on both sides." It was a love match, despite a big disparity in age, and Marie-Isabelle loved Belgrave Castle as much as the duke himself did, "helping him to add beautiful decorative pieces to his existing heirlooms." Unfortunately, she dies giving birth to Angélique, who is raised in happy seclusion by her doting father, adored by all. But Daddy dies, and her wicked half brother, the new duke, who hates her, exiles her from Belgrave to work as a nursery maid somewhere far away. She can inherit nothing, because of the entail, except for some jewelry of her mother's. But providentially, as her father is dying, he hands her a pouch containing £25,000 that he has squirreled away.

Bravely Angélique accepts her fate, and settles into her new life of service. But when she rejects the advances of a salacious young master, she's fired—without a reference! Therefore no domestic work for her in England, and when she tries France, she has no better luck there. Down and out in Paris and London, knowing no one and with nothing but her pouch between her and destitution, what does this pure, delicate flower of the aristocracy do? Just what you or I would do: Practically overnight, she opens what rapidly becomes the most elegant, successful bordello in Paris (preserving her own virtue, needless to say). Then on to America, marriage to a hugely rich lawyer who dies (of plot), leaving her with a dear little boy and a fortune. Meanwhile, her wicked half brother has overspent, so has to sell Belgrave Castle, which she secretly buys . . . and so forth.

The entire preposterous story is predicated on Angélique's not grasping what anyone in her place would certainly know—that £25,000, even cautiously invested in the famous 4 percents, would have provided her with a sizable income for life: no need to be a nursemaid *or* a madam. But we (and she) would have missed all the fun.

This retro venture, flatly written like all Steel's books, is just further evidence of how romance can swing any which way. Regency, psycho-paths, wedding planners, ranchers, sadists, grandmas, bordellos, dukes (of course); whips, fish tacos, entails, Down syndrome, recipes, orgasms— romance can absorb them all, which suggests it's a healthy genre, not trapped in inflexibility. Its readership is vast, its satisfactions apparently limitless, its profitability incontestable. And where's the harm? After all, guys have their James Bonds as role models. Are fantasies of violence and danger really more respectable than fantasies of courtship and female self-empowerment? Or to put it another way, are Jonathan's Bolognese and Cam's cucumber salsa any sillier than *Octopussy*'s Alfa Romeo and Bond's unstirred martinis?

The New York Times Book Review
OCTOBER 1, 2007

The Book of Books

AMERICAN MUSICALS

URING THE GOLDEN AGE OF BROADWAY, people generally referred to musicals by the names of their songwriters: Seen the new Cole Porter? The new Rodgers and Hart? The new Gershwin? The songs were the thing. Or, if a major star was involved, it might be the new Ethel Merman or the new Mary Martin. Then, when the choreographer/director took over in the fifties and sixties, there was the new Jerry Robbins, the new Bob Fosse. And, in a category of its own, the new Steve Sondheim. But nobody ever labeled a musical by the author of its book. The phrase "Book by" in the credits was like a pathetic tail dangling from a dog.

And yet you couldn't have a musical without a book: something to hang a story, a situation, a conflict on; a trigger for the songs; an opportunity for actors to . . . act. A rotten book could (but didn't always) sink a show; a terrific book couldn't often (but sometimes did) keep a show from sinking. Yet who really took notice? Great songs from a show go on to a life of their own, and great performances are treasured long after they've become history. But books?

As part of its current strategy to pep up (some carpers might say dumb down) its weighty list, the Library of America has decided to throw light on the subject, publishing in two volumes, under the title *American Musicals*, sixteen books (including lyrics) from sixteen famous shows, ranging from 1927 to 1969. You could argue over some of the choices (and I will), but most of these sixteen would undoubtedly appear on anyone's list of the classics.

In fact, there's only one real surprise: the Irving Berlin–Moss Hart *As Thousands Cheer*, probably Broadway's most celebrated revue, its sketches and songs famously taking off from "today's" headlines and celebrities. All Broadway buffs know about it—the 1933 show that gave us "Easter Parade" and "Heat Wave" and "Supper Time" and "Harlem on My Mind," the last three sung by the showstopping Ethel Waters—and about the problems between Waters and her (white) co-stars, which Waters blamed on racism. But we haven't known what, exactly, those Moss Hart sketches were like. Printing this text, though it's far from a standard "book," is a real contribution.

And the news is that, even this early in his career, Moss Hart was right on target. Here he is observing the Herbert Hoovers evacuating the White House as FDR and Eleanor move in. (Mrs. H: "I'm not going to leave anything for those Roosevelts, I can tell you that. Did you bring that electric toaster up from the kitchen, Herbie?") And here's the breakup of the Joan Crawford–Doug Fairbanks Jr. marriage. (Joan to the press: "I want you to be sure to say that this divorce can never change our spiritual relationship. Douglas will always remain to me the lover eternal—the finest man I have ever known. I shall always keep and treasure his water colors.") You can see why *As Thousands Cheer* ran for a year.

The most striking thing about the shows with proper books— almost all of them postwar, when book shows really took hold—is that they're nearly all adaptations: some from a novel (*Show Boat*, *The Pajama Game*); some from a group of stories (*Pal Joey*, *South Pacific*, *Guys and Dolls*, *Fiddler on the Roof*, *Cabaret*); some from plays (*Kiss Me, Kate*, *My Fair Lady*, *A Funny Thing Happened on the Way to the Forum*, *Oklahoma!*). *Gypsy* was "suggested" by the memoirs of Gypsy Rose Lee; *On the Town* was based on Jerome Robbins's ballet *Fancy Free*. Only *Finian's Rainbow* and *1776* are totally new.

The adaptation closest to its original is *My Fair Lady*—so close that when I first saw it, when it opened in 1956, it felt to me like a performance of "Pygmalion" irritatingly interrupted by songs. Today the songs are more famous than "Pygmalion," but when you compare the text of the book with the text of the play, you realize (a) how closely (and wisely) Alan Jay Lerner followed George Bernard Shaw and the extent to which he simply recycled Shaw's dialogue (which is, of course, why

Ethel Waters singing "Heat Wave" in *As Thousands Cheer*

Lerner's book is by far the best of all), and (b) how unlike in tone Lerner's lyrics are from Shaw. Can you imagine Shaw writing "Someone's head resting on my knee / Warm and tender as he can be"? But Lerner deployed the songs brilliantly. And the glorious climactic "Rain in Spain" sequence is essence of Broadway.

The librettos of *Oklahoma!* and *Guys and Dolls* and *Gypsy* are very satisfying to read—they're cannily structured and strongly written and have persuasive individual voices preserved from their originals. The exuberant *Pajama Game* works on the page; *Cabaret* doesn't—it's disjointed, the characters barely sketched in. *Fiddler* seems somewhat mawkish in its special pleading. Oscar Hammerstein's moving *Carousel*, based on Ferenc Molnár's play *Liliom*, would have been a more convincing choice than his *South Pacific*, based on James Michener, with its heavy message of Tolerance. Not all the humor of *On the Town*, which as a teenager I found dazzlingly sophisticated, has worn well; *Pal Joey*, with its rat of a hero, isn't as daring today as it must have seemed in 1940; and *A Funny Thing Happened on the Way to the Forum* is so convoluted and dependent on physical comedy that it's hard to take in on the page.

The two originals are vastly unalike. The somewhat dated book of *Finian's Rainbow* is an unlikely mixture of Irish whimsy, anti-racism agenda, hillbilly comedy, and young romance, but somehow these all come together as the perfect spawning ground for an extraordinary number of first-rate songs: "Old Devil Moon," "Something Sort of Grandish," "Look to the Rainbow," "If This Isn't Love," "When I'm Not Near the Girl I Love," and, of course, "How Are Things in Glocca Morra?" Only *Show Boat*, *Oklahoma!*, and *Annie Get Your Gun* (not included here) can match it in this regard.

By contrast, *1776* didn't spawn a single lyric I recognize—I had to watch as much of the movie as I could bear in order to get a sense of what the score was like. Yet its book, by Peter Stone, has fanatic admirers for the way it dramatizes the struggle to get the thirteen colonies to vote for independence. Yes, it's cleverly structured and pumped for suspense, but the tone of much of it is so cute, cute, cute that it reduces the birth of the United States to a sitcom with powdered wigs. A sly Pickwicky Ben Franklin? A moony, lovestruck Tom Jefferson too busy humping his luscious bride to turn out the Declaration of Independence? There's so much speechifying that hours—days—seem to go by without a snatch of song, which may be just as well since the songs themselves are so mediocre. *1776* is a straight play pretending to be a musical.

Reading these books, however effective (or not) each of them may be, presents a common problem: responding to a lyric when you don't know the music. Or you can reverse it: responding to a lyric without being affected by the music you *do* know. Try reading "Oh, what a beautiful mornin'" or "I could have danced all night" without hearing it. On the other hand, try these obscure Lorenz Hart lines, chosen almost at random from *Pal Joey*: "Danger's easy to endure when / You're out to catch a beaut; / Lie in ambush, but be sure when / You see the whites of their eyes—don't shoot!" This is why reading *American Musicals* can be such an uneven experience: One moment you're caught up in a song you love, happy to be able to place it in its natural context; the next, you're floundering.

I'm not complaining, though—it's good to have these complete books, even when they're less than inspiring. They may be more rewarding as history or nostalgia than as art, but that doesn't mean they don't have a place in the Library of America, given that the classic American musical is one of our great cultural accomplishments. The Library could have done its part of the job a little more helpfully, though. The basic introduction by the editor, Laurence Maslon, is both thin and hyperbolic, although his later notes on each production are substantial. Worse, the credits for each show are tucked away in the back, almost impossible to locate when you want them: You have to fumble your way through hundreds of pages to discover the date of a show, or its cast.

And then there are the typos, particularly egregious when they mutilate lyrics. In "Wunderbar," from *Kiss Me, Kate*, the leads drink "To the join of our dream come true." And, Pal Joey himself, in the classic "I Could Write a Book," sings: "And the simple secret of the plot / Is that to tell them that I love you a lot." Come on, Library of America: Take yourself more seriously.

The Writer

SEBASTIAN BARRY

How did it come about that an Irishman, Sebastian Barry, has written one of the most illuminating and moving recent novels about America—and nineteenth-century America at that? And what odds would you have given that it would be published in the United States within weeks of that other superb novel set in the same period: George Saunders's *Lincoln in the Bardo*? (Please don't tell me that the novel is dead.)

Days Without End is Barry's eighth novel, a number that includes an early, ambitious, and pretentious Joycean effort called *The Engine of Owl-Light*, which is unavailable and which you can safely ignore. Every one of his other novels is luminous. Not one of them sounds like anyone else. In Britain, he's a major figure—he's twice won the Costa (previously Whitbread) Book Award, not only for best novel but for Book of the Year, the only novelist to be so honored. Two of his books have been shortlisted for the Booker; two have won the Walter Scott Prize for Historical Fiction. His reviews are almost unanimously rapturous. In America they're equally splendid—and have been mostly ignored; he has ardent admirers here but remains relatively unknown, although he's traveled and taught in America and knows it well.

This should change with *Days Without End*, a book of such feeling, charm, persuasiveness, and suspense that Barry's American audience will surely swell. Who could resist the voice of its narrator, the young Thomas McNulty, who has escaped famine-struck Ireland—his family dead of starvation—in one of the notorious "coffin ships" that carried hundreds of thousands of Irish emigrants to America in pre–Civil War days? Those ships were hell, and for many of the new Americans, life here was hell too. Thomas, blundering across the country, desperate for any kind of work, finds himself in Missouri—alone, in rags, and hungry. Ducking under a hedge in a sudden downpour, he runs into another untethered boy: Handsome John Cole, as Thomas likes to refer to him. Thomas is about fifteen but "wren-sized"; John Cole is a year or two younger but tall. From that first moment, they belong to each other.

Together they head out, ready to take on any menial job, however

degrading, that they may stumble upon. They find themselves in a small mining town, hired by a well-intentioned saloon owner to dress up as girls and dance (and only dance) with the miners in a place where there are no women to speak of. Thomas is completely comfortable in his new garb and in this role, until he and John just can't hide their boyness any longer and are back on the road. As for their sexuality, it's dealt with in one astonishing sentence, dropped into the narrative so casually that it's as natural as it is shocking: "And then we quietly fucked and then we slept." That's just about it for the sexual life of these two men, except for a casual affectionate kiss, through the twenty-five years or so that we observe their deeply happy union.

For want of any other suitable occupation, the boys join the Army and find themselves in California, participating in a berserk massacre of unresisting Native Americans—unprotected women and children. Later they will be fighting for the Union in the Civil War, Thomas taken prisoner and sent to the dreaded Andersonville prison camp. (More than a quarter of its forty-five thousand inmates died there; the photographs of the survivors are as horrifying as those taken eighty years later at Dachau.)

During the course of these dangerous and soul-searing experiences, the relationship between the two young men never falters, and indeed is strengthened when, through a series of quirks of history, they find themselves the self-appointed guardians—the parents, in essence—of a young Sioux child named Winona. There are perils to come: Thomas in mortal terror, about to be hanged for desertion; Winona in need of rescue from another devastating massacre. There is no mitigation of the ugly history of our nation during these convulsive times.

So how does *Days Without End* achieve its buoyancy, its air of hope, its joyousness? Partly through the convincing goodness of its central characters, as revealed to us through Thomas's half-naive, half-acute, always generous perceptions. Partly through Sebastian Barry's response to the beauty of the natural world and, most important, to the beauty of life itself. "Sweet life," Thomas reflects.

> I was sore in love with all my labouring in Tennessee. Liked well that life. Up with the cockcrow, bed with the dark. Going along like that could never end. And when ending it would be felt to be just. You had your term. All that stint of daily life we sometimes spit on like it was something waste. But it [is] all there is and in it is enough.

Will Thomas and John and Winona survive the traumas of their youth? Since *Days Without End* is told in retrospect, set down when Thomas has reached the grand old age of forty or thereabouts, common sense reassures us that he, at least, does survive. But such is the pull of the narrative, and our feeling for him and his, that our apprehension doesn't let up. Nor does our affectionate concern for this openhearted, unselfconscious, practical, Irish American hero, who is at once an exemplary soldier and a cheerful farmer; a virile man who finds himself more and more comfortable in the guise of a woman; an orphan for whom family is everything.

DAYS WITHOUT END is the only one of Barry's novels set in the nineteenth century, but it is linked to certain of his other books in various ways, one of them literally. Once or twice in those that deal with the McNulty family in the twentieth century, we hear of a long-ago McNulty who emigrated to America and about whom no one knows anything. Barry himself, in interviews, tells us that there was such a figure in his own family's distant past, but "all my grandfather ever said about him was that his great-uncle had been in the Indian wars. That's it."

So Barry was free to *invent* his Thomas. In *The Temporary Gentleman* (2014), the central character refers to "my great uncle Thomas McNulty, who was scalped by a band of Comanches in the central grasslands of Texas." Barry in an interview mischievously remarks, "That's not true, I don't think," and more soberly explains, "It's when books contradict each other that gives me the most joy. That to me sounds more human. In later generations, everything is a story. History is surmises and good sentences."

Far from denying the connections between his life and his art, Barry is ready to point them out. The relationship between Thomas and John Cole, he has said, was inspired partly by his son Toby, on whose behalf he wrote an open letter supporting the Yes vote in Ireland's recent same-sex marriage referendum. In an extended interview in *The Guardian*, he reports: "My beautiful son came into our bedroom one morning when he was 16, and said, 'Dad, I'm gay.' I said 'Oh, thank God, because now you can go around all that ghastly heterosexual thing that we've been struggling with all our lives.' It just seemed like freedom." Observing Toby's relationship with his boyfriend, he discerned something quite distinct from his own "bonkers" early love life:

> There's an area of wonderment that I didn't expect. They were kids but they knew something that I didn't know. It was the beginning of

thinking, well, we're being asked as straight people to be tolerant towards gay people but maybe that's wrong, maybe what we should be is envious.

This perception of homosexuality is a reflection of Barry's overriding belief in the centrality of family to life, not a by-product of the culture wars or of identity politics. *Days Without End* is no more a gay novel than it is a war novel or, for that matter, a historical novel. In fact, you could say that Thomas McNulty, happily washed up on a hardscrabble farm in Tennessee, floats away from history. Because history, for Barry, is Ireland—a history that none of his other protagonists ever really escapes from.

THE SIX NOVELS that precede *Days Without End* divide neatly between two families: the McNultys and the Dunnes—Barry's mother's and his father's. The hero of his first mature novel, *The Whereabouts of Eneas McNulty* (1998), gets as far away from Ireland as his drifting life can take him—to Galveston, Texas, when he's still a youngster sailing around the world with the British Merchant Navy and learning about drinking and whores; later, to a French vineyard, where a peasant has taken him in after he's missed the Dunkirk evacuation; then to the port of Grimsby, where he spends years drudging as a herring fisherman; and on to West Africa, where he finds himself employed digging canals. He can't go home again, because at one point in his youth he joined the Royal Irish Constabulary and found himself on the wrong side of Irish history—a "peeler," a "tan," a traitor to the revolutionary cause of Irish freedom. It made him a marked man, a ruined twenty-year-old, pursued relentlessly by men obsessed with punishing such traitors to "Ireland."

Several times he sneaks back to see his parents and his younger siblings, and he finds that the girl he adored and hoped to marry has moved on. During one furtive visit, he peers through the window of his brother Jack's home and

sees his niece and his brother and feels the bareness of his own life. . . . No children, no wife, no picture house where human actions unfold

and are warmly enacted. He can barely remember why his life is so
bare, he is that used to it, the bloody life of a lone seal out in the un-
knowable sea. . . .

That he finds, eventually, a home and a family of sorts is a miracle; that
it cannot last is inevitable—finally, Irish history catches up with him.

Barry's novels give us lives, not plots—that is their power. Perhaps
it isn't coincidental that his most successful book until now, *The Secret
Scripture* (made into a movie with Vanessa Redgrave, Rooney Mara, and
Eric Bana that Barry has disowned), is the most plot-driven. Roseanne
Clear is a century old, living out her life in a benign if crumbling old-
people's institution where a Dr. Grene has been in charge of her forever.
She is secretly writing down her life; he is hoping to discover what that
life has been. He is mourning his wife; Roseanne is remembering her
ex-husband, a twentieth-century Tom McNulty, who cast her out. (She's
also remembering Fred Astaire: "Not a handsome man. He said himself he couldn't sing. He was balding his whole life. He danced like a
cheetah runs, with the grace of the first creation. I mean, that first week.
On one of those days God created Fred Astaire.") *The Secret Scripture* is
a beguiling book that I would have found even more beguiling if I hadn't
sensed too early on that it was moving toward a climactic and somewhat
predictable revelation.

Tom, Eneas, and Jack are the three sons of this generation of
McNultys. (Their only sister, Teasy, has become a mendicant nun in
England.) After shedding Roseanne, Tom has settled into a fulfilled second marriage and a solid middle-class existence. Eneas, as we have seen,
has his own book. Jack, whom we've only half-glimpsed in the earlier
novels, is the protagonist of *The Temporary Gentleman*, set in 1957 Ghana.
He's a retired U.N. observer, a washed-up expat planning on going
home to Sligo, the seaport in northwest Ireland where the McNultys
come from. But his memories and feelings are focused on reliving his
marriage to the once-radiant—the adored—Mai, who has slowly disin-
tegrated into alcoholism, despair, and early death (Jack blames himself),
leaving behind two daughters and a great rupture in his soul. It is of his
daughters that he is now thinking, hoping "to use all my skill whatsoever

I possess to build bridges at last of some coherence and solidity between myself and them." And particularly with his actress daughter, Maggie, who is a re-imagining of Sebastian Barry's mother, the celebrated Irish actress Joan O'Hara, with whom he had a tumultuous, often troubled relationship, and who died all too young. Somehow, Barry again manages to transform all this personal history and pain into invented lives; there's never a moment when you feel he's merely reporting. His family's past is his material, not his subject.

BUT, AS ALREADY MENTIONED, his family's past—and his Ireland's past—is not only the past of his mother's clan, but also of his father's: the Dunnes (that is, the Barrys). The three Dunne books—*Annie Dunne* (2002), *A Long Long Way* (2005), and *On Canaan's Side* (2011)—seem to me his consistently finest. Again, each of these books centers on one of the siblings of a single generation of a family, and as with the McNulty novels, each of them is meant to be read separately: They aren't linked sequentially, they don't overlap. (Completely apart from these is 1995's *The Steward of Christendom*, Barry's most successful play—he was a well-known playwright before he became a novelist—which focuses on the dominant member of the Dunne family, the father, as he holds forth, in and out of his right mind, in the institution where he is living out his last years. Thomas Dunne had been a great man: the head of Dublin's Royal Constabulary, the highest position a Catholic in his line of work could achieve in Ireland at that time, before history dislodged him from his eminence. It is Thomas whom his children first look up to, then look back on.)

The oldest Dunne daughter is Maud, who marries an artist, bears him four children, and then "put herself to bed one autumn morning and never arose again in any purposeful way." Next comes Annie, whose modest hump bars her from marriage. Then the one son, Willie, so much shorter than his father's six and a half feet that he isn't eligible to join the Constabulary. And finally Dolly, the live wire, the charmer, who abandons home and country for the New World.

Annie Dunne is quietly perfect: the story of a woman of sixty or so whose world is gone—her father dead, her siblings scattered, now living with Sarah, a distant cousin, on a little farm with nothing much to sustain them other than a flock of chickens, two milk cows, a pony, and the most resolute discipline. Years earlier, when her sister Maud retreated from life, Annie raised Maud's three boys, who are now grown men and leading lives of their own. But one of these men brings his two young children to the farm, for Annie and Sarah to look after for a summer. The children are city-bred, delicate, needful. For the two aging cousins, these children are life itself. "I love you, Auntie Anne," the little girl says, and Annie tells us, "The wolf of pride smiles in my breast."

The summer brings its difficulties, its anxieties—its dangers, even—and then it is over and the children are gone. "Will they remember anything of these days? Will they hold in their hearts the love I have for them, or will it all pass away like all the things of childhood?" The novel cannot answer such questions, but in a "conversation" that is printed in the back of his book, Barry does remember that "the woman I had in my mind and have carried in mind all my life, could love a child, and practiced that love faithfully and without stint when her brief time was given her." In the same autobiographical passage, he remarks that he is "just beginning a book set during the First World War. Oddly enough it is about Annie's brother Willie, who died in Flanders."

That book, *A Long Long Way*, is another masterpiece, though of a very different kind. As a war novel, it's as devastating as *The Red Badge of Courage* or *All Quiet on the Western Front*; its descriptions of the carnage in World War I are almost unbearable. Willie hangs on through four horrendous years as an Irishman soldiering in the trenches for the British army, making him a traitor to his erstwhile friends back in Dublin. He is frightened the entire time; he loses the girl he's loved since she was thirteen ("She wasn't so wedded to the idea of his erection as perhaps he was"); he is badly wounded; but rather than dehumanizing him, his fearful experiences do the opposite: They broaden his sympathies.

It was not just the Ulstermen of the 36th, not for a moment. It was Scottish Highlanders (some of them hailing oddly from Canada, Willie noted), black Africans, great clumps of Chinese workers incinerated while they worked, Australians and New Zealanders, in violent teems of youngsters faithfully plodding across acres to receive machine-gun bullets in their eyes, their brains, their cheeks, their breasts, their legs, their stomachs, their ears, their throats, their backs (more rare, unless the Boche came in behind them), the small of the back, the small of the knee, the small of the heart. There was no town or village on the anatomy of the human body—if the body could be considered a country—that had not tried the experiment of a bullet entering there.

Yet the greatest wound Willie receives is a rent in the fabric of love between him and his father. Home on leave, Willie blunders into the fatal Easter Rising of April 1916. He sees Irish killing Irish in the name of revolution, and British killing Irish in the name of law and order. A man dies in his arms. His father, representing the law, does his duty and is proud of it, and when Willie questions him, he turns on his adored son. Even so, in his last letter to his father from the front, Willie writes, "I believe in my heart that you are the finest man I know. When I think of you there is nothing bad that arises at all. You stand before me often in my dreams and in my dreams you seem to comfort me. So I am sending this letter with my love, and thinking of you." History has done its best to destroy their mutual devotion, but for once history doesn't prevail.

Our final view of the Dunnes comes in *On Canaan's Side*. Dolly Dunne, renamed Lilly Bere, has fled Ireland for America with her beloved new husband to escape yet another would-be fatal reprisal from political zealots. "Livin' on Canaan's side, Egypt behind / Crossed over Jordan wide, gladness to find," the epigraph reads. But there is to be no gladness. Lilly's husband is murdered in front of her, and now, looking back at the end of a long life, she contemplates "the colossal ungenerosity of it, implacable eternal hatred of it, that they wouldn't let us go, forgive us our trespasses. That they wouldn't allow us to cross into Canaan, but would follow us over the river, and kill him on Canaan's side. The land of refuge itself."

Lilly, in danger, has herself had to flee, slowly fashioning a new existence with a second husband, a son, a grandson, all now lost to her. Her circumstances are comfortable, but she is eighty-five years old, and there is nothing to live for. As she prepares to end her life she reflects:

> I knew, I exulted in the fact that when I was done, there would be something so slight lying there in the dress I wore. That the infinite gap between two points, in this instance between being alive and being dead, that the mathematicians tell us cannot be closed, would be closed. I would not have any distance at all to go to nothing.

Somehow, Barry has once more made us believe that, through the power of memory and language, a scarred and painful life can reveal itself as a triumph of humanity. Only in the great films of Ozu—*Tokyo Story, Late Spring, Early Summer*—have I come across such a fusing of tenderness and realism, suffering, endurance, and acceptance.

IN 1999, there was a long and wise review in *The New York Review of Books* by Thomas Flanagan of three new Irish novels, of which *The Whereabouts of Eneas McNulty* was one. "It is wonderful and a wonderfully strange book by a fine writer," he wrote; "too ambitious, perhaps, at times too portentous about history and Ireland, but in these times ambition is too rare to require apology." The ambition has only strengthened in the nineteen years between then and now, although it has partially masked itself by telling less far-ranging stories. Only *On Canaan's Side* extends itself as capaciously, but it is written in the domestic first-person voice of its protagonist, Lilly Bere, whereas Eneas's more mythic journey—it's surely not by accident that his name echoes that of Virgil's hero—is narrated in the third person.

Flanagan also remarks on Barry's "curious voice, one which commands an elegance which at times comes close to inflation, but wedded to the cadences of ordinary Irish country speech." I would have said that the voice at times turns somewhat lyrical, even poetic, though that is truer of the earlier books than of the later, as Barry evolves from the poet and dramatist he began as. His writing, in fact, is somewhat spare, but with an overlay of Irish panache. Well, he's Irish.

His great subject—the effect history has had on Ireland's men and women—has never worn thin, but it may have worn itself out as Irish history has taken such a dramatic turn in the past decades. Think of the disgrace of the church over pedophilia, contributing to its already waning influence; the economic miracle; the open border between the north and the south; the loosening of old moral imperatives: Not only did the bill on gay marriage pass by a strong majority but opposition to abortion has been steadily declining.

This is a brave new Ireland. Perhaps Barry's decision to set his latest novel in nineteenth-century America is an acknowledgment of that reality. But if his subject has left him behind, in *Days Without End* he has taken an astonishing step—backward chronologically but forward artistically. Who knows where his sympathies and imagination will lead him next?

The New York Review of Books
APRIL 5, 2018

Anatomy of a Publisher

THE STORY OF FARRAR, STRAUS AND GIROUX

W HAT MAKES A PUBLISHING HOUSE GREAT? The easy answer is the consistency with which it produces books of value over a lengthy period of time. That would include in our day, beyond the obvious candidates, houses as unalike as Oxford University Press and New Directions. But there's also the energy and flair with which it brings its books to the attention of the general reading public, so doing justice to its authors. And there's its loyalty to those authors. And its overall conviction that books matter. And, of course, turning a profit.

A new book—*Hothouse* (Simon & Schuster), by Boris Kachka—takes as a given that its subject, Farrar, Straus and Giroux, has been and remains a great publisher, and without any question that's the case. FSG, as it's generally called, has brought us more than half a century of distinguished books, rarely slipping below the level of distinction it hoped to achieve. How it did so is certainly worth both parsing and paying tribute to, but a degree of disillusionment with this project sets in when we get past the cute title to the even cuter and more hyperbolic subtitle: *The Art of Survival and the Survival of Art at America's Most Celebrated Publishing House.* The tone is set: This vigorous and often diverting trot through the history of an important cultural institution is frequently slapdash and overwrought in its determination to show just how hot the house was—in fact, "hands down, the hottest house in New York." I've been in the business close to sixty years, and there's never been a single hottest house; neither FSG nor any other publisher has ever been perceived as one—except perhaps by the central character in Kachka's account, Roger Straus, the crucial "S" of FSG and, to put it mildly, an accomplished blower of his own horn.

Roger (which is how he's referred to throughout the book—we're on a first-name basis here) drifted into publishing, as so many of us have done, though not by the usual route. Here was no wet-behind-the-ears idealistic book lover, recently out of college, scratching at the door of opportunity—no Dick Simon and Max Schuster, no Bennett Cerf and Donald Klopfer of Random House. Roger Straus came from the union of two of the most prominent German-Jewish families in America, the Strauses and the Guggenheims. The Strauses had been members of Our Crowd longer, and they had the more illustrious background: not just big money but serious government service. Roger's grandfather Oscar had served as minister to the Ottoman Empire under Cleveland, McKinley, Teddy Roosevelt, and Taft, and as Roosevelt's secretary of labor and commerce. The newer—and therefore slightly tarnished—Guggenheim money came from the American Smelting and Refining Company. But it was very big money indeed.

It was Oscar's son, the first Roger Straus, who married Gladys Guggenheim. "Rarely, outside glorious Temple Emanu-El, was so much of New York's new elite gathered in one room," Kachka tells us. This Roger was dragooned into the Guggenheim family business, and made a considerable success and a great deal of money but preferred to lead a relatively modest existence—an estate of "a mere thirty acres" in Westchester County, as opposed to the new Guggenheim spread of 250 acres in Sands Point, Long Island: Scott Fitzgerald's East Egg. *Our* Roger—Roger Jr.—spent his childhood and youth shuttling between these two principalities, concentrating on sports and girls. He didn't finish high school—some private tutoring plus serious pull eventually got him admitted to Hamilton College, from which he also never graduated. However, he spent summers working as a copy boy at a local newspaper, and "the cocky teen" was "turned on." During this period, he grew close to a young woman named Dorothea Liebmann, an heir to the Rheingold brewing fortune, whose parents had "stormed their way into the haute bourgeoisie," and who was far more literary than Roger would ever be—known later for her stylish writing and for rereading Proust almost every year. They were married in 1938. He was twenty-one and without real occupation, but fortunately "he and Dorothea had two trust funds to tide them over."

Roger went to work as a journalist, wandered into a magazine called *Current History*, and started a book-packaging firm. After Pearl Harbor, he was disqualified for active service because of osteomyelitis (which luckily didn't affect his ferocious tennis game), and landed, thanks to a rich pal, in something called the Branch Magazine and Book Section of the Navy's Office of Public Information; he did six weeks of training at Cornell and emerged an ensign—with a fetching uniform. On the job, he met and worked with a number of writers and made endless contacts—making contacts was one of his lifelong gifts—including one crucial to his future: a Navy lieutenant, in civilian life an editor at Harcourt, Brace, named Robert Giroux (the future "G" of FSG), who, "hair prematurely white at age thirty, outranked the handsome, grinning twenty-seven-year-old flack."

By the time the war was over, in 1945, Roger knew that he wanted to be a publisher—that is, he wanted to have a publishing house of his own. The money was found, some from his family, some from outside sources, and an appropriate editorial partner was found as well: John Farrar, who had been one of the founders of Farrar & Rinehart, the Rineharts being the sons of the formidable, best-selling Mary Roberts Rinehart. But when Farrar came back to New York after a distinguished war career, he was instantly and unceremoniously ousted from the company he had helped found. He needed a job, Roger needed a partner with editorial experience, and, in the fall of 1946, Farrar, Straus & Company launched its first list.

Despite Farrar's experience, what was determining for the company's success was the character, the temperament, the psyche—and the talent—of the young Roger. The talent wasn't primarily editorial, although he was a canny reader, and he had taste (he liked to say that his favorite FSG book was Marguerite Yourcenar's *Memoirs of Hadrian*). And although he was certainly shrewd on a day-to-day basis, his core strength was strategic: He knew what he wanted in the long term, and he knew how to move toward it. Roger needed to be a very big frog in whatever pond he was going to be in, and he needed as well to be in total charge, which meant not joining one of the established houses. The question was how to impose himself on the book world with a newly hatched, undercapitalized company that had no backlist and no really prominent editor on board.

Farrar did acquire a number of established writers (Theodor Reik, for one), and he presided over several best-selling novelists, but the FS list was somewhat schizophrenic. The first book published was an interior-decorating how-to called *Inside Your Home*, and close behind it came *Francis* (he was the Talking Mule). The book that was a harbinger of things to come was Carlo Levi's *Christ Stopped at Eboli*, a critical triumph and best seller in 1947, and it was Roger who had acquired it—through a scout. His famous days of personally descending on Europe in search of major writers didn't begin until twelve years after the firm came into being, although he preferred to forget that detail. But his instincts for commercial publishing were already sharp: In 1950, on a tip from another scout, he published *Look Younger, Live Longer*, by the health guru Gayelord Hauser, which sold half a million copies—a huge number in those days—as well as Judge Samuel Leibowitz's sensational *Courtroom*, another commercial triumph.

BUT COMMERCIAL SUCCESS, alas, can lead to serious difficulties. Despite almost demented penny-pinching—starvation wages for the staff, the office run on Draconian principles (the martinet supplies manager made the out-of-town salesmen turn over all their stolen hotel soap for use in the company bathrooms)—over-optimistic expansion threatened the health of the business. Later, Straus would sum up the situation in the fifties: "Success almost bankrupted me once." From then on, Kachka says perceptively, he became a more conservative publisher, "one who focused less on his company's growth than on its identity—less on market share than on a market niche."

One advantage Roger had when capital was low was that banks, aware of the family fortune, took for granted that he was solvent and were willing to accommodate him. On the other hand, even when books were selling, the company was not perceived as a real money-maker. Despite further commercial successes along the way, like Sammy Davis Jr.'s *Yes I Can*, and several major best-selling novelists (Scott Turow,

Tom Wolfe), there was a sense in the industry that FSG was having to scramble, a perception that actually contributed to Roger's astute—and highly vocal—positioning of the company as a plucky, somewhat beleaguered firm of quality prevailing in a world of ruthless commercial big boys: the Simon & Schusters, the Random Houses, the Doubledays. His particular, and loudly proclaimed, bugbear was Richard Snyder, of S. & S., who had dared, in Roger's view of things, to snatch several of his authors. This kind of feud, even when one-sided, clearly amused him—it suited his swagger—and did no harm to his targets.

Roger couldn't pay writers the big bucks, but he recognized that in post-war New York there was an intellectual and artistic ferment that could be harnessed if not organized. One of his brilliant maneuvers was to inaugurate a Great Letters Series, for which prominent figures of the present edited the correspondence of important figures of the past: Lionel Trilling (Keats), Jacques Barzun (Byron), Lillian Hellman (Chekhov), et al. "This was another ploy," Roger boasted, aimed not at selling books but at the "entrapment of authors." And then these eminences, and *their* connections, would be beguiled by the Straus social life—"scoring invitations to literary soirées" at the elaborate East Side town house ("where you might eavesdrop on Leonard Bernstein, Mary McCarthy, and Jerzy Kosinski"). And then certain of these stars would become informal editorial advisers to the firm: Trilling, for one, and, more important and longer lasting, Edmund Wilson, to whom Roger gave endless (needed) support and for whom he had endless (needed) patience. It all worked, until eventually "you didn't have to score a party invite to know where the vital center of books could be found."

Another particularly clever and successful strategy of Roger's was the acquisition of small imprints that had valuable authors or backlists but were failing—conspicuous among them Horizon, Pellegrini & Cudahy, Hill & Wang, and Noonday, which had not only a paperback line but a handsome fish colophon, which Roger swiped, and about which Kachka makes too much of a fuss. The FSG logo is elegant, but it's never had the same level of recognition as the Random House house, the S. & S. sower, or the Knopf borzoi. (Alfred really promoted that borzoi, convincing a lot of people that "A Borzoi Book" guaranteed quality.

Readers couldn't know that the Knopfs thought borzois were a particularly stupid breed of dog.)

Beyond occasional best sellers and takeovers and bank leniency and industry perceptions, what consolidated the success of the company was the arrival of Bob Giroux, in 1955. As John Farrar was slowly receding from the business, Roger turned to a stockholder who was also a well-known writer and critic, Stanley Young, for financial and editorial help. That was the brief era of Farrar, Straus & Young. Then came the meatpacking heiress Sheila Cudahy, who brought herself, along with her foundering publishing venture, to Roger, so inaugurating the marginally longer era of Farrar, Straus & Cudahy.

It was Cudahy, at a point when Roger was urgently looking for a major editor, who suggested Giroux—at the very moment when Giroux, about to be forty-one, and now editor in chief of Harcourt, Brace, had decided to leave the firm because of the Old Guard's conservative editorial policies. (They wouldn't, for instance, let him acquire *The Catcher in the Rye*.) Giroux was a quiet, modest, passionately literary man whose homosexuality was known and disregarded; he shared his life with the same man for more than half a century, until they died, within a few months of each other, in 2009.

As an undergraduate at Columbia, he had made close friends with a number of writers-to-be, including John Berryman and Thomas Merton, who famously became a Trappist monk, and whose *The Seven Storey Mountain* sold six hundred thousand copies for Harcourt, Brace in its first seven months. Among Giroux's responsibilities at Harcourt had been the care and feeding of such weighty figures as T. S. Eliot, whom he became close to, and Edmund Wilson ("He needed no editing. My only function was to praise the writing"). Among his own discoveries were Robert Lowell (who took him to Washington to meet Ezra Pound, in St. Elizabeths Hospital), Jean Stafford, Flannery O'Connor, Bernard Malamud, and Hannah Arendt, whose *Origins of Totalitarianism* he published in 1951; almost all of them followed him to FSG. Among the many writers he later signed were Elizabeth Bishop and Walker Percy.

New publishing houses tend to flourish best when their two leading personalities are in sharp contrast to each other: owlish, bookish Max

Roger Straus and Robert Giroux

Schuster and marketing genius Dick Simon; Random House's glad-handing, savvy jokester Bennett Cerf and distinguished, gentlemanly Donald Klopfer; panjandrum Alfred Knopf and his fierce and exigent wife, Blanche. As for Straus and Giroux, what a curious pair they were: "the Jewish prep school jock and the Jersey City Jesuit," as Kachka snappily puts it. That they were so unalike made the arrangement workable—until their differences eventually made it unworkable. Although Giroux immediately helped the company to a new level of visibility (and profitability), it was nine years before he outlasted both Y and C to become the "G" in FSG.

AS THE KINGDOM EXPANDED, Roger moved toward empire: Finally braving Europe, he quickly became a central figure at the Frankfurt Book Fair, hosting dinners and parties, establishing close relationships with the major foreign publishers (though oddly not with the English; the FSG list has always been weak on British literature), and scooping up an extraordinary list of important writers, alerted to them by his editors or unofficial advisers (Philip Roth, for one). His passion was for publishing Nobel Prize winners, and between 1978 and 1995 ten of the eighteen laureates were FSG writers, including Isaac Bashevis Singer, Joseph Brodsky, Czeslaw Milosz, Elias Canetti, Derek Walcott, and Seamus Heaney. An astounding record, which to a large extent he owed to his most important writer/friend/adviser/maybe lover, Susan Sontag.

Practically from the moment Sontag turned up at FSG, in the early sixties, she and Roger formed an almost conspiratorial alliance, and everybody was aware of it:

> By 1965 . . . Sontag was in a category of her own. When she swept into those grimy offices to work on a manuscript, "everything had to stop for her," says a former copy editor. "We would put aside whatever else and we would work with her." During the long stretches Sontag spent in Europe, FSG received and sorted her mail, looked after her apartment, and paid her bills—sometimes even her rent and Diners Club card.

There were minor bumps in the road, but "my loyalty to you, my gratitude to you, and my love for you, Roger, are absolutely unchanged" (Susan), and "Dearest, Dearest Susan . . . Please don't brood about us. Everything should be so good" (Roger). "Neither Straus nor Sontag was naïve about the utility of their friendship," as Kachka tactfully puts it, "but they seemed genuinely to adore each other." Why? "Both were preternaturally vital, social, and restless. They loved gossip and actively sought out people who were brilliant or beautiful, preferably both. Out on the town at One Fifth or the Brussels, in matching leather jackets, they were a power couple. The question of whether or not they were ever an actual couple still divides industry gossips today." It does?

Here Kachka is in his element. Gossip about Roger's sexual life (and everyone else's) is a dominant feature of *Hothouse*—yes, FSG was hot in this way, too. Not only was Roger the Emperor of Frankfurt, but in New York, in the office, he was the Sun King—complete with deer park. The chief doe, Peggy Miller, arrived in his life around the same time Sontag did. She was an experienced executive secretary who went to work for Roger in that capacity and stayed on until the end, a major force at FSG. ("I'm . . . grateful to Peggy Miller," Kachka writes, "the living soul of independent FSG, for giving me so much of her time.")

For decades, Roger would pick up Peggy on his way to work every morning. And for years Peggy was with him at the Frankfurt fair, making arrangements and acting as hostess—and before the fair going with him for weekends to Bavarian spas (where "Peggy indulged in her favorite dessert, a delicate seasonal plum cake") and, after the fair, on to London for meetings and theater. Some of the Europeans "who didn't know him well thought she was his wife. Some of those who knew her better, in the halls of 19 Union Square West, speculated on the extra spring in Miller's step come September, trilling: 'Peggy's gonna get laid in Frankfurt!'" (That "trilling" is a quintessential Kachka touch.)

But Peggy Miller was only one of the FSG women to receive Roger's personal attentions. "By the early 1960s, he was probably sleeping with three of his female employees. At the very least there were a switchboard operator and a publicity director. They were opposite physical types, but that didn't seem to matter. 'Roger would fuck a snake if you held it down,' says one employee from that time period. These two women, who were good friends, went shopping together and bought Roger matching bathrobes so that their boss would feel equally at home having 'lunch' at either of their apartments." Now, *that's* team spirit.

Others exhibited the same team spirit. "Everybody was fucking everybody in that office," Kachka quotes Leslie Sharpe, "a former FSG assistant who occasionally slept with Roger" after leaving the firm. Top editors were having conspicuous affairs. Husbands left wives for younger colleagues. "People were having sex in the mailroom after hours." No wonder Dorothea Straus referred to FSG as a "sexual sewer."

How did any work get done? And how did Dorothea deal with all this? To a large extent, she led her own life, although she was always an elegant hostess in her black silk dresses and big hats with veils (her son remarked, "I think my mother saw an Aubrey Beardsley drawing when she was young and never recovered from the experience"). And her talk, Kachka assures us, "was always of the highest order."

Clearly, like many others she was in some kind of thrall to her husband, that potent combination of grand seigneur and buccaneer.

ROGER, WHO LIVED THE HIGH LIFE as a rich man born to riches, seems to have had something like contempt for those who weren't so fortunate. His failure to pay his staff sufficiently, let alone generously, was notorious in the industry. One young woman, confronted by Roger after being caught stealing books to sell to the Strand, said to him, "I'll stop if you give me a raise."

This stinginess applied at every level. In 1964, he and Giroux brought in the considerably younger and highly talented (and well-regarded) Henry Robbins to modernize the list. Robbins came through spectacularly: Tom Wolfe, Joan Didion, John Gregory Dunne, Wilfrid Sheed, Grace Paley, and Donald Barthelme quickly signed on, although Wolfe, whose snobberies were compatible with Roger's, soon became a Roger man. (Wolfe letter to Roger: "Your splendid dinner Friday really did restore my soul.") But Robbins was not the amenable Giroux—he found Roger's editorial interferences enraging. Besides, his health was insecure: He had suffered a serious heart attack in his mid-forties, and he couldn't support his complicated family life on his salary of twenty-five thousand dollars. By 1973, he was desperate.

At that time, I was running Alfred A. Knopf (where Robbins had once worked), and I remember him coming to see me for advice: Should he leave FSG for Simon & Schuster (where *I* had once worked)? S. & S. was offering him much more money, and he also felt that, as a strong commercial house, it would present his authors more aggressively: He was distressed by FSG's somewhat sluggish (and cost-saving) publishing. My view was that he clearly had to improve his situation, but that S. & S. as it was then would be a personal disaster for him. Alas, that is what it turned out to be. After two unhappy years there, and a less painful short stretch at Dutton, he died of another heart attack, a major loss for American publishing. Bob Giroux spoke lovingly at his funeral; Roger not only didn't attend, but when he heard that Bob was going he "threw a fit."

The next editor in chief to try to *be* editor in chief at Roger's publishing house was the much-admired Aaron Asher, who brought Philip Roth to the company but after half a dozen years bowed out, from then on, according to Kachka, always referred to by Roger as "the late Aaron Asher." Other talented and productive editors—Pat Strachan, Michael di Capua—for the most part managed not to antagonize the boss, and so could enjoy long and fruitful careers at FSG.

The most complicated relationship Roger had with a colleague was with his and Dorothea's only child, Roger III, known as Rog. Everyone who knew Rog back then, including me, liked and respected him, and he was in publishing not only because it was the family business but because he loved it. When he came into the company, Rog said, "I was twenty-one, and it was easy and comfortable to do it his [Roger's] way. But by the time I was thirty-one, I started having ideas of my own, which were sometimes not his ideas." He decided to move to Harper & Row. "I wanted more oxygen. I wanted to flap my own wings, or whatever. And also, since marketing had become my thing, I wanted a place where I had more money to spend, a more diverse list to market." At that point, in 1975, he was sure he would never be back.

By 1985, he was back. But a final confrontation between Roger and Rog, in 1993, led to the younger Straus's definitive departure. Rog: "He said a bunch of things and I said a bunch of things and I said, 'If that's the way you feel I'm gonna quit,' and he didn't say anything and I quit." Roger gave Rog a final chance. "You're not coming back, are you?" Rog said no. Philosophical conflicts? Temperamental conflicts? Oedipal conflicts?—it hardly matters. Roger and his son were fated to suffer the same clash of wills, and the same ultimate breach, that Roger had experienced with his own father, who had assertively challenged Roger's choice of publishing as a way of life.

Roger's unmediated temperament led to his being at odds not only with his father and with his son but with his brother and, eventually, with Bob. Toward the end of his life, Giroux explained that he wasn't going to write a book about his publishing life because, as Kachka puts it, "he couldn't find a way to write it without speaking ill of Roger Straus, and he didn't think that would serve anyone well." Unsurprisingly, the main cause of his disaffection was a justifiable resentment at the way Roger had dealt with him financially.

There were those who loved Roger and those who hated him: Not many people were neutral. A buccaneer of his own stamp, the notably aggressive agent Andrew Wylie, with whom Roger had an ambivalent (mostly antagonistic) relationship, spoke at Roger's memorial service, summing him up as "a magnificent character: vindictive, raucous, willful. A wonderful man." His energy, his charm, his single-mindedness, his nerve, his ruthlessness, his remarkable instincts propelled him to the top of the book world, yet he wasn't an intellectual; he was an un-ashamed autodidact. He was almost abnormally competitive, relishing public brawls. He was funny, he was foulmouthed, and he could be cruel: His very talented editor Michael di Capua, who was gay, once came back to the office after a stay in the Hamptons "with his balding pate bright red. 'Hey, Mikey, did someone suck your head off on the beach?' " Was this the man whose favorite book was *Memoirs of Hadrian*? Or was he showboating—enjoying shocking people and happy to be adding to his reputation for outrageousness?

What seems to me a sadness about him was his lack of capacity for intimacy. Once a week for fifty years he played tennis with a man named Roger Hirson. Their friendship, we're told, consisted almost entirely of their tennis dates, yet Straus made Hirson a co-executor of his will. "He didn't have a lot of personal friends," Hirson says.

When Roger died, an Italian publisher pronounced, "He was not a great publisher, but he was a great man." I think he got it exactly backward. From the story Kachka tells, Roger emerges as a truly great publisher but very far from a great man.

THE HISTORY OF FSG CONTINUES, of course, after Roger Straus's death, and therefore so does *Hothouse*. The firm had begun to change before he died, when concern for the future led to his finally deciding to sell it. Immediately after his son left, Roger called his Frankfurt pal Dieter von Holtzbrinck, the billionaire chairman of a company whose hold-ings in America were the publisher Henry Holt and the magazine *Scien-*

tific American. The deal—for about thirty million dollars—was concluded over the phone. Having inveighed endlessly about the awfulness of publishing conglomerates while congratulating himself on not being part of one, he had capitulated: FSG had become part of the second-largest consortium in German media; only Bertelsmann was larger.

By that time, however, a potential successor was in place. The editor Jonathan Galassi, a refugee from Random House, had all the intellectual qualifications of a Bob Giroux, but was both tougher and more ambitious—as well as more tactful than a Robbins, an Asher, or a disaffected son. ("Ductile," Scott Turow called him. "He's supple in his dealings with very strong personalities, and knows how to get around them.") Galassi brought to the firm writers like Jonathan Franzen, Jeffrey Eugenides, and Thomas Friedman, and he steadily rose to become editor in chief and executive vice president. Unlike Giroux, he was a first-rate publisher as well as an editor; unlike Rog, he was a first-rate editor as well as a publisher. He himself says he was "the good son, [Rog] was the bad son." That the two "sons" have remained good friends is a tribute to both their characters.

In the first decade after the sale, Holtzbrinck kept most of its non-interference promises—the most important to Roger being the promise of continuing editorial independence. Meanwhile, inch by inch, he ceded authority to Galassi, while suffering (or ignoring) the modernizations on the business side, essential for survival, that were being quietly implemented. (Only after his death did the company move into handsome modern offices that made day-to-day life for the staff not only bearable but pleasant.) He had become an old lion now, but not a toothless one—and he was still The Chairman. When Galassi suggested to him that his feuds and grudges might be counterproductive, he snapped, "Don't give me any of that Christian forgiveness, Galassi, I'm a vindictive Jew." Even so, he was mellower, and his health had grown shakier. By the time he died, in 2004, at the age of eighty-seven, FSG had, without losing its unique distinction, been transformed.

Given the new technologies, the past ten years have, as everyone knows, been traumatic for the publishing business. FSG, under Galassi, seems to have ridden out the storm as well as any of its rivals, owing to a combination of things: the rationalization of its business practices following the sale to Holtzbrinck; the richness of the backlist that Roger so carefully nurtured; and the success of its editors in acquiring impressive and profitable newer authors. Of course there have been compromises, but FSG has not been compromised.

Kachka doesn't have much to say about writers as writers, but when there's gossip in the air he's on top of it—pages and pages, for instance, are devoted to the notorious Jonathan Franzen–Oprah Winfrey spat. On the whole, though, it's the early history that's freshest and most instructive; particularly welcome is the detailed portrayal of Bob Giroux. But Kachka really doesn't grasp what things used to be like in publishing, what the relationships and struggles and personalities were—he lacks context. This is feature journalism masquerading as history.

Another difficulty is the tone of the writing, which is again and again overexcited and/or inexact. "The old bookman [Donald Brace] said he couldn't overrule his trusted hire." Columbia was "a cauldron of passionate, callow strivers." The Strauses' decorator died soon after completing his work on their New York house, "never to see it resonate with the contentious exclamations of Susan Sontag, Tom Wolfe, or Joseph Brodsky." "His relationship with Susan only grew more enmeshed after her recovery." When Rog decided to leave for Harper & Row, he "spun it to Dad like a stifled boyfriend." "Profits were nothing to drool over." Three hundred and forty-five pages of this kind of thing is hard to take.

Even so, and despite all its flaws and confusions, *Hothouse* is a valuable effort. No one has previously anatomized a publishing house in such depth, and publishing is fascinating—at least, to those of us who are in it. Farrar, Straus and Giroux, moreover, is well worth anatomizing. It's had a larger-than-life central character, an amusing cast of secondary characters, and a history replete with drama. Most important, it has maintained an amazingly consistent level of quality: It's better than "hot," it's good. And it's now a happy place, for both writers and staff. Take it from one who knows: I'm an FSG author.

The Maestro

ARTURO TOSCANINI

O N THE NIGHT OF JUNE 30, 1886, Arturo Toscanini—recently turned nineteen—arrived, barely on time, at the imperial opera house in Rio de Janeiro, where the touring company for which he was the principal cellist was about to perform *Aida*. Pandemonium. The unpopular lead conductor had resigned in a huff. His unpopular replacement had been shouted off the podium by the audience. There was no one else. Toscanini, who was also assistant choral master, was thrust forward by his colleagues. "Everyone knew about my memory," he would recall, "because the singers had all had lessons with me, and I had played the piano without ever looking at the music." He was handed a baton and just started to conduct. A triumph! Typical of the glowing reviews: "This beardless maestro is a prodigy who communicated the sacred artistic fire to his baton and the energy and passion of a genuine artist to the orchestra." For the remaining six weeks of the tour, Harvey Sachs tells us in his biography *Toscanini: Musician of Conscience*, the maestro led the orchestra in twenty-six performances of twelve operas, all from memory. No one offered him a raise, and it didn't occur to him to ask for one.

It was almost sixty-eight years later, in April 1954, that he conducted his final concert, an all-Wagner program, at Carnegie Hall. He was eighty-seven and decades earlier had established himself as the world's most famous conductor—the world's most famous musician; a "genius," in fact, alongside such names as Einstein, Picasso, and, with a backward glance, Thomas Alva Edison. Nor was this a new notion: Back in the conservatory in Parma, his hometown, "Arturo's fellow students teased him by calling him *Gèni*, the dialect word for 'genius.'"

Genius or not, he unquestionably *was* a prodigy. At school he had been assigned the cello as his instrument, and he quickly mastered it—by the time he was fourteen he was playing in the Parma opera company's orchestra. He taught himself to play the piano, the violin, the double bass. He sang, he composed, he organized and led groups of his fellow students. Everyone was aware of his astounding photographic memory and his immense powers of concentration. In his final year he was named the school's outstanding graduate, and he was liked as well as admired. "When I look back at the years of my adolescence," he would reminisce, "I don't remember a day without sunshine, because the sunshine was in my soul."

Music happened to him by accident. His good-natured if rather feckless father, Claudio—whose heart lay in his years of campaigning with Garibaldi's army of the Risorgimento, and who made a somewhat precarious living through tailoring—and his cold and distant mother, Paola, were "musical," but not exceptionally so. It was an elementary school teacher who spotted little Arturo's strong response to music and advised his parents to send him to Parma's music conservatory, where once he was accepted as a live-in student all his expenses were taken care of—a boon to the financially strapped family.

Word of Toscanini's South American success quickly got around, and soon he was a busy itinerant opera conductor: Turin, Bologna, Venice, Genoa, Palermo, Pisa, Rome—he was working everywhere, though undoubtedly his greatest satisfaction in those early days was playing cello for Verdi, his hero, at the 1887 premiere of *Otello*. After some years at Turin's Regio Theater, where in 1895–96 he conducted the world premiere of *La Bohème* (he'd done the same for *Pagliacci* in Milan) and the first Italian production of *Götterdämmerung*, he was wooed away, inevitably, by La Scala, where he reigned on and off until in 1908 he left Italy to lead the Metropolitan Opera in New York. In Milan he had worked with (and disciplined) the young Caruso and Chaliapin, had forced audiences to accept darkened auditoriums, instituted a bitterly opposed policy of no encores, and had the orchestra playing in a pit rather than at stage level. He had mounted and conducted the first Italian performances of *Siegfried*, *Pelléas et Mélisande*, and *Eugene Onegin*.

And he had married. When Arturo met Carlotta De Martini in 1895, he was twenty-eight and she was eighteen, a pretty, vivacious girl whom he pursued with all his intensity and tenacity. They married in 1897, and he liked telling people that their son Walter was born exactly nine months after the wedding: "in tempo, like a good conductor." Two girls and another boy would follow. You could say that it was a successful marriage but not a happy one. Arturo and Carla would stay together until her death in 1951, both of them loyal to the idea of family but increasingly distanced from each other emotionally. Her messiness maddened him ("For *41 years* I've suffered from this disorder of hers!!!"), and his serial philandering deeply wounded her. He came by his life of compulsive adultery honestly: Claudio, Arturo would say, "was a good-looking man. Women went after him. And what's a young man to do? Some say yes, some say no." Claudio said yes often, and Arturo, notably short though equally good-looking, said yes as well—many, many times, both as a young man and as an old one.

The most damaging of his extramarital relationships was a prolonged affair with the leading soprano Rosina Storchio. The relationship was an open secret—one night when she was singing Cio-Cio San, one of her finest roles, a breeze ruffled her robes and a member of the audience shouted out, "Butterfly is pregnant with Toscanini's child." In 1903 Rosina gave birth to a son, Giovanni, but a mishap during the delivery left him brain-damaged, and Giovanni died at sixteen. Rosina never married.

In a dismaying echo of that tragedy, Arturo and Carla suffered an equally devastating loss. Their second boy, Giorgio, not yet five, died of diphtheria while they were all in Buenos Aires, and Carla—not only drowning in grief but wildly angry because she believed her husband had been with Storchio as Giorgio was dying—packed her trunks to leave for Italy. She relented, though, as always torn between her love for her husband and her distress at the circumstances of her marriage. Besides, she had her other children to consider, Walter and her daughter, Wally. Despite her grief—or, as Sachs suggests, perhaps because of it—she determined to have another baby. But with the birth of Wanda, when Carla was thirty, all sexual relations between husband and wife came to an end. As for Wanda, whose difficult disposition reminded her father of his difficult mother, she went on to marry the profoundly neurotic (and homosexual) piano virtuoso Vladimir Horowitz.

Toscanini's relationship with Geraldine Farrar, the reigning diva of the Metropolitan Opera, was hardly a secret. She was determined to marry him, he had no intention, then or ever, of leaving Carla and the children, and it's generally assumed that he resigned his leadership of the Met after seven years in order to escape her importunities. Among the dozens of other women with whom he was involved were other famous singers like Lotte Lehmann and Alma Gluck (and, some said, Gluck's daughter, the writer Marcia Davenport). Carla put up with all of it—and, in fact, befriended a number of the mistresses.

ONE OF THE THINGS that led Sachs to write a second biography of Toscanini, more than twice as long as his first (published in 1978), was the new availability of huge archives of documents and letters—in 2002 he edited *The Letters of Arturo Toscanini*. The letters cover an immense range of musical, political, and personal matters, but the most astonishing ones are passionate love letters that sometimes go beyond the erotic to the pornographic. From a typical letter to Elsa Kurzbauer, with whom he was in love for many years: "Your kisses, your lips (oh! sweetness) your mouth inflame ever and evermore at the utmost my frenzy to have you under my libidinous caresses—kisses—suckings—lickings—bitings, all over your *girlisch* body—I am dying and lusting for every part *nook—crevice—hole—holy hole* of *your lovely person*." Their relationship would pick up, though not quite where it had left off, twenty years later, when Elsa had escaped from Vienna to New York. "Don't *lose time*," the septuagenarian Arturo wrote to her. "Maybe *before long* God will take away even the *little bit* of *virility* that's left me. And then? What misery!"

The fullest correspondence, though—almost a thousand telegrams and letters from Toscanini, adding up to something like 240,000 words—was with Ada Mainardi, a pianist with whom he was besotted for seven years, beginning in 1933. They met rarely—she was in Italy, with her cellist husband, and he was mostly in America—which may explain why the relationship in all its intensity lasted so long. These letters are a revelation of his day-to-day doings, his ideas, his feelings. And he wrote, compulsively, of his passion: "I'm like a madman, I could commit a crime!! . . . When, oh when, will we be able to possess each other completely, clinging together, deep inside each other, our mouths gasping, united while *awaiting the supreme voluptuousness* at the same moment? When—when?" His erotic impulses toward Ada grew ever stronger—and stranger. Sachs tells us that "he had begun to send her a fresh handkerchief each month, with increasingly insistent requests that she stain it with her menstrual blood and send it back to him so that he could suck it—or so he claimed—'since I can't quench my thirst directly at the *delightful fount.*'" Apparently, "she often complied, and he gleefully and blasphemously described each handkerchief as the Holy Shroud." To each his own.

What eventually undermined the relationship was not their geographical separation but his increasing distaste, then disgust, for her political leanings and casual anti-Semitism. "You hurt me when you say that you don't love the Jews. Tell me, rather, that you don't love the *human race,*" he wrote to her in 1939. He had been deeply moved by his experience three years earlier, when—at no fee and paying his own expenses—he inaugurated what would become the Israel Philharmonic. By that time, he was famous throughout the world for his implacable hatred of Fascism and Nazism. One of the many ways he demonstrated his hostility to Mussolini was his defiance of the law that the Fascist Party's anthem, "Giovinezza," be played at the start of every public performance. In response, in 1931 he was beaten by Fascist thugs outside the opera house in Bologna, and his passport was taken from him. Only in the face of an international outcry was it returned.

In 1933, after several extraordinarily successful seasons at the Bayreuth Wagner festival—Toscanini was the first non-German conductor to perform there—he informed Winifred Wagner, Wagner's English daughter-in-law now in charge (and a close friend of Hitler's), that given the conditions obtaining in Germany since the Nazis had taken over earlier that year, and despite a flattering personal letter from the Führer himself, he would not be returning. "For my peace of mind, for yours, and for everyone's, it is better not to think any longer about my coming to Bayreuth." Nothing could better demonstrate both his unbending loyalty to principle and the astounding position he held on the world stage.

In the same spirit, early in 1938, after having triumphed for the third time at the annual Salzburg Festival, he decided that with the Germans poised to overrun Austria, he would not return. Mussolini again had his passport impounded, and again worldwide indignation forced the Duce to change his mind. On the very day that the passport was suddenly returned, the Toscaninis left Milan for America. "To flee, to flee—that was the consuming thought!" he wrote to Ada. "To flee in order to breathe freedom, life!"

He would not see his country again for eight years. Sachs tells us that when, at seventy-nine, he presided over the post-war reopening of La Scala, tens of thousands gathered outside the opera house and millions listened around the world: "For Toscanini, it was the culminating moment of his life as a musician." Yet even at this moment of exaltation he kept his sense of humor. As he was walking from the stage entrance into the auditorium, someone offered to hang up his hat for him. "Thank you," he replied, "but I'm not the prima donna—and I'm not even the baritone."

THE TRAJECTORY OF TOSCANINI'S ARTISTIC PATH constitutes the main body of Sachs's biography, and he gives us an extremely thorough chronicle of his activities and achievements. Here are the early galvanizing effects he had on opera in Italy and at the Met (where he led the world premiere of Puccini's *La Fanciulla del West* and the American premiere of *Boris Godunov*); the endless triumphs in Europe and South America; the revitalization of the New York Philharmonic; and on to the final seventeen years leading the NBC Symphony Orchestra. Sachs frequently steps over the line and in his ardor for his subject and his addiction to detail tells us more than most of us need to know. (For example, extensive lists of programs should have been relegated to footnotes or supplied as addenda rather than woven into the narrative.) And then there are nuttily detailed references to completely irrelevant matters, such as this passage about the villa the Toscaninis rented on the Isolino San Giovanni: "Through much of the first half of the twentieth century, it was rented to various wealthy people, including Vittoria Colonna di Sermoneta, the estranged wife of Leone Caetani, Prince of Teano; she had a passionate affair there with the painter Umberto

Boccioni." But these are failures of excessive zeal rather than failures of judgment. Sachs's account of Toscanini's career is persuasive and compelling in the important ways.

He also gives us the man, with all his contradictions. Famous for his tantrums in rehearsal (breaking and flinging batons, shouting imprecations at musicians he found lazy or unprepared), he was unfailingly kind in person. He never fired musicians, even those he disliked; he was a warm host; and he was personally generous—donating his services and his orchestra to countless causes and instructing Carla to help out any musician in need of funds, no questions asked. Money was never of importance to him. The evidence makes it clear that everything he did was in the service of music, not of ego or success. He gave almost no interviews, had no press agent, shied away from applause, and conducted calmly and simply—he admired Leonard Bernstein but deplored what Sachs tactfully calls Bernstein's "emotive podium style." Typical of his lack of self-regard are remarks such as "Every time I conduct the same piece I think how stupid I was the last time I did it," and his response after his retirement to someone who addressed him as Maestro: "Do not call me Maestro. I am no longer a maestro."

His self-deprecation is especially telling in light of the torrent of praise that from the start he received from almost every contemporary conductor. Let Pierre Monteux stand for all: "I had before me, simply, a man of genius, a conductor such as I had never seen in my life, a true revelation in the art of conducting and interpretation." And from Stravinsky, although he found Toscanini's choice of repertory sadly oldfashioned: "I have never encountered in a conductor of such world repute such a degree of self-effacement, conscientiousness and artistic honesty."

For those who want to comprehend how Toscanini inspired and affected the musicians who played or sang for him, I recommend B. H. Haggin's *Arturo Toscanini: Contemporary Recollections of the Maestro*, in which almost a score of his musicians speak about him. It's a unique and moving tapestry of fear, awe, and devotion, though Caruso anticipated them all when in 1909 he said, "Experience has taught me that I don't know if I know a role until I sing it with the *Grande Omino* [great little man]!"

Of course there were naysayers along the way, particularly about matters of repertory. Toscanini had been a trailblazer in his earlier years, championing composers like Berlioz, Debussy, Ravel, Puccini, and Strauss. Later, he dabbled in Bruckner and Shostakovich but resisted Mahler, Bartók, Schoenberg, *Wozzeck*. "I can't get modern music to enter either my head or my heart! I'm too old, and my faculties have *calcified*," he wrote to Ada. He would instead "keep conducting the *same music*!"—Beethoven, Wagner, Brahms, Verdi—and continue to deepen his understanding of it. And although he performed Gershwin (he admired *Porgy and Bess*—"a true American opera"), Grofé, and Barber, he was often reproached for neglecting American composers. (He did conduct Copland's *El Salón México*—once.) Charles Ives, Sachs tells us, "reviled 'Toscaninny'" for his conservatism, and the brilliant critic/ composer Virgil Thomson never ceased complaining about the retro nature of the maestro's tastes and his reliance on superb execution rather than depth of interpretation.

ON THE OTHER HAND, Toscanini approved of many of the young postwar artists. He had launched Renata Tebaldi on his return to La Scala in 1946, and he very much admired David Oistrakh and Kathleen Ferrier ("that divine voice"), while in 1951 he had this to say: "I find this Callas woman very good, a beautiful voice and an interesting artist, but her diction is unintelligible. . . . You *must* hear every word, otherwise it's a concert." Nothing had changed since in 1908 he offended the young diva Frances Alda by asking her politely, after a rehearsal of *Louise*, "In what language were you singing?"

By the post-war period, his fame and authority were so great that nothing could get between him and his adoring public, a vast popularity that had been pumped up by the blaring publicity machine of NBC and RCA, whose president, David Sarnoff, had lured him into leading the new NBC Symphony Orchestra. Toscanini was *news*— three times on the cover of *Time*; subject of spreads in *Life*; received by presidents. Yet he was never grand when off-duty, as when in 1950 on a six-week tour across America with his orchestra some of his musicians spotted him coming up the ski tow in Sun Valley. (He was eighty-three.) One of the more daring of them said, "Maestro, you are a brave man." Without hesitation he replied, "I've never been afraid of anything in my life."

The most scathing attack on him appeared in 1987, in Joseph Horowitz's *Understanding Toscanini* (in which I had a hand), although it was more an attack on the "commodification" of him by NBC, RCA Victor records, and the reviewers who glorified him. Toscanini was "the priest of beauty." "He has shown us, as St. Francis did, the startling and terrible beauty of that which is forever kindling and alight: that pure flame of the imagination, 'burning in the void.' " Et cetera, et cetera. Horowitz was expanding (though with reservations) on the fierce views of Theodor Adorno about the commercialization of culture, and his examples are all too convincing, climaxed by the cult of personality created around Pavarotti and encouraged by him with remarks like "With all due respect, I do not agree with Maestro von Karajan's remarkable comment that my voice is greater [than Caruso's]." Well, no one ever claimed that tenors were modest.

There is, however, a disturbing antidemocratic slant to this assault on the popularization of musical culture—on, for instance, the simplicities of "music appreciation" for children. ("I'm sorry to say that Mr. Beethoven wasn't a kind father at all and that was one of the reasons why Ludwig grew to have a strange, unhappy disposition.") Yet better to be exposed to nonsense like this than that children grow up never having heard of Ludwig, or heard his music. It didn't harm my eventual love of Schubert that in the fourth grade we were taught to sing along "This is . . . the sym-pho-ny . . . that Schu-bert loved but never fin-ished." Horowitz's book, when it isn't strident, is invaluable in many ways, both historical and sociological, but Toscanini is its innocent victim: *He* didn't want a cult; what he wanted was to make music. It was David Sarnoff who wanted glory—and profits.

Today, Toscanini is receding from our consciousness, notwithstanding his many recordings. (Can there be a greater live opera recording than his 1937 Salzburg *Falstaff*, despite the questionable quality of the sound, or greater orchestral recordings than those with the New York Philharmonic from 1936?) Creative geniuses can survive for centuries, even millennia; interpreters inevitably go over the cultural cliff. But that doesn't detract from the crucial—the central—role Toscanini played in our musical culture for well over sixty years. Nor from the almost universal regard he was held in as a man. To Isaiah Berlin, for instance, he was "the most morally dignified and inspiring hero of our time," and, closer to home, Walter Toscanini, who had for many years taken responsibility for his father's welfare, is quoted by Sachs as saying that although he knew his father's personal failings intimately, the "human side" of his character was even "greater than his musicianship."

As for that musicianship, let Virgil Thomson, his most perceptive and persistent critic, have the final word. At the end of a "Birthday Salute" written for the maestro's eightieth, he wrote: "We must enjoy him and be thankful for him and cherish him. For when he leaves there will be little left save a memory and a few gramophone records; and these give hardly any idea of his electric powers as a public performer. By a miracle we have him with us still and, by a greater miracle, in full possession of his powers. That those powers are without peer in our time cannot be denied by anybody. That they may long be preserved to him and to us is the prayer of every living musician and lover of music."

The New York Times Book Review
JULY 2, 2017

Lenny!

LEONARD BERNSTEIN

I N 1966, Leonard Bernstein conducted *The Rite of Spring* and Sibe-
lius's Symphony no. 5 with the London Symphony Orchestra, and
just recently that BBC event has been released on DVD for the first
time. It's a fascination—not only for the strong performance, but even
more so for the chance to watch "Lenny" in action, close-up. Yes, all
conductors have highly personal characteristics, but has there ever
been one as theatrical, as showy, as hammy as he was? Or as exciting, as
persuasive, as dedicated?

There's the Lenny problem: Is he for real or is he an act? Do we love
him or do we want to kick him in the ass? Is his heart only on his sleeve,
or is there another one inside him? And do those of us who grew up with
him in all his avatars respond to him the same way as those coming to
him for the first time, with no history and perhaps no expectations?

Look at him up there, facing a cadre of highly disciplined, impeccably groomed Englishmen. (Not many women in the LSO in those
days.) They watch him closely, of course—is it my fantasy that they
watch him as if they were in striking distance of a dangerous tiger? His
behavior to them is totally cordial and respectful—in fact, remarkably
generous: hands shaken, pats on the shoulder, warm smiles. If he isn't
happy with their playing, you'd never know it.

But have they ever worked with a conductor not only this legendary but this over-the-top? It's not just his notorious bouncing up and
down. He grins, he grimaces, he thrusts and spasms; the emotional
climaxes of the music are reflected on his face—he's thrilled with excitement one moment, anguished the next. He nods and sways. He
sweats. He mouths along with the music. Since he conducts without a
score—his musical memory is famous—his inner concentration is un-

broken. If a tragedian performed *King Lear* this way we'd probably hoot him off the stage. But just when we're ready to find the whole thing risible, we begin to believe it. No, he's not a charlatan; no, he's not a joke. He's a believer. It's for real.

And yet . . .

The mystery of who and what Leonard Bernstein was is what draws us to accounts of his life, and now to a large collection of his letters, *The Leonard Bernstein Letters*, edited by Nigel Simeone. Surely the letters of such a well-educated and literate man, a practiced and effective writer—author of best sellers about music, important lectures, successful television scripts—will be revealing? Alas, it is not so. Despite his cleverness and charm, which definitely come through, we're left knowing no more, really, than we knew before. The confusion between genius and narcissism, heroism and self-pity, generosity and exploitation, remains unresolved. His astounding energies both made him everything he was and undermined him. Was he a composer or a conductor? Was he "serious" (the *Jeremiah* Symphony, *Chichester Psalms*) or "showbiz" (*On the Town*, *West Side Story*)? Was he straight (his beloved Felicia, and their three cherished children) or gay (just about everyone else)? Was he loyal to his friends and benefactors or careless with them? Was he deeply emotional or merely sentimental? Did he use his extraordinary powers wholesomely or did he dissipate them? And what really mattered to him?

He's not going to tell us, but the *Letters*, read in conjunction with Humphrey Burton's excellent 1994 biography, *Leonard Bernstein*, suggest that there were three things that motored him: music, of course; his family, despite (or because of) the conflicts; his Judaism (and his belief in Israel). The money, the celebrity, the sex were front and center, but not, in the long run, central.

LETTERS CAME EASILY to the young Bernstein—he's as fluent a writer as he's fluent at everything else—and he understands how self-centered he is. (To his great pal Kenny Ehrman, he once said, "Who do I think I am, everybody?" To Helen Coates, first his piano teacher, later, and for decades, his assistant, guide, life-support system: "Before I forget myself and write an 'I' letter, I want to wish you a very pleasant summer." He pours out his heart to just about everybody. He's met the perfect girl (boy). He's written this, he's done that. So-and-so complimented him, so-and-so is giving him a hand up. Always there's the assumption that anyone he's writing to wants to know everything about him—a narcissism that's normal, even touching, in a young man, but less so in a (supposedly) mature one. Think how he would have taken to blogging!

He needs, obsessively, to be appreciated, to be admired, to be loved. He needs people. "You may remember my chief weakness—my love for people," he writes Ehrman in 1939 (he's twenty). "I need them all the time—every moment. It's something that perhaps you cannot understand: but I cannot spend one day alone without becoming utterly depressed. Any people will do. It's a terrible fault." He needs to be witnessed—at bottom, he's a performer, and his letters are performances. Only to a few people—his sister and brother, for instance— does he talk straight: When he tells them what's been happening and that he loves and misses them, it's the real Lenny who's talking—if there *is* a real Lenny.

THERE'S A SPECIAL CATEGORY of letter in his early years—the flattering cries for attention of a young man on the make. By the time he was twenty, he had cast a spell over a series of major musicians. Of course, they were also responding to his extraordinary abilities, apparent to everyone from the very start—the music world knew at once that he was a prodigy and a future leader. And they were drawn by his good looks and intelligence and personal magnetism. But their partiality was certainly enhanced by the way he approached them. To Aaron Copland, the first of his formidable mentors, in April 1942: "It would have been wonderful to see you. God, yes. On our first beautiful spring day. And we would have walked in all Boston's parks and spoken long, quietly & with heart. Such gab. Can't you come anyway? We must have a session on the Copland youth opera, you know. The master's interpretation. Hell, I miss you so."

This relationship, which either did or did not begin as a love affair, was probably the most durable and nurturing of Lenny's life. There were ups and downs, but Copland always cared about his younger friend, and Lenny always revered him. One of his most persuasive pieces of writing was the speech of introduction he gave at the Kennedy Center Honors in 1979, which ended:

Usually men of such restraint and moderation, who also harbor such tumultuous inner passions and rages, are sick men, psychotics who are prone to unpredictable and irrational explosions. Not so Aaron. . . . The man is sanity itself—and that is why the first moment I met him— on his thirty-seventh birthday—I trusted him instantly and relied completely on his judgment as gospel and have done so ever since. It is my honor to present him to you, my first friend in New York, my master, my idol, my sage, my shrink, the closest thing to a composition teacher I ever had, my guide, my counselor, my elder brother, my beloved friend—Aaron Copland.

His exchanges with the formidable conductor Dimitri Mitropolous, a tormented (gay) man, are painful. Mitropolous is so lonely, so needy, that the attentions Lenny paid him became essential to him. He wrote to Lenny, "And, dear boy, I need your appreciation, your respect, your love! It is of great importance in my life.... May I ask a small picture of you to be my companion on my Europe trip?" And a month later:

> Can you imagine for a moment, I thought I lost your love, and then, I was asked me [*sic*], perhaps I am not right to ask anything, to expect anything, from anybody, that my destiny is to be alone with myself and my art. But you my dear friend, tell me, it is not so, I am something for you, yes . . . don't forget me. Goodbye dear, Dimitri.

Humphrey Burton believes that the relationship was not sexual, that "theirs was essentially a spiritual friendship." But Dimitri's language is the language of love, and although Lenny venerated him, he also took advantage of the conducting opportunities Mitropolous afforded him. Was it conscious advantage? Lenny simply could not help being seductive, and the older man could not help being emotionally seduced.

Lenny was also wooing Fritz Reiner (Pittsburgh) and Artur Rodzinski (New York Philharmonic), both of whom boosted his career. Later, he even captivated the greatest lion of them all, Toscanini, who in 1949 wrote to him, as quoted in Burton's biography, "Your kind visit and dear letter made me very, very happy.... I felt myself 40 years younger." (Alas, we do not have the "dear letter.")

THE MOST INTENSE BARRAGE of Bernsteinian flattery was aimed at the man who more than anyone else forwarded his career, America's most influential conductor, Serge Koussevitsky (Boston Symphony, Tanglewood). One example, from 1943, early in their relationship:

> Dear Doctor, Every once in a while I am appalled at the idea that I never see you—and I feel that I must write to you, or talk to you, if for no other reason than my constant warmth of affection for you. No matter how much time elapses without seeing you, you are always with me, guiding my work, providing the standards by which I measure my progress in our art. And today I feel simply that I must communicate with you, out of love and friendship—that is all.

Not long afterward, it's love from "Lenushka." And in 1945—he's conducting around the country—

> Every time I lift my arms to conduct I am filled with a sense of wonder at the great insight that has flowed from you to me. . . . It is something for which I thank you every day of my life—something which has freed me and given me a welcome bondage—as Prospero to Ariel . . . and when I feel this way, I always find I can express it best to you and through you to the Universal Creative Mind, to which you are closer than I.

It's clear that Koussevitsky's ego was as formidable as Bernstein's powers of flattering it, and by 1946 the maestro is growing touchy. There's a disagreement over programming a concert that Lenny is to conduct for Dr. K's Boston orchestra, and Lenny has, apparently, taken liberties. Dr. K snaps at him and instantly Lenny—"deeply grieved"—recants, apologizes, grovels. "Is there an evil element in my nature that makes me do and say immoral things? Is it that I say one thing and mean another? Or is it that communication between two people who are as close to each other is so difficult?"

The breach is repaired, but things are never again as they were. Because by this time, of course, Bernstein is no longer the eager beginner, grappling for a foothold in the world of classical music, but a public phenomenon: He's enjoyed the triumph—front-page headlines (BOY

CONDUCTOR GETS HIS CHANCE)—of his last-minute substitution for
Bruno Walter conducting the New York Philharmonic; he's written his
Jeremiah Symphony; and his score for Jerome Robbins's smash-hit
ballet *Fancy Free*, followed by the musical based on it, *On the Town*, has
made him not only a star but a celebrity. One of Lenny's finest qualities
was his loyalty, and he never fully turned away from Koussevitsky or
his family, but he no longer needed him.

His esteem for great conductors was real, even fervent. Consider
the genuine outpouring of respect and affection expressed in the letter
he wrote to the dying almost-ninety-year-old Karl Böhm in 1981, ending:
"You are young. Please stay so, for me, for my colleagues, for the holy art.
What you have done in music has already made you immortal; does
that not encourage you to remain with us, and teach us forever? I pray for
you, as does the whole world of music. With devotion, Bernstein." Alas,
Böhm died the day after this letter was written, but the important thing
is that Lenny obviously means it all—at least at the moment of writing.
He may be carried away by his feelings, but being carried away by one's
feelings, however fleeting, isn't as great a crime as not having any.

LENNY'S TONE with his early showbiz friends is naturally more relaxed,
more a matter of equals chatting with equals. He first met Adolph Green
when they were both working at a summer camp, and Adolph was instantly smitten with his brilliance. By the time Adolph was joined at
the hip with his lifelong partner, Betty Comden, and was working with
their other great friend Judy Holliday in the nightclub act called the
Revuers, Lenny was on hand, playing the piano for them down at the
Village Vanguard. (On the occasion of an experimental telecast in 1940,
as noted by the columnist Leonard Lyons, the distinguished page-
turner for Bernstein was Aaron Copland.)

Only a couple of Lenny's letters to Adolph, and none to Betty or
Judy, are included in this volume—maybe none has survived—but their
letters to him over the years punctuate and enliven the book. Comden
in particular remained a loving friend, sensible and honest and concerned.
Adolph is bouncy, gregarious, eager: "Dollink Lennie, What is there

to say? You are brilliant, brash, you (28)—I am fat, old (49½) and feeble. In short, what is there to say?" (Actually, Adolph was thirty-two.)

The two musicals Lenny and Adolph and Betty wrote together—*On the Town* and *Wonderful Town*—were big hits, but although there was endless talk of their working together again, it never happened. Adolph and Betty were off in Hollywood writing *Singin' in the Rain,* among other movies; he was off in Europe conducting Maria Callas in *La Sonnambula.* Lenny had his Hollywood episodes, too, ranging from a two-night fling with the young Farley Granger to a serious scheme at Paramount for him to star in a film opposite Garbo: He would be Tchaikovsky, she would be his patron Madame von Meck. Think of the music Lenny and Greta could have made together—even if, in real life, composer and patron never met.

ONE OF THE MOST TELLING EXCHANGES of letters over the decades is that between Lenny and the woman he would marry, the beautiful and talented Felicia Montealegre. She was a well-born Chilean actress, also a musician, whom everybody adored, including Lenny. It is obvious that she worshipped him, and soon they were talking marriage. An early letter from her signs off "Boss darling—goodnight," not necessarily a happy omen. Marriage receded, then was back on the front burner, then happened. Felicia knew the score. They hadn't been married long when she wrote to him, speaking of what she refers to as "our 'connubial' life":

> *First:* We are not committed to a life sentence—nothing is really irrevocable, not even marriage (though I used to think so).
>
> *Second:* you are a homosexual and may never change—you don't admit to the possibility of a double life, but if your peace of mind, your health, your whole nervous system depend on a certain sexual pattern what can you do?
>
> *Third:* I am willing to accept you as you are, without being a martyr or sacrificing myself on the L.B. altar. (I happen to love you very much—this may be a disease and if it is what better cure?) . . .

As for me—once you are rid of tensions I'm sure my own will disappear. A companionship will grow which probably no one else may be able to offer you. The feelings you have for me will be clearer and easier to express—our marriage is not based on passion but on tenderness and mutual respect. Why not have them?

They *did* have them, and he had known they would: In a letter about Felicia to his sister, Shirley—always the person he was most open and honest with—just before the die was cast in 1951, he wrote, "I feel such a certainty about us—I know there's a real future involving a great comradeship, a house, children, travel, sharing, and such a tenderness as I have rarely felt." It worked, except when it didn't. When he was in New York, they enjoyed a rich domestic life. Then he would be off on his endless conducting tours, writing long gossipy letters to her, occasionally meeting up with her. She was able to do some acting; she was raising the children.

But by the 1970s, his life as a homosexual had become flamboyantly open, to her increasing distress. He was now immensely famous and powerful, and he cast off all restraints—the self-regard he had always exhibited had hardened into unmitigated narcissism. Burton reports that Paul Bowles, a very old friend meeting him after many years, thought that "he had become 'smarmy' and 'false'; 'a small crumb of what he once had been.' His success had been 'painfully destructive' of his personality. It was," Burton remarks, "a chilling assessment," and the letters validate it.

In 1976, Lenny left Felicia for a young man named Tom Cothran. It was a public break, devastating and humiliating her. Eventually he returned to her, but it was too late—soon afterward, in 1978, she died of lung cancer, and it was his turn to be devastated. Despite everything, she was certainly the great love of his life. "He never recovered from her loss," Burton concludes, "and he never forgot the curse she uttered when he told her he was leaving her for Cothran. She had pointed her finger at him in fury and predicted, in a harsh whisper: 'You're going to die a bitter and lonely old man.'"

THE SMARTEST DECISION made by Nigel Simeone was to include scores of letters *to* Lenny. Again and again they're more interesting than his own letters—possibly because so many of them seem refreshingly direct and sincere, in contrast to his performances. I've mentioned Comden and Green's letters to him—they're fun, they're witty, and they're true. The letter Jackie Onassis wrote thanking him for arranging the music for Bobby Kennedy's funeral at St. Patrick's reveals this enigmatic woman at her most open and heartfelt. One passage from her long letter, written at four in the morning the night of the funeral:

> When your Mahler started to fill (but that's the wrong word—because it was more this sensitive trembling) the Cathedral today—I thought it the most beautiful music I had ever heard. I am so glad I didn't know it—it was this strange music of the gods who were crying. . . . The only thing that mattered in the world was that Ethel should have what she wished as music for her husband. . . . Dear Lennie—you were so tender and gentle and understanding—and tactful and self effacing—so she had *everything* she wanted.

The letters from Martha Gellhorn—a seemingly odd choice of friend for him—are engrossing. He writes to her that he had met her onetime husband Ernest Hemingway

> and was taken totally by surprise. I had not been prepared by talk, photos, or interviews for a) that charm, and b) that beauty. God, what goes on there under his eyes? What's that lovely adolescent tenderness? And the voice and the memory, & the apparently genuine interest in every living soul: fantastic.

In response, she writes:

> Interested about Ernest. Tenderness is a new quality in him; but people do luckily change all their lives and the luckiest ones get better as they grow older. His main appalling lack was tenderness for anyone.

I longed for it in him, for myself and for others. I'd almost have settled for others. . . .

He was interested in everyone but there was a bad side. It was like flirting. (Like you, in fact, he has the excessive need to be loved by everyone, and specially by all the strange passing people whom he ensnares with that interest, as do you with your charm, though in fact he didn't give a fart for them.) . . .

By the time I did marry him (driving home from Sun Valley) I did not want to, but it had gone too far in every way. I wept, secretly, silently, on the night before my wedding and my wedding night; I felt absolutely trapped. . . . You will also be surprised to hear that I have never been more bored in my life than during the long long months when we lived alone in Cuba. I thought I would die of boredom.

And there's Saul Chaplin—raw from the experience of helping to produce the film of *West Side Story*—writing about Jerome Robbins, with whom Lenny had a lifelong relationship, mutually beneficial but, like most relationships with Robbins, fraught:

Jerry, of course, is wildly talented. He is also wildly destructive of people and relationships. For me, one doesn't compensate for the other. He is easily the most reprehensible person I've ever known. And so, when the golden day dawns when I will, at last, be freed from *West Side Story*, I will make it a life's work never again to mention his name or think of him. That, indeed, will be a time for wild celebration.

Jerry was, indeed, a tough customer. How interesting that, as Simeone tells us, quoting Lenny's longtime record producer, "Felicia was vital to his stability as was Jerry Robbins, the only two people who could make Lenny sweat." Yes, Felicia could be a tough customer, too.

THROUGHOUT THE VOLUME, moments of Lenny's wit and insight flash out:

To Copland, about Anton Bruckner: "Impossibly boring, without personality, awkward & dull, masked in solemnity."

To Felicia, about Lillian Hellman: "I had forgotten what a charm Lil has: speaking to her over the phone reminded me of why one sticks to her through thick: she has a real attractiveness in spite of everything, and a kind of combination of power and helplessness that in a woman is irresistible."

To Felicia, about Herbert von Karajan: "My first Nazi."

Alas, Simeone has diluted the gold in his book with pointless letters—notes, often—from and to Lenny. Here's a telegram from 1957: "Dear Lenny, I hear glowing reports about your new show [*West Side Story*]. All my congratulations to you and Jerry. Best, Cole Porter." Seemingly anyone with a celebrated name is automatically thrown in. And Simeone's editorial apparatus is erratic—some notes tell you things everyone knows, others don't exist where you want them. Where the letters involve serious discussion of music, they're absorbing—the serious Lenny peeks out—but there should be more (if they exist). Certain friendships—as with the composer David Diamond and the clarinetist David Oppenheim (Judy Holliday's first husband)—are fully explored, others are not. One wants more to and from his parents and siblings. There are almost no letters between him and his three children—their decision, I assume.

Simeone tells us that there are more than 10,000 (!) Bernstein letters extant, and making a selection of a mere 650 must have been a daunting challenge. The results are uneven, but the basic problem stems not from the editor but from Lenny himself: He so often comes across as fatally facile rather than deeply probing. His friend the legendary musician Nadia Boulanger tactfully put it this way when he sent her the score of *West Side Story*: "*Merci*—I am enchanted by its dazzling nature—perhaps facility is a danger, but it is enough to be aware of that and follow it. . . . I often think of you, of the problems and temptations that your gifts give you—divergent and convergent." Lenny was aware of the danger, but he was helpless before the temptations.

Yes, he wanted to be everything to everyone, but we have to remember how well he succeeded at being so much to so many. He was one of the most acclaimed conductors of his day. He was a successful composer, though we tend to take his light music—the musicals— more seriously than we take his serious music. I mean, wouldn't you rather be listening to *On the Town* or *Candide* than his *Kaddish* Symphony, his *Dybbuk*? He was an ardent advocate for the music of his day. He was a potent and highly influential proselytizer for music in general, both in his writings and on television—his impulse was relentlessly pedagogical. ("I don't really possess my own feelings until I've shared them.")

And whatever his emotional vagaries, he was a consummate professional. I worked with him only once, in the 1960s, as the editor of his book *The Infinite Variety of Music*. He was an accommodating author— late on deadlines sometimes but, considering his schedule, how not? He was serious about his writing and responsive to suggestions. In other words, his ego didn't get in the way of his meeting his responsibilities. And he was appreciative. A few months after our book was published, he sent me a Christmas present. Why was I not surprised that it was a copy of *The Infinite Variety of Music*?

The New York Review of Books
DECEMBER 19, 2013

At the Top of Pop

CLIVE DAVIS

C LIVE DAVIS, the mogul of moguls of pop music through the
past half century, published a relatively fluent and interesting
memoir called *Clive*—in 1975. In 335 pages it carried him from
his (not too) humble beginnings to the traumatic moment when he was
fired, without warning or mercy, from his top job at Columbia Records,
which he had taken to the heights of the industry. (The first casualty of
his abrupt departure, after he was escorted out of the corporate building by security guards, was that Columbia suits scotched the deal he
had painstakingly crafted to keep Bob Dylan with the company. They
lived to regret it.)

Now, almost forty years later, he gives us this story again, though in
only about 170 pages of the staggering 551 it takes him to give us all of
The Soundtrack of My Life. Unfortunately, the earlier version of his rise to the
top is far more lively than the current one. Back then he was telling a
story; now he's establishing the official version. Also, he had a more spirited collaborator back then (James Willwerth) than he does now (Anthony DeCurtis). Perhaps "spirited" and "official" are mutually exclusive.

Here's that early story. Clive Davis was born, in 1932, in the Crown
Heights section of Brooklyn into what he reports to have been a warm,
sociable household—not much money, perhaps, but affording him a
full life centered on the Dodgers, radio (Jack Benny, Fred Allen, and
Burns and Allen), double features, ice cream, and girls. Music didn't
mean much to him, although he did like Bing. As he put it in *Clive*, "My
'act' was schoolwork. I was your basic, garden-variety, ambitious, up-
wardly mobile, hard-working Jewish boy from Brooklyn. I was bound
to go beyond my parents. It was simply the way things were." Of course,
he was especially smart and capable: Not every ambitious Jewish boy

from Brooklyn was always at the top of his class in elementary school and at Erasmus Hall High School, or was awarded a full scholarship to New York University (where he was president of the freshman class and then of the student council), and then another scholarship to Harvard Law. As he puts it, "I just seemed to have a self-starting drive from birth."

After Harvard, his hard work, ambition, and eye for the main chance propelled him into and out of the prestigious law firm headed by Sam Rosenman, adviser to Roosevelt and Truman, and then to the legal division of Columbia Records, where he flourished, fascinated by the music industry if not by the music itself. His great conversion experience was hearing Janis Joplin at the 1967 Monterey Music Festival; until then he'd been successfully negotiating new contracts with Dylan, Barbra Streisand, and Andy Williams, and signing the Scottish flower-singer Donovan. Now he was overwhelmed by a phenomenal new singer and her "vital, seething, raw talent . . . a force so compelling that it rode down fatigue, strain and the limits of endurance, to reach the very core of human capacity. Few artists have ever mattered so much to me as Janis." You believe it, and you get here the clue that explains how the Brooklyn student council president turned into the great impresario of cutting-edge rock. While remaining a shrewd, even ruthless businessman, he had been born again as a true believer.

Passionate enthusiasm combined with prodigious know-how carried him ever upward in the pop music business, as he built an unparalleled reputation for spotting and nurturing talent, plotted brilliant promotional campaigns for singles and albums, and snatched success from the jaws of other clever—but less clever—record producers and executives. His account of the expertise he and his colleagues deployed to convince disc jockeys (the crucial element to success back then) to air *his* products is fascinating. Ditto his understanding of how crucially important a defining hit single was to the success of an album.

Among the many examples he offers is the way he insisted that Barry Manilow—whom he took on when he started Arista, his own company—add a strong song to his upcoming album in order to jump-start it. The song Davis chose was "Mandy" (née "Brandy"). Barry would have preferred a song of his own, but he acquiesced and "Mandy" zoomed to number one on the singles chart, the album sold a million copies, and Barry was launched on the career that has lasted forty years or so. You may feel ambivalent about the art of Barry Manilow, the phoenix who rises and rises again, but numbers are numbers.

This story gets told again and again. Perfectly fine singers see themselves as creative artists and insist that their own songs dominate their albums. But not all singers are writers like Bruce Springsteen, whom Davis also helped develop, or Patti Smith, whom he was knocked out by at first sight ("she just gave me chills"), signed up at the start of her career, and whom he totally trusted through the quarter century of their collaboration, as she did him. No Brandy-Mandys for Patti. In 2000, when he was inaugurated into the Rock and Roll Hall of Fame, it was Patti Smith who introduced him, and Davis quotes liberally from her flattering remarks about him. Yes, his ego permits him to do this, but he also displays his genuine awe of talent: "I marvel at Patti's spirit and I can only say I'm one lucky guy to have been in her corner watching that spirit soar and letting her vision take her where she was destined to go." Finally, it's that awe of talent that keeps us rooting for Clive Davis, despite all the reasons he gives us not to.

IT'S IN THE NEW BOOK that we see a real eruption of the ego, or what, more generously, you might call a kind of naive self-regard—Davis is just so pleased with what his life has turned out to be! This is how he begins *The Soundtrack of My Life*: "Perhaps my favorite time of the year is the period at the beginning of February leading up to my pre-Grammy party." It doesn't occur to him that all of us may not be aware of his pre-Grammy party, though we certainly learn about it quickly—and at length. We hear how Clive and his son Doug and "other family members and party-planning strategists" hole up in "the bungalow at the Beverly Hills Hotel that is my second home" and that, for the duration, is "the Grammy Party War Room."

We're told about the historic moment when an infuriated business attorney kicks a chair out from under fellow mogul David Geffen, prompting Paul Simon to exclaim, "You can't do that—that's David Geffen!" We share the excitement of the unforgettable moment of "watching the likes of Gwen Stefani and Donald Trump leap to their feet as Aretha Franklin, backed by Whitney Houston and Toni Braxton, tears into 'Respect.'" And we share in the anxiety about the fire department holding things up for half an hour while "several tables were dismantled in order to bring the ballroom in compliance with the fire code." (Don't worry: "Robin Williams spontaneously quieted the crowd and launched into a hilarious stand-up comedy improvisation.") There are five pages about the party (it premiered in 1976), and throughout the book we come back to it again and again; it's a defining element of Davis's view of himself.

Just as defining, and far more irritating, is his assumption that the world needs to hear every detail of everything that ever happened to him. There's simply no inner censor. "Two school friends lived nearby in Bayside. One was Harold, who was in my house plan, and the other was a girl named Lola Fiur, whom everybody called Rusti because of her fiery red hair. I dated Rusti for a while, and she and I and Harold and his wife, Ruth, remained bonded over the years. . . ." When he decides to write *Clive*: "I rented a suite at the Hotel Ruxton on Seventy-second Street between Central Park West and Columbus Avenue, just a few blocks from my apartment." And try this for mind-numbing business minutiae:

> I had a great group of executives in place. Roy Lott stepped into the position of executive VP and GM with exceptional savvy and tenacity; our head of promotion, Rick Bisceglia, had come up under Donnie [Ienner] and shared his go-for-the-kill approach; and there were very skilled senior executives in place in marketing (Richard Sanders, Marty Diamond, and Tom Ennis), publicity (Melani Rogers), creative services (Ken Levy), international (Eliza Brownjohn), urban promotion (Tony Anderson), and really across the board.

I'll spare you the five "top guys" in the A&R department. Maybe this is gripping stuff to readers who were in the industry twenty-five years ago, but *The Soundtrack of My Life* is meant for the general public—and is being snapped up by it. Or at least by that portion of it that is fascinated by inside stories of the pop music world: the lowdown on the artistic, financial, and personal ways of the stars and the star-makers. No unsavory gossip, though, about drugs, alcohol, or irregular sexual conduct. In Davis's version, the industry (and he himself) is more or less squeaky-clean.

IT'S NOT SURPRISING that Davis comes across as knowing what he's talking about. He was at the heart of the action for half a century. Again and again he identifies salable talent, grabs it for whatever label he's in charge of, steers it, and tries to protect it—often against itself. Anyone can be lucky, but a track record like his has to reflect a deep understanding of the field. And an ability to change with the times. Here is a lawyer-turned-businessman-turned-producer-turned-mogul who starts off working in a world of Mitch Miller sing-along albums and is still going strong in a world of Alicia Keys, Pink, the Foo Fighters, and Sean "Puff Daddy" Combs, by way of such major players as Dylan, Streisand, Springsteen, Simon and Garfunkel, Sly and the Family Stone, Chicago, Aerosmith, Billy Joel—all during his Columbia (CBS) days alone.

After he's ignominiously dismissed from his job on false suspicion of illegitimate expense accounts, he founds Arista, where among other things he propels Whitney Houston into the stratosphere (perhaps his most spectacular success).

He takes more than thirty pages to tell her story—*their* story—in all its mutual generosity and eventual sadness. He loved her remarkable ability, and we are convinced that he loved her, too. He straightforwardly chronicles the explosive rise to fame—she was the first singer to have seven consecutive number-one singles, surpassing the record shared by the Beatles and the Bee Gees—and the eventual downward spiral that was so painful and so public. And then, when she seemed to be recovering, the sudden death (on the eve, wouldn't you know it, of the annual Grammy party). Davis includes in his account a letter he wrote to

Houston analyzing a concert she had given the night before. It's micro-managing at its best—calm, brilliant, disinterested, and utterly persuasive. Here is Clive Davis doing the job better than anyone else did it, and making it clear to us why his level of success was no fluke: It was laboriously earned and richly deserved.

Responding as always to the changing musical climate, when country makes a comeback, he launches a Nashville branch of Arista that comes up with such superstars as Alan Jackson, Brooks and Dunn, and Brad Paisley, and when the corporate situation changes, he starts up newer successful labels, like Jive, under the BMG (Bertelsmann) umbrella. Through an association with *American Idol*, he oversees the rise of Carrie Underwood and undergoes excruciating travails with Kelly Clarkson, *Idol*'s first winner, to which he devotes thirteen pages. Along the way, with his almost infallible instinct for reigniting careers in decline, he rescues Aretha Franklin, Carly Simon, Rod Stewart, Dionne Warwick, and most dramatically, he engineers the amazing comeback of the guitarist Carlos Santana. Santana's 1999 album *Supernatural*—number one for twelve weeks, twenty-eight years after his last number-one album—sold thirty million copies worldwide.

Triumph after triumph, though occasionally an artist slips through his fingers (Tom Petty) or slides from the heights, usually through ignoring his counsel (Melissa Manchester, Taylor Dayne). Among his big successes—and we have to exercise charity and forgive him for it—was Kenny G, the sort-of-jazz sax player to whom he devotes six somewhat defensive pages. But even the greatest successes fade away, so let's end this catalog of Clive Davis's achievements with his account of the fading of Kenny—a passage that will also alert you to the quality of the Davis/DeCurtis prose style. As his career started to go sour, "my relationship with Kenny became a little contentious." And then more contentious:

> When you reach that point, you have to break apart professionally, which was very painful. You've been through so much and reached such heights. You try to keep it warm and cordial, try to focus on the

really incredible shared experience you've had, but nearly all endings are sad endings. You've been like family for many years. I had been to Kenny and Lyndie's wedding, had shared their joy when their son Max was born. Kenny always performed for me whenever a special occasion arose. So I wanted to keep it going but just knew I couldn't. Without the opportunity of working on a new album with an artist, your lives do separate. . . . I know that what we did together was exceptional, and from my perspective it always will be.

AND WHAT ABOUT CLIVE'S OTHER LIFE—the nonprofessional life, the inner life? He takes us very lightly through marriage number one (two kids) and marriage number two (two kids), and into the present. Lest we think that he has

little or no life outside work, let me correct that notion right now. First, I love my family, and since I don't believe in loving a stranger, I make every effort to spend time with them. Each week I have dinner in New York with three of my kids, Fred, Lauren, and Doug—along with Fred's two sons, Austin and Charles, Fred's wife, Rona, and Lauren's husband, Julius, and their son, Matthew, and daughter, Hayley. . . . My son Mitchell, his wife, Clare, and their son, Harper, and daughter, Sloane, live in Los Angeles, so when I'm there, which is about six times a year, we share at least one or two meals together on each visit.

Then there are the twenty or so special friends who spend weekends with him at his house in Pound Ridge, in Westchester. ("We gather on Friday night at one of the excellent restaurants in the area, and brunch on Saturday and Sunday, and dinner on Saturday, are catered for up to forty of us.") Best of all are the big family-and-friends summer vacations. "Whether it's a house in St. Tropez for one group or a boat cruising the Mediterranean with another, I do fill my annual five weeks of vacation with family members and family friends with the bonding that truly makes life a joy." It's an idyllic life, and he loves it.

And, oh yes, as marriage number two is failing in the mid-1980s, he's "openly approached by a young man of about twenty-five who happened to be a huge music fan," and one thing leads to the next thing until "on this night, after imbibing enough alcohol, I was open to responding to his sexual overtures, my first such encounter with a male." Nontraumatic divorce, gratifying relationships with this man and several women, until in 1990 (he's fifty-eight) he enters into a thirteen-year monogamous relationship with a male doctor. And a year after that ends, he begins another monogamous relationship with a man that has lasted until now.

What are we to make of this startling turn of events? (It emerges on page 545 of his 551-page text.) What he's most eager to have us make of it is that, although he had no previous homosexual experiences (or impulses?) before the awakening, since then he has been as sexually happy with men as he had been with women; that there really, truly are bisexuals, and he is one of them. It's also important to him that we know that everyone in his family has been totally supportive, except that one son "had a tough adjustment period," but "that after one very trying year, the issue became totally resolved between us." As to why he didn't go public with his new life, a primary reason "was my strong feeling that I didn't want to be typecast."

He didn't have to worry: There's no way Clive Davis can be typecast. I say hats off to his venturesome sexual/emotional life—hetero, homo, or bi; he wants to make it clear that he's as comfortable with his sexuality as he appears to be with all other aspects of his life, so why should we be uncomfortable with it? What I'm uncomfortable with is the way the reader is sandbagged with this information so late in the book, without the slightest preparation, and without real reflection or insight. But Davis's insights have always been directed outward, toward his work.

In the final pages of his book he takes a quick look at the condition of the music business today, and he's optimistic, although, given the new technology of streaming and iPods, "audiences seem to have lost interest in artists and what they have to say." He's pleased that his

Grammy party is now an official Grammy-week event, co-hosted by the National Association of Recording Arts and Sciences (NARAS), and "is still going strong—more exclusive, more unique, and more festive

Janis Joplin and Clive Davis

than ever." He's proud of his philanthropies as well as of his achievements. He's gratified when former colleagues "make sure I know of [their] continuing high regard and deep respect."

And he hasn't forgotten the people who he says have been inspirations to him. There was the imposing (and crafty) Goddard Lieberson, his early mentor at Columbia, who not only taught him the corporate ropes but was a model in many things, including dress:

> Goddard was elegant, informed, incredibly witty, and very articulate, as attractive a figure to the high-end media as many of the artists on the label. He was always very handsomely turned out. Matching his pocket handkerchief with his English-made shirts was a signature element of his style, a touch I have adopted to this day.

And then there was what you might call the anti-Goddard in his life—the wild reckless talent and lifestyle of Janis Joplin, whom he recalls in his final sentences:

> I think often of that day in June 1967 at the Monterey Pop Festival—the pulsating excitement of Janis Joplin's performance, the sense of possibility in the air, the exhilaration of realizing what a life pursuing your biggest dreams might be like—when a door opened to what the rest of my life would be. That so much came from the events of that one day has been an incredible gift, and the passion I felt then is with me still.

Another man might have found it painful to harbor these apparently contradictory influences, but Davis doesn't register them as contradictory—because for him they haven't been. He had to be Goddard in order to be able to hatch Janis; he had to have Janis to spark his life into meaning. Given his irrepressible vigor and adaptability, his relentlessly positive response to necessity and possibility, can we fault him for his almost touching complacency and self-congratulation?

BUT THERE ARE MYSTERIES, the most perplexing of which is his relationship to music itself. As we have seen, it didn't mean much to him as he was growing up. There seems to have been no classical music in his background, and although he took so much from Goddard Lieberson, he didn't absorb his passion for it—no Stravinsky connection, for instance, although he did once take the Vladimir Horowitzes to a disco blasting Motown all night. ("They loved it.") In *Clive*, he speaks at length about his relationship with Columbia's major symphony orchestras—that is, about their contract negotiations, never the music. Jazz doesn't really have a grip on him, although he seems to have enjoyed his ruffled relationship with Miles Davis. (*All* relationships with Miles Davis were ruffled.) He hardly ever refers to the wonderful pop of his time that wasn't in his immediate line of sight: Elvis, the Beatles, Motown. What does grip him is performance—far more than what is being performed. And most of all the industry itself: "My *love* of the business dominates all my memories."

This frame of mind stands out even more clearly when seen in contrast to the impassioned response to music of Davis's younger rival Tommy Mottola, whose autobiography, *Hitmaker*, was published only weeks before *The Soundtrack of My Life*. Tommy came from the Bronx, not Brooklyn; was Italian, not Jewish (although he converted to Judaism to marry his first wife). His book is personal in the best way—it winningly conveys Mottola's exuberant, generous, impetuous personality, his directness and sometimes unnerving honesty. But the chief difference between the two moguls is that for Mottola, everything started with the music. His family made music, the streets he grew up in were filled with music.

> Music was around me from morning till night. From the time I was two years old I would climb on the stool and bang on the keys of our family piano. But there *was* one single defining moment that ran through me like a bolt of electricity when I was eight years old: that was the first time I heard "Don't Be Cruel" blasting through my sisters' AM radio. The beat and the rhythm of that song branded me forever and was everything that motivated and inspired me to become what I became.

He became a (failed) musician himself. He then started in the trenches at the very bottom of the industry, and went on to the very top. His artists are a roll call of fame—Hall and Oates, John Mellencamp (not Mister Nice Guy), Gloria Estefan, Celine Dion (it was he who masterminded her singing "My Heart Will Go On" on the *Titanic* soundtrack). His account of dealing with Michael Jackson's dementia and megalomania is chilling and pitiful. And central to his story is his professional and personal relationship with Mariah Carey—his Whitney Houston—whom he helped propel into superstardom and, famously, married. It was a mistake, which he manfully acknowledges: He was twenty years older and should have known better; and he *did* know better when he entered into a third, and happy, marriage.

His book, then, is a chronicle of professional and personal success, yet it never seems ego-driven. Because it's music-driven.

But even if Tommy Mottola is a very different kind of mogul from Clive Davis, he recognizes and salutes Davis's accomplishments. "When I first started out," he says, "I could only hope to come close to achieving some of Clive's success. His work in this industry is unrivaled. Everybody in this business looks up to him." This tribute, as it happens, appears not in *Hitmaker* but is quoted by Davis himself in *The Soundtrack of My Life*.

The New York Review of Books
JUNE 20, 2013

Sizing Up Sinatra

O NE OF THE ODDER BYWAYS OF NONFICTION are the dishy memoirs by those who have served the great or the near-great. Think of all those books by former White House staff members: seamstress Lillian Rogers Parks's *My Thirty Years Backstairs at the White House*, chief usher J. B. West's *Upstairs at the White House*, kennel keeper Traphes Bryant's *Dog Days at the White House*. England has a long tradition of royalty rip-offs, most famously *The Little Princesses* (1953), the royal nanny's best-selling tell-all. The Queen was not amused.

We, of course, don't have royalty—even presidents don't qualify—but we do have Hollywood. And now we have Frank Sinatra's onetime valet, George Jacobs. With the help of William Stadiem, Jacobs has given us a vivid account of his many years serving The Voice, and of the tragic (to him) denouement of their relationship. *Mr. S: My Life with Frank Sinatra* is a curious and convincing portrait not only of Sinatra but of Jacobs himself, and of the kind of mentality that breeds such passionate attachment to a man so spectacularly unworthy of it.

George Jacobs, now seventy-six, was born in New Orleans. Although black, he had Jewish blood on both sides—hence his last name. After a stretch in the Navy, during which he became aide to an admiral and learned to cook Mediterranean style, he married, moved to Los Angeles, and, through a series of maneuvers and accidents, found himself Man Friday to agent Swifty Lazar's Robinson Crusoe. Which in turn led to Sinatra snatching him from Swifty—needling Lazar was one of Sinatra's favorite pastimes.

It was love at first sight: "I loved the guy, and I assumed he loved me, too." From 1953 to 1968, George was Frank's shadow. He cooked for him—the Italo-American food Frank craved; he dressed him (orange was Sinatra's favorite color); he ferried Frank's lady friends and call girls to and from the Residence; he palled around with the Rat Pack; he watched over Ava (long after she had bounced Frank) when she needed looking after; he became a link to Sinatra's family—big Nancy and the three kids—and stayed on close terms with Dolly, Sinatra's bar-owning, ward-heeling, midwife/abortionist mother, even after Sinatra booted him; he knew Marilyn ("the girl Dolly wanted her son to marry") and the Kennedys, the notorious Judith Campbell and the dangerous Sam Giancana. And he dealt as best he could with Mia Farrow (when she was Mia Sinatra), whom he clearly despised, even before she became the engine of his fall from grace.

A summer night in L.A. George has the evening to kill before going over to Ava's bungalow, where they would "get plastered, and ... sing to each other until daylight." Looking for action, he stops off at a place called the Candy Store for a few drinks, and along comes Mia. "I thought she was high, high as a kite. 'Dance with me, Georgie Porgie,' she insisted, dragging me out to the floor. . . .'" After they dance "for what seemed an eternity," George slips away to meet Ava. When Frank reads about their dancecapade in Rona Barrett's gossip column, it's over in a flash: George's key suddenly doesn't fit the compound door, and a letter from Frank's lawyer tells George that he's been fired. "I was not to re-enter the premises, nor telephone, nor in any way approach or try to contact Mr. Sinatra. . . . There was no explanation, no apology, no severance pay." And indeed, the two men run into each other only one more time, in 1978, at Don the Beachcomber. "I took one look at him and broke down into tears. I couldn't stop crying. Mr. S put his arm around me. 'Forget about it, kid,' he said. 'It isn't so bad.' I guess I couldn't forget about it, because the tears didn't stop. Mr. S gave me one last squeeze and was gone. . . . I was sad he wasn't as sentimental about us as I was."

There are telling discrepancies between what George Jacobs says here and what, in the early 1980s, he told Kitty Kelley when she interviewed him for her no-holds-barred Sinatra bio, *His Way*: "After fourteen years together, he dropped the net on me just like that, and he couldn't even look me in the face to do it. He couldn't fire me in person. He had to have his prick lawyer do it for him. I was so mad afterwards that I threw away everything he'd ever given me—two-thousand-

dollar watches, suits, sweaters, shirts, shoes, coats, cameras, radios—
everything. I didn't want anything from the bastard around. I got twelve
thousand dollars in severance pay and blew it, and then I sold all my
shares in Reprise Records." It's not only the wasted severance pay that
stands out here, but the anger that's generally absent or veiled in the
new book. Time does heal all wounds.

There was clearly a blurring of lines in the relationship between
the two men, as there often is between master and servant. George was
definitely more to Frank than a valet, unless your definition of valeting
includes procuring, getting chummy with gangsters and presidents,
and babysitting Ava Gardner and Marilyn Monroe. We're not talking
Jeeves here. To George, Frank was a hero—not only "the most powerful man in the entertainment business" ("the folks in show business
feared Sinatra the same way the folks in Communist Russia had feared

Stalin"), but also "my best friend, my idol, my boss." What George was—actually—was an adoring courtier to a member of Hollywood's royalty. "It feels great," he tells us, "to be the right hand of a king."

It doesn't feel great, though, to be expelled from paradise. What George Jacobs suffered at Sinatra's hands is the old story of Prince Hal and Falstaff, and of a million less famous examples of favorites being abruptly shed: You think you're a "we" and discover you no longer even exist; the king doesn't need you anymore, and wants you out of his sight and off his conscience. Some cast-offs fade gracefully into oblivion; some shriek with rage (*The Devil Wears Prada*); and some put a good face on it, which is what George Jacobs has done in *Mr. S*. It helps that he has humor and a certain wit, and it's a relief to the reader, who comes to like him, that he managed to make a life for himself after Sinatra, despite the dismal fate of several of his children and an appearance on *The Gong Show*.

What we discern about Sinatra—and it jibes with other accounts—is that he was a man with profound feelings of inferiority about everything but his music. He was a shrimp; he had scars and a damaged ear from a difficult birth; and he never got over his unlovely background. Hoboken was hardly "class," and no concept was more important to this man who aspired so desperately to be accepted by what he saw as the elite: Fred Astaire, Humphrey Bogart, Bing Crosby, Edie Goetz (Louis B. Mayer's daughter, and supposed doyenne of social Hollywood), the Kennedys. "Mr. S craved class like a junkie craves a needle." But his social aspirations were undercut by his blatant weaknesses—an almost pathological anger and blasts of unforgiving coldness: Tommy Dorsey, Lauren Bacall, his godfather, and many others who had been faithful and loyal were brutally banished. He was a serial hater. "Everything about Mr. S had to do with paying debts and settling scores"—the Sinatra family needn't have left Sicily.

Sinatra pursued women voraciously, but did he ever really love anyone except Ava and Dolly? Certainly he cared as a friend for some of his occasional conquests—Marilyn, Judy Garland, Peggy Lee, Natalie Wood, Dinah Shore, and a hundred more—and he was generous and gallant to his bought women. After all, they gave him what he most wanted: control. He was fun, yet abusive; free from prejudice, yet consorting with and admiring some of the most repellent criminals of his day. And, of course, he was a very great singer.

It's hard to feel sorry for Frank Sinatra, and yet he was crushed by two traumatic defeats. One was the loss of Ava. The other was being dropped by the Kennedys after Jack made it to the White House (with Sinatra's crucial help). By then, Frank's criminal connections were too rank for Bobby and for Ambassador Joe, and Frank in turn became the Falstaff figure, banished by the prince. It was a public humiliation. Indeed, the severest portraits in Jacobs's book are of Bobby (Sinatra called him "the weasel") and of Dad—Joe Kennedy is probably the one man in the world George Jacobs could be said to have hated. Vile about blacks, Joe was even nastier about Jews. "The Jewish jokes didn't stop. The worst one I can recall: 'What's the difference between a Jew and a pizza? The pizza doesn't cry on its way to the oven.'" "Mr. Ambassador," Jacobs sums up, "if anyone had the guts to spit in his face, a bravery that my boss sadly lacked, should have been called Mr. Asshole." As for Bobby's assassination at the hands of Sirhan Sirhan, the unforgiving Sinatra could only mumble, "It wasn't even one of us." Peter Lawford? "Cheap, weak, sneak, and freak."

Jack was a different matter. "As much as I disliked his father, that's how much I was crazy about John Fitzgerald Kennedy." Jack was "handsome and funny and naughty and irreverent as Dean Martin," insisting that George call him by his first name and obsessed with Hollywood gossip and Mr. S's love life. According to George, the senator "was far more in awe of Mr. S than Mr. S was of him." Why? "Because Frank Sinatra controlled the one thing JFK wanted more than anything else: Pussy! Mr. S was the Pope of Pussy, and JFK was honored to kiss his ring." After all, Mr. S could "bestow" not only a Judy Campbell but a Marilyn Monroe. There's a hilarious scene in which Kennedy is being massaged by George while they "talk pussy." The talk has its effect, leading to the punch line: "We better get you laid, Jack."

About Frank himself close up, George is specific and admiring. Ava, weighing up her "one-hundred-twenty-pound runt," put it most succinctly: "There's only ten pounds of Frank but there's one hundred and ten pounds of cock!" On the other hand, Jacobs may be the only witness to how Sinatra dealt with the problem of size. For Oscar night—the night he won Best Supporting Actor for *From Here to Eternity*, the night that revived his career—he "had special underpants made, a cross between a panty girdle and a jock strap. The idea was to hold down that big thing of his, so it wouldn't show through his tuxedo pants." Everybody's got problems!

I only wish I'd known about this cunning device the one time I met Sinatra. Among his closest friends were Bill Green (chairman of the Clevepak Corporation) and his wife, Judy, an old school pal of mine. Judy was determined that Frank and I should meet, God knows why, and she set up a formal dinner party. One night during the 1970s, my wife and I drove up to the Greens' house in Mt. Kisco with Swifty Lazar—Sinatra, by the way, was still on Swifty's case—and I found myself at the end of a long dinner table on one side of Judy, with Sinatra on the other. If I'd known about the dick-suppresser, it might have gotten the conversational ball rolling, but as it was, I was as much at sea as Sinatra about what to say. Finally I blurted out some bland question about Hollywood, and Frank lit up: Here was a subject he could safely address. Leaning over Judy, he looked at me directly for the first time. "You know, Bob," he said, "sometimes Hollywood can be the loneliest town in the world."

The New York Observer
JUNE 30, 2003

American Ballerina

MARIA TALLCHIEF

THERE ARE CERTAIN PUBLIC FIGURES so important to us that we welcome everything that those who knew them can tell us, no matter how marginal or anecdotal. Ballet lovers like me, for whom George Balanchine has been the central artistic figure of our time, have reason to be especially grateful in this regard: During his lifetime and especially since his death, in 1983, an entire literature has grown up around him. His first and third wives, Tamara Geva and Vera Zorina, and his second, "unofficial" wife, Alexandra Danilova, have published autobiographies, as have a number of his leading dancers, including Suzanne Farrell, Edward Villella, Peter Martins, Merrill Ashley, the apostate Gelsey Kirkland, and, most recently, Allegra Kent. There have been many substantial interviews, including those in Francis Mason's essential assemblage of reminiscences, *I Remember Balanchine.* There is the profound commentary on his work—another kind of biography—by our finest dance critics, Edwin Denby and Arlene Croce. And, of course, there is the brilliant testimony, over a period of fifty years, of Balanchine's partner at New York City Ballet, Lincoln Kirstein. What we have not had until now is an extended account of one of the great turning points in Balanchine's life—the middle 1940s to the late 1950s—by his fourth wife, Maria Tallchief, who not only witnessed the beginnings of City Ballet but was instrumental to them. In the face of resistance to Balanchine by large sections of the ballet public, to say nothing of the dance critic of *The New York Times,* John Martin, Tallchief's personal success was a crucial element in the company's survival and eventual triumph.

Elizabeth Marie Tall Chief was born in Fairfax, Oklahoma, in 1925, to an Osage father, whose family was financially comfortable through oil rights, and a mother of Irish-Scottish extraction, who was both beautiful and "determined"—a quality her older daughter was to inherit. (The younger daughter, Marjorie, also grew up to be a dancer of distinction.) Betty Tall Chief, who had perfect pitch, was trained as both a concert pianist and a dancer—she began lessons at three and soon was performing at community events, country fairs, even rodeos. But this was not the career their mother envisioned for her children, and when Betty was eight, Mrs. Tall Chief moved the family to Los Angeles and proper teaching—eventually from the demanding Bronislava Nijinska, choreographer of *Les Noces* and *Les Biches* and sister of Vaslav Nijinsky. In Nijinska's studio Betty "became committed to becoming a ballerina, and Madame understood I was serious," and by the time she was seventeen she was in the corps of the Ballet Russe de Monte Carlo. It was then that Agnes de Mille suggested that "Maria" might be a more appropriate name for a dancer than "Betty Marie," and, "Tall Chief" having become "Tallchief" in high school, Maria Tallchief was born.

It was not until 1944, when she was nineteen, that she encountered George Balanchine professionally. The first thing she grasped about him was that he "approached a score like a musician.... He broke down the inherent rhythm of the music to make the steps more exciting.... When I saw what he had done, I was astonished.... The musicality of the man was magical." Undoubtedly it was Tallchief's own musicality, and her understanding of his, that focused Balanchine's attention on this young dancer. That and her capacity for hard work, combined with her ready acknowledgment of her technical deficiencies. He saw what she could become and she was prepared to become it, at whatever cost: "I virtually had to retrain myself, work harder than ever before. But... I knew he was right." She had already learned from Nijinska how to present herself, to "fill the stage with my presence." Now, "dancing with confidence and authority in his ballets allowed me to show people exactly who I was and what I could do." No wonder that soon after they began working together, Balanchine startled her one night by saying, "Maria, I would like you to become my wife." The idea was so new to her (and to others) that the next day, when she told a fellow dancer, "George asked me to marry him," her friend replied, "George who?"

Francisco Moncion and Maria Tallchief in George Balanchine's *The Firebird*

The story of their marriage and collaboration is, naturally, the heart of this book—and Tallchief lovingly chronicles their domestic as well as their professional life together. (How moving are his little notes to her, most of them beginning "Hi Darling!") Balanchine is always calm, courteous, affectionate, reasonable—interested in her clothes, her perfume (he chose L'Heure Bleu for her—she still uses it), her increasing fame. But "work took precedence over everything. . . . Passion and romance didn't play a big role in our married life. We saved our emotion for the classroom." Dryly, she informs us that "he made sure we slept in twin beds, perhaps to conserve his energy." Nevertheless, she wasn't disappointed. "I was half George's age and didn't know what to expect. . . . Our relationship fulfilled me." Until it didn't, and she went on to further marriages and motherhood and he went on to marry Tanaquil Le Clercq.

Meanwhile, Tallchief's tremendous abilities and Balanchine's deployment of them resulted in a series of great ballerina roles, among them the revised version of the first movement of *Symphony in C*, never danced by anyone else with her dazzle and command; the pyrotechnical *Firebird*, City Ballet's first great popular success; Eurydice in the Stravinsky-Balanchine *Orpheus*; Odette in Balanchine's *Swan Lake*; and the Sugar Plum Fairy in his *Nutcracker* (in its first season she danced every Sugar Plum—no second casts in those days). In Tallchief, Balanchine had found a ballerina who through these central dozen years of his life was able to embody and extend his artistic ambitions. It was the combination of choreographer, ballerina, and sponsor (the City Center) that—fifteen years after Balanchine's arrival in America—made possible a full-scale company with continuity and a dedicated audience.

Tallchief's autobiography provides us with many stories, insights, even passing remarks that shed light on both this crucial moment in dance history and Balanchine's elusive personality. Some of it we've read before, in Tallchief interviews, and certain stories have been told and retold—for instance, her dropping the boiled potatoes on the kitchen floor as the Stravinskys toil up the stairs for dinner. (Is there such a thing as a new ballet anecdote?) But such repetitions don't matter; what does is that Tallchief has now given us her definitive and convincing account of Balanchine as choreographer, teacher, husband, friend.

As for Tallchief herself, her book's title, *Maria Tallchief*, accurately reflects the woman in its rejection of metaphor or allusion to a role or an event; she had, indeed, learned how to present herself. Nor does her subtitle—*America's Prima Ballerina*—suggest any ambiguity. She was—is—deeply American and deeply proud of her Osage background (Balanchine was fascinated by it). She was a "ballerina" in the classic sense—grand, glamorous, authoritative: a diva. And she certainly was "prima," until she couldn't be any longer, at which point (and at only forty-one) she retired.

The book itself, written with Larry Kaplan (and sadly under-illustrated), is an apt expression of her nature—forceful, assertive, tough on herself as well as on others, suffering few people gladly. She is not introspective, certainly not literary, and Kaplan's prose is hardly distinguished. But there is a positive side to his lack of polish: The flatness of much of the writing underlines her directness. We know exactly what she thinks, with no holds barred and no mitigation for reasons of modesty, tact, fanciness, or apology. Perhaps she doesn't tell us everything about her marriages (why should she?) or her relationships with Erik Bruhn and Rudolf Nureyev. But we feel we can trust what she *does* tell us. And when she is disapproving, as she is about the current state of the Balanchine repertory at New York City Ballet, she is relentless. "I'm afraid the pure classical technique George demanded from his dancers isn't being asked for anymore" is a mild example of half a dozen such remarks. Some of her onetime colleagues agree with her about this (if less outspokenly); others do not. But it is certain that no one—not even the great dancers who succeeded her—can ever know Balanchine's Eurydice, Firebird, Sugar Plum the way she does, because they were created not only for her but *of* her. Tallchief's testimony about such roles as these, and their maker—whether on paper, on film, or in the studio—should be eagerly embraced by today's Balanchine dancers, by dance historians and critics, and by those of us who were there.

Russian Ballerina

MAYA PLISETSKAYA

MAYA PLISETSKAYA: her father (a loyal Communist) executed in the Stalin purges of the 1930s; her mother (a onetime silent film star) exiled to Asia; Jewish; close relatives in America; and perceived, always, as a rebel, a troublemaker, and, worst of all, a potential defector. Oh, yes—she was also undertrained, her ballet schooling interrupted by the terrible traumas of her childhood. How, then, did this woman with so many strikes against her not only survive but prevail, becoming the Bolshoi's leading ballerina for decades, dancing on and on to celebrate her forty-seventh anniversary on the Bolshoi stage and, at seventy-six, still going strong? At its best, her autobiography, *I, Maya Plisetskaya*, is the fascinating story of how this artist of implacable will confronted and defied the Soviet regime—and eventually had her way.

Russian dancers of the twentieth century had three choices: get out, accept the regime and its restrictions while enjoying its favors, or stay and struggle. Only Plisetskaya took that third route and triumphed. She was talented, of course, and wonderful-looking, with her thin body, long legs and arms, and flaming red hair. From the first she stood out: Hers was not a slow ascendancy; she was always headed for great things unless she self-destructed or was destroyed by others. She was partly protected by association with her mother's family, the Messerers, who constitute a dancing dynasty in Russia; and eventually she had the unconditional support of her husband, the composer Rodion Shchedrin.

But all that was secondary. What drove her past all obstacles and hazards were her unbending determination and her refusal to do things any way but her own.

Maya Plisetskaya as Kitri in *Don Quixote*

She began as she meant to go on: "I was a willful child, and they called me *neslukh*, the 'not-listener.'" And: "Everything in me, in my nature, resisted 'socializing.'" They want her to attend Komsomol meetings and learn about dialectical materialism? She goes twice, and that's it. Advisers want her to leave the KGB and the "vileness of the Bolsheviks" out of her book? "No, I won't change anything. I won't touch things up." She's always on the barricades; defiance is not only a principle and a tactic but also an essential element of her nature.

Her credo: "I don't want to be a slave. I don't want people whom I don't know to decide my fate. I don't want a leash on my neck. I don't want a cage, even if it's a platinum one.... I don't want to bow my head and I won't do it. That's not what I was born for." It's admirable, it's heroic, but it's not very cozy; I would think it would be easier to be in love with her than to love her.

The strongest parts of her book are, indeed, those that deal with the KGB and "the vileness of the Bolsheviks." Of course we have encountered this story many times before, and in truly great books, like Nadezhda Mandelstam's *Hope Against Hope*. But as with the Holocaust, each telling is different, and each is worth listening to.

Plisetskaya's is unique in that her story is that of an artist who loathes her circumstances ("Endless suffering and humiliation fill my memory") yet overcomes them without (too much) compromise. And who chooses not to defect—a decision she provides a number of reasons for, ranging from pride in her position as prima ballerina at the Bolshoi to love for the Bolshoi Theater's stage. (Besides, she promised Khrushchev she wouldn't.)

Nothing that was to follow compared in horror to what she witnessed when they took her father away. Maya was eleven—"skinny, scared, not understanding what was going on." They came for him at dawn. "My mother, unkempt, pregnant with a big belly, weeping and clutching. My little brother screaming, rudely awakened. My father, white as snow, dressing with trembling hands. He was embarrassed. The neighbors' faces were remote. The witness, the blowsy janitor Varvara, with a cigarette between her lips, didn't miss a chance to suck up to the authorities: 'Can't wait for all of you bastards to be shot, you enemies of the people!' " And finally, "The last thing I heard my father say before the door shut behind him forever was, 'Thank God, they'll settle this at last.' "

When they sent her mother to Kazakhstan, all that stood between Maya and an orphanage was an aunt who took her in, somewhat grudgingly. But it was ballet that really saved her. She had great natural gifts—in particular a dazzling leap. ("Nature had not passed me over when it came to jumps.") What she lacked was solid technique. Just as she is wise and generous in her estimation of other dancers—particularly her exalted coeval and rival Galina Ulanova—she is honest about her own deficiencies.

In Paris, she tells us, referring to an overwhelming triumph (twenty-seven curtain calls) in *Swan Lake*, her friends agree that "I had forced the audience to switch its interest from abstract technique to soul and plasticity. When I danced the finale of the second act, people's eyes were glued to the line of the swan's arms, the angle of the neck; no one noticed that my bourrées were not so perfect." She even reports that when she met Balanchine in New York, in the early 1960s, he said to her, "Being your own boss isn't bad. But, don't be angry, Maya, you need a good teacher." As usual, he had seen and understood everything.

She was kept from the West for years—a matter of supreme frustration and rage—and when she was finally allowed to come, the conditions were onerous: not only unrelenting KGB watchdogs, but barely enough money for food; all earnings went back to the bosses in Russia. In 1959 she received forty dollars a performance, and on days when she didn't dance, "Zero." The corps de ballet got five dollars a day.

Bizarrely, before setting out for America, the touring dancers would stuff their luggage with food. Then, when their supplies ran out, "cat and dog food were particularly popular. Cheap and vitamin-rich. You felt very strong after animal food. We fried canine beefsteaks between two hotel irons." (When not munching canine beefsteaks, Plisetskaya was hobnobbing with the great, including Robert F. Kennedy, with whom she had a mystifying palship.)

Despite being undertrained and underfed, she made an indelible impression here. Although, as she acknowledges, her fouettés were erratic, she was an outstanding Odile in the Black act of *Swan Lake*, a cold and blazing dominatrix. Her Odette, for me, was always more about being a bird than being a vulnerable captive princess, but *Swan Lake* remained her signature ballet: She danced it more than eight hundred times. Her *Dying Swan* likewise seemed to me more about undulant arms than about death. (I once saw her "die," then respond to the applause with a second "death" and then a third. Why not? It was all showiness. When Ulanova's swan died, she was dead.)

But her passionate, flirtatious, swirling, seductive Kitri, in *Don Quixote*, remains unparalleled. And her dramatic power in such Soviet pieces as *The Stone Flower* and *Spartacus* was incontestable, though all in the service of kitsch. (Does she realize that?) When she gets to commissioning ballets and ultimately choreographing her own, they're all diva vehicles: *Carmen, Anna Karenina, The Lady with the Dog.* I don't think it ever occurred to her that she was more suited to some roles than to others. Only blinders—or undifferentiated ego—could have led her to write, "I have been endlessly asked why I didn't dance Giselle. . . . I could have done it, but something in me opposed it, resisted, argued with it. Somehow it just didn't work out." Plisetskaya as a fragile peasant girl betrayed in love? It's inconceivable—except to her.

I, Maya Plisetskaya has the virtues of candor and directness, and it has a real story to tell. She may have her vanities, but what star doesn't? And how many stars have had to exhibit such an indomitable spirit? She insists that she wrote her book herself, and it reads as if she did— or rather, as if she had dictated it into a tape machine. (It's as if she was her own ghostwriter.) In Antonina Bouis's energetic translation, she comes across as the same person we knew on the stage: glamorous, exciting, voracious. Larger than life. Not always pleasing but never to be ignored and certainly never to be trifled with.

Los Angeles Times Book Review
NOVEMBER 4, 2001

The Coach

ELENA TCHERNICHOVA

IT'S NOT ONLY STAR DANCERS and choreographers and impresarios who contribute significantly to the art of ballet. Crucial, too, are the teachers, coaches, and ballet masters who keep classical technique—and classical dancers—honest. In our day, Elena Tchernichova, who was trained as a dancer in the Soviet Union and later immigrated to the United States, has been a conspicuous example of a person who has performed all three roles. Her *Dancing on Water* is an important account of "A Life in Ballet," as its subtitle has it: a book as illuminating as it is interesting, revelatory about how ballet works, and fascinating as an account of a life devoted to an art—and to survival.

The immediate interest stems from the extraordinary arc her life has followed, and the clearheaded intelligence with which she (and her excellent co-author, Joel Lobenthal) recounts it. For someone who has experienced the tragedies that have fallen her way, she's remarkably free of self-pity and, more remarkable, of self-dramatization. Which doesn't mean she's free of self-regard. But why should she be? She has more than fulfilled her early promise. That she's not a household name only reflects her uncommonly early understanding of where her talents really lay and of how she might best deploy them, rather than spending her considerable resources pursuing a fame and fortune that didn't attract her.

Elena Tchernichova was born in Leningrad in 1939 as the war broke out in Europe, and her childhood was all too typical of many others who lived in that place at that time. When she was three, her father, of German origin, who oversaw a munitions factory, was summoned by the KGB and never returned from the meeting; there was never a definitive account of his fate, but Elena distinctly recalled him muttering,

"I don't want to go; I just don't want to go!" Her mother, Maria, was a beauty, an aspiring actress, an indulged young wife: "She liked to bake, do needlepoint—and of course dress flamboyantly."

Then, with her husband having vanished, she was on her own during the siege of Leningrad, trying to keep herself and her little girl alive: "Government rationing had dwindled to one scrap of bread a day. We were forced to eat anything we could snatch, uproot, or improvise. We crowded around my grandmother as she fried pancakes from a batter of rice-based face powder."

Maria took a lover, then when the war ended got a job managing a warehouse, but by this time she was an alcoholic. One day she slashed her wrists and Elena, aged eight, came home early from school and found her just in time. On her thirtieth birthday Maria threw herself a "farewell gala," and that night took poison and died. Elena's aunt forced her to go to the morgue to identify her mother's body—an ordeal she never forgave or forgot.

Elena was now officially an orphan, although she was living with her grandmother, and a distinguished family wanted to adopt her. The mother was Evgenia Vecheslova-Snetkova, a leading teacher at the Kirov's school, by far the most important ballet academy in Russia, among its graduates Fokine, Pavlova, Nijinsky, Karsavina, Danilova, Balanchine, Ulanova. Elena refused to leave her grandmother—"As long as you're alive I'll be with you"—but she often visited the family. Snetkova saw a future in ballet for the child, brought her into the school to be auditioned, and Elena was accepted. She was ten.

Her account of her training is consistent with other accounts we have (like Danilova's): "Our school was something like a cross between a naval academy and a British public school, with a bit of Dickens peeking around the edges of our ruthlessly regimented lives. Punishment followed misbehavior as inevitably as night follows day.... Our teachers weren't really cruel, but oh, were they tough!"

It was a nine-year course, and for all those nine years Elena's teacher was Lidia Tyuntina, who had been a favorite of the great Agrippina Vaganova, after whom the school was eventually renamed.

Elena Tchernichova coaching Susan Jaffe and Andris Liepa in *Swan Lake*

ELENA WAS CLEARLY TALENTED, but she wasn't easy. "The other kids obeyed me. I was never afraid of teachers or directors, and they respected that.... Sometimes I would just have a fit, running out of a class and out of the building while a teacher screamed, 'Where do you think you're going? Don't you realize that class isn't over yet?' 'I have to see the sun!' I cried, and threw myself into the street."

She got into serious trouble when her briefcase was stolen, and with it her Komsomol notebook—her membership passport for the Communist Youth League. Essentially, she was put on trial, threatened with expulsion—"Your Komsomol book is the most important document in your life. You must carry it with you all the time. An enemy could use this to spy on us!"—but she remained defiant. "What secrets can they get from our ballet school?" "Don't be smart. They can use it to show that they're a citizen of this country." "There is my name and my picture and my age. I don't think they have spies who are fifteen." She more or less got away with it, "but so great was my disillusionment that I don't think I was ever again the same person."

She drove Tyuntina crazy by appearing to be lazy—dancing off pointe, neglecting her studies. But when the final examinations were coming up, she rallied and did well, and she had a real success dancing the *Raymonda* dream pas de deux at her graduation performance on the Kirov stage. There were supposed to be two more performances, but she announced that she was injured. "I preferred to observe.... I thought I had done my job already. Why suffer through two more *Raymonda*s when I could be watching and enjoying?" Invited to join the main company, she accepted, but by then she had realized that she didn't want to dance professionally. "I lacked a true performer's mentality and concentration. Dancing in the studio was for myself and I could enjoy it sometimes. But dancing on stage was living up to my responsibility to others."

By this point in her story we realize that what she had been doing through her years as a student was observing, judging. She was, for instance, reaching conclusions about the Kirov's ballerinas, most importantly Natalia Dudinskaya, who with her husband, the company's artistic director, Konstantin Sergeyev, ruled the roost and who with her amazing allegro technique dazzled the world but "knew that she didn't have the line, the cantilena, for adagio, and so she danced the Shades [in *La Bayadère*] faster than any other ballerina in history." And in contrast the magnificent but ill-starred Alla Shelest: Elena's page-and-a-half description of Shelest in *La Bayadère* should be required reading for every dancer who assumes the role of Nikiya. We also grow aware of how Dudinskaya (that "inveterate intrigante") managed to block her rival's career. The Sergeyevs, here as in other accounts, emerge as the Macbeths of the Kirov.

Elena was also observing her extraordinary classmates, who included Nureyev, Natasha Makarova, Alla Sizova, and Yuri Soloviev. About Nureyev in particular she has a good deal to tell us—about his willfulness, his obsessiveness, his defiance of authority. "Don't ever show them you're afraid of them," he tells her, "and then they'll become afraid of *you*." The only person he fully respected was his teacher, the great Alexander Pushkin, who would afterward be responsible for Baryshnikov as well. But even with him Nureyev could be naughty. Once, Elena reports, he snapped a rude word at his teacher, "but after class Rudi jumped on Pushkin like a monkey and kissed him, pleading, 'Don't be angry with me! Thank you, thank you!'" "What a strange relationship," she noted. She realized not only how driven Nureyev was but how different—how special: the vanguard of the future.

She also appreciated Makarova's special qualities. Makarova had started late and had only five years of schooling behind her when she joined the company. "Her first years onstage were a trial by fire. Her technique lagged well behind her emotional and her interpretative depth. Yet for me it was always ten times more interesting to watch Makarova fall off her pirouettes than to see some other ballerinas execute every step perfectly."

The dancer who interested her the most, however, was Igor Tchernichov, a couple of years older than she was, with whom she fell in love as a teenager and married—after three years of a passionate but unconsummated relationship. Even then she wasn't sure she wanted to marry, but he was determined, and by the time she was twenty they had a son, Alyosha. While still at school she had been asked by Tyuntina to teach some classes. Now, although she was performing in the company, she was more focused on coaching the highly ambitious Igor, who had become a leading dancer and an aspiring choreographer. When he was invited to take over the ballet company in Odessa, she went with him to help stage his *Nutcracker* (they were given a two-year leave of absence from the Kirov), and soon she was the principal ballet mistress there. "I rehearsed everything and staged all the classical ballets." The company was lax. "The girls were lazy and overweight; they approached their job as a hobby." She started teaching company class to the corps de ballet girls, and during

the first month they went to the Opera House supremo and complained about me. He called me to his office. "Maybe you could be a little bit nicer to them, and give an easier class."

"Absolutely not," I told him. "I'm being honest with them. If they don't want to take the information that I'm giving them, without playing games, too bad, they're stupid. I'm not going to make myself stupid, too." But within two or three months I felt as though I had them in my hands. We all got along very well.

Perhaps. What's certain is that although the Odessa company was now doing very well (a big success at a Moscow festival, touring), she and Igor weren't doing very well. He "became more and more full of himself and more dictatorial, more high-strung and volatile. . . . And yet if it hadn't been for his drinking, we might very well have stayed married." Deciding that life with him was no longer possible, she returned alone to Leningrad, where the head of the Kirov told her that if she didn't want to dance, he would make her a ballet mistress. She accepted, and went back to work in the company. Later, her mind on the future, she succeeded at being accepted at an elite choreographic institute in Moscow, and was soon creating dances for television and the theater. Her career was on track.

BUT IN THE EARLY 1970s, her thoughts were focusing on America. In 1962, New York City Ballet had made its historic first visit to the Soviet Union, bringing Balanchine back to his native country for the first time since his departure in 1924. The old guard was skeptical and critical of what Balanchine was doing; they despised his innovations, they declared he was unmusical. Igor's mother had been in Danilova's class at the Kirov school and she

was baffled when Balanchine returned triumphant to Russia with his company. A great choreographer? A genius? And so many Western wives? But he always chased the most beautiful girls in the school . . . and they didn't want him. . . . Balanchine wasn't a great classical dancer, [Igor's mother] said; once she had offered him half an apple if he could do a double tour. He tried and failed and received no apple.

Besides, his face was covered with pimples, she recalled. Someone so gauche, so afflicted couldn't possibly have become famous!

But the students and the other younger dancers "were skylarking with joy." Elena was overwhelmed—by Balanchine's genius, by his personal modesty, and most of all by Allegra Kent as the Sleepwalker in *La Sonnambula*. "I saw every performance she gave; I wanted to somehow impress irrevocably on my brain every single step of hers." By the time Balanchine was gone, "I was ready to follow him to New York."

The year before, Nureyev had defected to the West. Makarova followed in 1970, and four years later, Baryshnikov. Elena wasn't surprised: After a performance of *Giselle*, he had taken her aside and asked her whether his performance was "on an international level." "Yes, absolutely," she replied. "That phrase 'international level' had an odd sound. As I reassured him, his eyes were X-rays searching for any false flattery. I now was sure that he was making plans." Two days before he left on the tour from which he defected, she was talking with him in his apartment and told him that she was hoping to emigrate. "I wish you would stay there" (i.e., abroad), she said. "But it's your life." "I will be back," he said. "Of course he wasn't going to drop any hints," Elena remarks. "Misha would have been insane to have told even his own shadow anything out of the ordinary."

Several of her close friends had succeeded in getting to New York, and were pressing her to join them. But how to get there? "In those days the bulk of emigration from the Soviet Union was granted to Jews. Since my father's father had been born in Dusseldorf, there was some credibility to claiming that I was Jewish, even though my passport didn't say so. . . . I wasn't officially listed as Jewish, I told them, because my mother was Russian."

It wasn't easy, even after she was granted an exit permit. There were last-minute dramatic (and dangerous) moments before she was on the plane to Vienna. But the most traumatic crisis had come when Alyosha, now sixteen, under pressure from his father, decided not to accompany her; he would, he said, come on his own in two years, when he would no longer need his father's permission. It would be twelve years before they saw each other again.

IN ROME, where Tchernichova waited for an American visa, she was receiving an émigré allowance from the Tolstoy Foundation and earning some money by teaching. It was six months before the visa came through, and when in 1976 she finally reached New York, a limousine sent by Baryshnikov was waiting at the airport to collect her. That night she watched him and Makarova in *The Sleeping Beauty.* "ABT looked like an immature company. I had the distinct impression that many of the dancers did not entirely know what they were supposed to be doing. Stylistically, they weren't academically clean or refined." When Makarova in her dressing room insisted on hearing her opinion, "since she seemed to really want to know, I did tell her diplomatically that I didn't think her arms were very correct and her extension wasn't as high as before."

Soon she was giving Natasha private classes, teaching at the Harkness Ballet School and elsewhere, becoming part of the international ballet community. Inevitably, she was invited by Lucia Chase to work for ABT, where Misha, Natasha, and the young Gelsey Kirkland were the greatest stars. Her observations of them and others—their strengths, their weaknesses, their differences—are significant as testimony and delicious as gossip. Her judgments are cool—severe yet generous:

Whenever Natasha danced, improvisation always co-starred with structure; she invited impulse, the imperative of the moment, to guide her as she lived and breathed her roles. . . . The slate was blank for every performance, and that meant extraordinary excitement for the audience—but torture for some of her partners.

Makarova never compromised with a partner; her personality was too vehement, her artistic impulses too sure. . . . No approach, however, could have been farther from Natasha's than Misha's. He was disciplined, programmed. What he rehearsed, learned, and planned in the studio he did on the stage. Natasha nettled him because she was so utterly unpredictable. When they danced together, he might feel abused and she might feel thwarted, her fabulous expressiveness a little pinched.

In some ways Natasha and Misha were made for each other on-stage. Their training, their bodies, and body language blended perfectly. But there was more rivalry than rapport between them.

Kirkland was another matter:

For me, her Giselle was a revelation. . . . What she did was perfect for her; I wouldn't have changed anything.

Kirkland couldn't be a medium for Giselle the way Makarova was; she didn't feel the character so deeply inside. Yet Gelsey's elfin appearance was perfect for this heroine, and whether moving or poised in arabesque, her body was a portrait of infinity. If in *Giselle* her style was Russian-influenced with a British accent, her statement was altogether American. Gelsey's rebel spirit manifested itself in sublime revisionism. I loved the way she broke rules that were inviolate in Russia. Altering the musicality and timing of familiar passages, she produced effects that were startling, freshly expressive. In the spectator they produced the emotion that Gelsey herself did not experience.

THE ISSUE of American versus Russian approach—of being American versus being Russian—is a subtle theme of *Dancing on Water*. From the time of that first Balanchine visit, in 1962, Tchernichova is comparing and contrasting. When she arrived in New York, it was immediately apparent to her that Baryshnikov had changed: "The influence of Western classes and dancing Balanchine's repertory at ABT had already made Misha faster and crisper than he'd been at the Kirov. He had honed his attack; he now pointed his feet extra hard, as if to give his line a Manhattan dynamism."

Her own ideas begin to modify. ABT's physically commanding ballerinas Cynthia Gregory and Martine van Hamel didn't conform physically to the Kirov belief that *The Sleeping Beauty*'s Aurora should be short and slight, but the audience believed they were Auroras, "and so did I. Perhaps that was the beginning of my reconsideration of some needlessly stringent parameters of Russian casting."

On the other hand, she deplored the backstage behavior of the American dancers—the environment at the Kirov was "more respectful and more hierarchical." Everyone at ABT was talking in the wings. "Corps de ballet members in a crowd scene could be late for their entrance, or even fail to show up at all without any penalty. . . . Once I walked into the wings and saw dancers who were supposed to be on stage, drifting in from the cafeteria. 'What is the matter with you?' I screamed." She was also dismayed by the quality of ABT's orchestra and conducting.

The latter sections of her book are punctuated with the gossip, intrigue, alliances, and resentments that are the daily stuff of the ballet world. Elena assisted Baryshnikov in staging his *Don Quixote* and Makarova with her *La Bayadère*. When Baryshnikov became the head of ABT, her situation grew even stronger. (After a terrible fight with Kenneth MacMillan over his new *Sleeping Beauty*, MacMillan tried to get her fired. "I can't fire her," Misha told Kenneth, "she *is* ABT.") But when Baryshnikov left, she was no longer ABT—"Overnight it seemed as though ABT was a different company. A race to erase the prior decade and put the clock into reverse had begun."

Her account of these ABT years is not as disinterested as her memories of her Russian years. Slights are recorded, blame is accorded, scores are settled, triumphs are registered. There's more detail about certain second-tier dancers than any but the most ardent balletomane (or critic) requires. But always her trenchant grasp and passionate application of important principles continue to enlighten. This is why she's against girls taking entire classes in pointe shoes; this is why the lower back is so crucial to strength and to style. ("There wasn't a single dancer in ABT who used his or her lower back completely correctly. Dancers trapped their tension in their shoulders and neck. That became their center, and as a result their gravitational stability was off-kilter.") Class has to be varied:

> If the whole class is very fast, muscles will spasm and they can't respond, can't develop anything. Too much tension stays in the thighs

and behind, and circulation to the feet is blocked; it stops at the knee. If too much of the class is slow, then dancers never learn speed and attack and their muscles become overblown.

Others may not agree with all her principles, but unquestionably they bore fruit over the years; the results were up there on the stage, for all to see.

TCHERNICHOVA'S PERSONAL LIFE, naturally, changed through the New York years. She married a dancer fifteen years younger than herself—it lasted four years. Alyosha finally reached America, where she had the joy of working with him. (After twenty-five years he's still in the West.) She made close friends, among them Joseph Brodsky, whose thoughts about her appear as the moving afterword to her book. After ABT she was for several years the embattled new artistic director of Vienna's state ballet, and brought it back to life. She worked with the Trocks—the wonderful all-male Ballets Trocadero de Monte Carlo. (It's to be regretted that she doesn't talk about her experience with them—about teaching *Giselle* to guys. Vaganova's school surely hadn't prepared her for that particular assignment.)

In recent years, she coached the brilliant international star Diana Vishneva—another story replete with tensions and rivalries. Vishneva was returning to the Kirov to dance *Swan Lake* despite active resentment from the administration. "The idea that it was all right to let any teenager contort her way through Odette/Odile on the Kirov stage, but letting Vishneva dance the role was somehow going to violate hallowed traditions was nothing less than delusional." Whether writing about New York, Vienna, or St. Petersburg, Elena Tchernichova remained outspoken, confrontational, and honest.

Toward the end of her life, she was back in St. Petersburg, where she died in 2015, working to the end.

Dancing in the Dark

FLESH AND BONE

W HAT DID BALLET EVER DO TO THE WORLD to deserve the way it's always being represented by writers and film-makers? Poor ballet! It's so hard to get right; it's so fragile an enterprise; it's so battered by economic and sociological realities. Why does this fiendishly demanding but deeply rewarding process have to be distorted into an orgy of sadism, masochism, and misery? The latest avatar is the eight-part TV series *Flesh and Bone*, produced by the cable network Starz and starring the dancer Sarah Hay.

Yes, Nijinsky went mad, but he was a troubled young man—was it really Diaghilev and his Ballets Russes who pushed him over the edge? Yes, the great Olga Spessivtseva cracked up and was hospitalized for more than twenty years, but she seems always to have been unstable.

Meanwhile, the vast majority of the twentieth century's leading dancers—from Pavlova and Karsavina through Markova, Danilova, Ulanova, Plisetskaya, Makarova, Fonteyn, Nureyev, Baryshnikov, Tallchief, and Farrell—led gratifying, untormented lives. They did not cut themselves, starve themselves (most dancers eat like crazy), commit incest, commit suicide, commit murder—they just applied themselves, day in, day out, to class, rehearsal, performance. "Tendu, tendu, tendu," "plié, plié, plié," then home to soak sore feet and sew ribbons on toe shoes. (Well, maybe a glamorous party or two—and in the case of Fonteyn, Diors and Balenciagas in the closet.)

One movie and one book paved the way for today's ballet psycho-dramatics. The movie, of course, is Michael Powell's incomparable *The Red Shoes* (1948), in which Vicky Page, played by Moira Shearer, cries out, "Why do I want to dance? Why do I want to live! Because I must!" And so she dies the death, torn between her love for her reliable com-

FROM EXECUTIVE PRODUCER MOIRA WALLEY-BECKETT
THREE-TIME EMMY® WINNER FOR **BREAKING BAD**

take no prisoners

flesh and bone
NOVEMBER 8 **starz**

poser husband and her obsession with ballet and the prodigious if
sinister Boris Lermontov (a libel on the prodigious but hardly sinister
Diaghilev). There have been other ballet movies, but nothing like this
one in its opulence and ambitions. From a slow start, *The Red Shoes*
became a tremendous box-office hit in both England and America (in
New York, it ran at a small art house for more than two years); there's
no way of estimating how many little girls demanded ballet lessons in
the wake of its gorgeous melodrama.

One of the most striking aspects of *The Red Shoes* is how over the
decades it's changed: not in its content, naturally, but in how we per-

ceive it. In its early years, the 1950s, Vicky Page seemed to be the victim of the Svengali-like Lermontov, who manipulates her into abandoning her husband and domesticity in order to return—fatally—to his company to perform the *Red Shoes* ballet. In our more liberated day, it's the husband who comes across as the bad guy: It's his selfish requirements of Vicky that stand between her and her artistic destiny, and so drive her over the brink. Either way, though, she's a victim—and victimhood is the heart of the quintessential ballet melodrama.

The literary version of all this is Gelsey Kirkland's notorious memoir of 1986, *Dancing on My Grave.* She's the victim of everyone and everything, starting with her perfectionist father (the author of the play *Tobacco Road*) and featuring the tyrannical George Balanchine, whose crime lay in rigorously training her and starring her at his New York City Ballet. And then there's her drug addiction, her self-loathing (horrible efforts to alter her looks), her eating disorders, the casual behavior of her most famous dancing and sexual partner (Baryshnikov), the drug death of her later dancing and sexual partner, Patrick Bissell, and most of all, her seething anger.

But why blame Daddy, Mr. B, Misha, or Lermontov, when you can blame the real villain: ballet itself? If Vicky, Gelsey, and other martyred heroines had never been bitten by the ballet bug, they could have led normal, wholesome lives.

TIMES HAVE CHANGED, however, and although terrible things continue to plague fictionalized ballet heroines, something different and up-to-date is also taking place: Claire Robbins, the heroine of *Flesh and Bone*, finally refuses to succumb to abuse. Being a modern liberated young woman, she learns to take charge of her life, to be her own woman, to say no to her oppressors, from her toxic family to her toxic artistic director, a two-bit Lermontov. In fact, the last word spoken in *Flesh and Bone* is her defiant "No!" Her significant progress hasn't been from corps girl to prima ballerina but from victimhood to assertion. Just in time, she's discovered her self-worth!

When we first encounter Claire, though, ballet is an escape route,

DANCING IN THE DARK

not a transcendence. She's climbing out of the window of the grim house in Pittsburgh in which she's living with her father and brother—presumably they would forcibly prevent her from leaving in a more orthodox way. Well, maybe they would: Daddy is a beer-chugging invalid, raging at the universe; brother is a violent ex-marine whose relationship with Sis has been, to put it tactfully, seriously unconventional. A few years ago, Claire was an up-and-coming apprentice in a local ballet company, but she dropped out—because, as we eventually learn, she'd been inconveniently made pregnant by Bro.

No matter. Claire hops a bus for New York, proceeds at once to an open audition at the "American Ballet Company," and though she apparently hasn't taken class for years, is exhausted by her bus trip, and has no particular glamour, she is immediately hired by ABC's volatile artistic director, who decides practically on the spot that she's the Future and dumps plans to open his new season with *Giselle* in favor of a cutting-edge new piece that's to be tailor-made for her.

This doesn't go down well with all the other girls, who are relentlessly bitchy, and it really gets under the skin of the company's leading ballerina—in fact, its *only* ballerina, so far as we can see. The very glamorous Kiira (effectively played by the former ABT dancer Irina Dvorovenko) is approaching the end of her triumphant career but—and this is the most realistic thing in the series—she's in denial: She's convinced that she can go on . . . and on. Fortunately for Kiira, when she finally has to acknowledge that the bell has tolled for her at last, she has an adoring rich husband, an assortment of past and present lovers, and her cocaine habit to cushion the fall.

There seem to be fewer than thirty dancers at the American Ballet Company, which is nevertheless presented as a major organization. The only visible principals are Kiira (until she's gone) and a single male (another ABT refugee, the estimable Sascha Radetsky). There's a talented black guy in the corps who's amusingly campy, though ruthlessly ambitious, but the rest of the corps are mostly undifferentiated.

Only two of the girls stand out: redheaded, promiscuous, deeply insecure Mia, Claire's roommate, who it turns out (are you ready?) is going blind; and self-assured rich girl Daphne, who buys a promotion to soloist but whose main function is to introduce Claire to the fancy strip joint where Daph enjoys performing with a pole when she's not back in the studio practicing her fouettés. Club Anastasia is run by a charming but vicious Russian thug who happens to be in love with ballet. His favorite is *Swan Lake*, and he arranges to have Claire, whom he instantly recognizes as a special soul, too fine for poles, dance the famous second-act solo before a throng of rich people on his large yacht out in New York harbor. Oh—I almost forgot: There's a mini-subplot about the Russian mafia that comes out of nowhere and disappears without a trace.

CLAIRE, WE'RE CONSTANTLY REMINDED, is a tremendous talent, a judgment confirmed by the cutting-edge choreographer Toni Cannava, a tall, rakish blonde who is hired to create the masterpiece that will pull the American Ballet Company out of its artistic doldrums. Yet Claire is somehow emotionally blocked. (She also has some bad habits, like self-mutilation.) She has to learn to expose her feelings. "Show the camera your marrow," dictates artistic director Paul Grayson. "Strip yourself bare. Let it devour you." She does her best, but even after Paul flicks his member at her to make his point, men (always excepting Brother Bryan) just don't get through to her.

Throughout the series we get to watch ABC rehearsing, and eventually performing, Balanchine's *Rubies* (a touch of class), but the focus is on the new ballet Toni Cannava is creating. It's called *Dakini*, a Tibetan Buddhist manifestation of some kind of spiritual progress (if I understand its Wikipedia entry), and somehow it mirrors Claire's progress from victimhood to womanhood. The actual choreography is by the brilliant ex-dancer Ethan Stiefel, but I'm afraid it's the usual crummy business of lifts, lifts, lifts: Up Claire goes, down Claire comes. It's about as cutting-edge as celery, and next to *Rubies* looks pathetically reductive.

It would be easy, and fun, to go through *Flesh and Bone* and laugh at all the blunders and misrepresentations, but I'll let one stand for all. Suddenly, in a fit of pique—his natural state—artistic director Grayson turns on one of the corps girls, shrieking the equivalent of "You're fired! Get out of here!" and the poor girl slinks off, never to reappear. Grayson has presumably internalized Donald Trump's management techniques from *The Apprentice*, but apparently neither he nor anyone else connected to *Flesh and Bone* has ever heard of contracts and unions.

Sarah Hay, a pleasing if not exceptional American dancer, was "discovered" to play Claire, and at the start there was a fuss about her cleavage, considered by some as excessive for a ballerina. But she stuck to her guns, and I'm certainly not complaining. Hay is perfectly adequate as both a dancer and an actress—it's not her fault that she's hardly the incomparable performer she's meant to be.

She even works convincingly with the series's remaining major (and most irritating) character, Romeo, a homeless literary schizophrenic, played by Damon Herriman, who hangs out at the brownstone where Claire and Mia live, benignly watching over them. Claire responds to his kindness, little knowing that at the very moment of her overwhelming triumph in *Dakini*, while the audience is standingly ovating, Romeo is stabbing Brother Bryan to death in Central Park. You may ask yourself why he's wearing a coat he's patiently fashioned for himself out of bottle caps. Just don't ask me.

All this plot—plus a lot of gratuitous sex (Bryan humping Mia, but only after tying her up; Paul humping his cute ethnic rentboy)—emphasizes the fact that *Flesh and Bone* is pure soap opera, masquerading as, or aspiring to be, an illuminating look at the world of ballet. The obvious comparison is to the award-winning movie *Black Swan* (2010), a confused psychodrama about deeply disturbed characters in a semi-surreal world. In a word, *Flesh and Bone* is merely ridiculous; *Black Swan* is inflated, arty pretension. Given the choice, I'd go the soap opera route any day. Besides, it's fun watching Dvorovenko go to town in *Rubies*. In soap opera as in real life, Balanchine comes off best.

The New York Review of Books
JANUARY 14, 2016

A Star on Pointe

S

O MUCH IS AWFUL about the blood-and-tutu psychodrama *Black Swan* that I perversely want to start with what's good about it. It really tries to be honest about what life is like for ballet dancers (female ones, that is; the guys are barely discernible in the movie's fictional ballet company). We see how hard the girls work, how they long for better roles, how they endure the physical pain that's an unavoidable component of what they do. And its star, Natalie Portman, is utterly game: Having had ballet training as a young girl, she looks plausible, even if there is nothing in the dancing she performs here (when her body double isn't doing the tough stuff) that proclaims her as particularly talented.

She's very pretty, of course, and her pale complexion, thin body, and one-note intensity suffice to give her a ballerina look. That her voice is tiny and monotonous isn't a problem—dancers don't have to sound like Sarah Bernhardt. That her acting is monotonous is a problem—but this isn't a movie that depends on acting of any depth; it's about shocking the audience, not persuading it.

What really matters is that *Black Swan* deploys and exaggerates all the clichés of earlier ballet movies, especially *The Red Shoes*, another tale of a ballerina driven mad and suicidal. The heroine of Michael Powell's classic suffers because she's torn between Life and Art. The heroine of *Black Swan* suffers because she has a destructive ballet mother (as if this were unique), because she has lesbian impulses (they emerge in one of her psycho-fantasies), and because she is frigid—a serious no-no to male screenwriters and directors, who seem to find frigidity personally offensive. Clearly, she has to die.

Before she does, however, the company's impresario-choreographer

(Vincent Cassel) does his best to unfreeze her, and when that doesn't work, he sends her home to masturbate—no doubt a tactic he learned from Balanchine and Ashton. Still game, she follows orders, but no go.

BLOOD IS THE LEITMOTIF of *Black Swan*. It's everywhere, beginning with Nina's skin—stigmata of some sort on her back; seeping from her self-mutilations. It pools out from beneath a closed door behind which, in one of her nightmare fantasies, she's stuffed the body of the friend/rival whom she's offed in a moment of irritation. And of course, at the

Natalie Portman in *Black Swan*

grand climax of the film and of the "perfect" performance of *Swan Lake* on which the film centers, it leaks out of her midsection as her Odette impales herself and leaps to her watery doom. It's so unfair—and so unrealistic: By killing herself, Nina misses out on her curtain calls.

So *Black Swan* is Grand Guignol with pretensions to class, and audiences are eating it up. Which wouldn't matter if it weren't recapitulating all the old, ugly misrepresentations about ballet. Dance is about suffering. Art is inevitably linked to madness. (Nina's predecessor, forced to retire, is another self-slasher.) You have to become a monster to succeed—or sleep with the boss. And to be an artist you have to feel . . . to live; talent and hard work aren't enough. Get out there, Nina, and have a drink, have some pills, have some sex. Throw those stuffed animals out of your bedroom. Then get up on that stage for one perfect performance and . . . curtains!

What did ballet ever do to deserve this?

Black Swan does what Hollywood movies have always done—it spends its energies on getting some surface things right while getting everything important wrong. Darren Aronofsky, the director, applies the same techniques and the same sensibility here as he did with *The Wrestler*, only with a prettier protagonist. (Mickey Rourke in a tutu is something I'd like to see.) The advance hype has been relentless. Some of the acting—notably Mila Kunis as Nina's nemesis—is a lot of fun. Portman, aiming for the Oscar rather than fun, is good enough. Why is it all so dispiriting? And are deluded ballet parents around the country going to expose their little darlings to this sadomasochistic trip? There are going to be tears.

The New York Observer
DECEMBER 7, 2010

Brilliant, Touching, Tough

MARY ASTOR

L UCILE VASCONCELLOS LANGHANKE was born in 1906. "Mary Astor" was born in 1921—that was the name that went up in lights for the first time, at Manhattan's Rivoli Theater, where, not yet sixteen, she was playing in a short film called *The Beggar Maid*. Soon her Madonna-like face was spotted in a fan magazine by the great John Barrymore and she was commandeered by him to play his love interest in *Beau Brummel*—as well as the (temporary) love of his life, and maybe the greatest love of hers. She missed out on the chance to play Mrs. Ahab to his Captain in *The Sea Beast*, but they were back together in *Don Juan*, the real first movie to include sound, even if it was only background music. Equally prestigious: she was Dolores de Muro, Douglas Fairbanks's love object, in *Don Q, Son of Zorro*.

Astor, after nearly forty feature-length silents, made the transition to talkies, although for a long time they were mostly junkies—*Ladies Love Brutes, The Sin Ship*—and while she showed no extraordinary talent, her astounding beauty and impeccable elocution kept her on the screen, and in the chips, until better roles started coming her way: with Ann Harding in the first version of *Holiday*; with Clark Gable and Jean Harlow in *Red Dust*. Then, in 1936, after a series of calamities like *The Case of the Howling Dog* and *Red Hot Tires*, she was featured in her finest role to date: as the noble Edith Cortright, together with Ruth Chatterton and Walter Huston, in William Wyler's *Dodsworth*. It was being filmed while she was also featuring in the greatest Hollywood scandal of the decade: the trial for custody of her daughter, which lasted for weeks and had to be conducted at night, since you couldn't expect a major studio to shut down filming during the day for a mere court case.

Among the movies to come: *The Prisoner of Zenda, Midnight* (she's married, ritzily, to Barrymore), *Brigham Young* (she's the great man's first wife), *The Great Lie* with Bette Davis, for which she won the supporting actress Oscar for playing a selfish concert pianist with a glamorous upsweep hairdo who gives her baby away for the sake of her career. Then her greatest role—as the ultra-noir Brigid O'Shaughnessy in *The Maltese Falcon*—and on to the man-hungry "Princess" who ends up with Joel McCrae's identical twin in Preston Sturges's glorious *The Palm Beach Story*, then soaked to the skin (along with Dorothy Lamour and Jon Hall) in John Ford's *The Hurricane*.

And then in 1944, at the age of thirty-eight—as she recounts dolefully in her two excellent memoirs, *My Story* and *A Life on Film*—she begins a long string of mothers: first (and best), Judy Garland's in *Meet Me in St. Louis*; then Gloria Grahame's, Dorothy McGuire's, Elizabeth Taylor's, Esther Williams's, Janet Leigh's; then Taylor and Leigh's again, plus Margaret O'Brien and June Allyson's, as Marmee in the 1949 *Little Women*; and on and on. Mercifully, it was a cameo in *Hush . . . Hush, Sweet Charlotte*—as a murderess, not a mother—that, in 1964, ended her forty-three years on the big screen.

ASTOR NEVER MADE A FLASHY COMEBACK because until her retirement she had never been far away. But now, thirty years after her death, she's back with a bang, thanks to Edward Sorel's endearing tribute to her, *Mary Astor's Purple Diary*, told in throbbing words and spectacular color. (Forget that the notorious diary was written in brown, not purple, ink; the press would have its way.)

The diary—she'd been keeping one since girlhood—purportedly revealed not only details of her torrid affair with the playwright George S. Kaufman but accounts of her affairs with countless other men, many of them top stars of the screen, whose sexual powers she was said to have rated and whose careers (and marriages) would have been destroyed if the news got out in those days of the strict Hays Code. Her ex-husband, whom she was challenging in court, had paid to have the purple pages snatched from her locked desk and had blackmailed her with them to

Edward Sorel's Mary Astor

gain total custody of their daughter, Marylyn. But now, in 1936, Mary
had decided to fight back at the risk of her own career: Mother love came
first, a standard Hollywood trope, though in this case real life proved
far more turbulent than it does in your standard weeper.

A few pages from the diary were leaked to the press, the more lurid
ones forged. The court battle raged on and on, the story dominating
the front pages not only of the tabloids but of the Los Angeles and New
York *Times* as Mary, demurely dressed, showed up in court day after
day after filming had ended. Eventually, Judge Goodwin ("Goodie")
Knight—who would go on to become governor of California—shut the
circus down, sequestered the diaries, and, based on what he believed to
be best for four-year-old Marylyn, essentially turned her over to her
mother. Kaufman slunk out of town rather than be subpoenaed, scurrying home to New York and his open marriage; Marylyn's daddy, a

fashionable gynecologist, went back to his own multiple affairs, one of them almost certainly a bigamous marriage; and both *Dodsworth* and Mary's career flourished. To everyone's relief, the far greater scandal surrounding the abdication of Edward VIII for "the woman I love" soon replaced the purple diaries as Subject Number One.

How had the Madonna-like Lucile, who had never even been alone with a man until Barrymore and *Beau Brummel,* turned into such a scarlet woman? Her childhood and youth present an unusual type of abuse. Otto Langhanke, her Prussian father—who had big ideas (raising fancy poultry, writing German textbooks), little common sense, and a lot of bad luck—determined that Lucile was to be the family breadwinner. Perhaps through music? She was force-fed singing lessons. And she was made to practice the piano up to six hours a day, growing so competent that when, decades later, she had to impersonate a concert pianist performing Tchaikovsky's first piano concerto while a professional pianist played off-camera, her hands on the keyboard were so convincing that even as experienced a musician as José Iturbi was fooled.

But music was not to be the family's financial salvation. Movies were the great new thing, and Otto decided to cash in on Mary's beauty. He staked everything on acting lessons, then scraped up the money to get the three Langhankes to New York, where they had no contacts and no road plan. Yet it happened, and at fourteen Mary was before the cameras.

She had had no real childhood, apart from school (which she loved). There were no physical demonstrations of affection. Her father frightened her with his relentless, brutal criticism. She was allowed no friends, no amusements other than reading and wandering alone in nature. She had no money of her own—in her late teens, when she was earning up to four thousand dollars a week, she was getting by on a weekly five-dollar allowance. Her mother was with her all day, every day, at the studio. Any letters she received were vetted by her parents, and she couldn't write openly to anyone since she wasn't allowed even to walk to the corner alone if she wanted to post a letter. There were no parties, no dates, no girlfriends. And no privacy: Her bedroom door had to be left open, even at night. Meanwhile, her father made all her deals with the studios she worked for and spent all the money she earned.

But even downtrodden victims can turn on tyrants, and eventually, urged by Barrymore to assert herself, she escaped from her bedroom late one night, climbing down a tree and walking to a nearby hotel. She was nineteen.

No wonder that when this all-work, no-play girl started playing, she played hard. But to get fully away from her parents, she needed to marry, and at twenty-one she married Kenneth Hawks, younger brother of the director Howard Hawks. They shared tastes and interests but not sex—every night on their honeymoon he kissed her chastely on the forehead and retired to his own bed. Although they were happy with each other in other ways, their sexual life remained close to nil, and Mary, whose needs had proved to be considerable, began an affair with a Fox executive, got pregnant, and had an abortion. Meanwhile, Ken's health was deteriorating, not helped by being informed of Mary's affair—by her mother. In 1930, after two years of marriage, sweet, sensitive Ken died in a plane crash while directing aerial scenes for a movie.

She had loved him, but life goes on, and Mary went on to marry Dr. Franklyn Thorpe, who fathered Marylyn and with whom she was to battle so fiercely in court. The great romance with George Kaufman— she was really crazy about him—ended abruptly when he ran home to Mrs. Kaufman and Broadway, but there were to be many other men, two more marriages, and one more child. Even so, after the scandal died down Mary and Thorpe stayed on good enough terms that for a number of years he remained her principal physician; there was even brief talk of remarriage. As for Marylyn and her father, to whom she was never very close, she has reported: "After I married he became our family doctor and delivered all my children. That's when I saw him." Well, he may not have been a good father, but he must have been a good doctor.

THROUGH ALL THE TURMOIL of her private life, Astor was working assiduously to become a better actress. From the beginning she was determined to learn, but there was no one to teach her, once Barrymore was out of her life. He had wanted her to come with him to London to play Ophelia in his famous production of *Hamlet* and Lady Anne in *Richard III*, but her father nixed it: "It was 'impractical.'" "Of course it was," she would remark; "no money in it." Earlier, Otto had ruined her chance to work with D. W. Griffith, an opportunity her friend Lillian Gish had provided. After Griffith turned Mary down, Lillian explained that he had taken one look at Daddy, and that was enough. "The man is a walking cash register," Griffith said. "I would never have any freedom to develop the girl."

No one developed her. She was beautiful, she was likable, she was tractable, even though, as she was to say, half the time she didn't know what she was doing. And she was in constant demand, for movies she despised. As she would one day write: "There was never any reality . . . just real big [troubles] that never happened to anyone—avalanches, suffering at the hands of the Huns, or being shot at or starving to death. And everything always came out right in the end." No surprise that a young woman of her intelligence would end up saying, "I was never totally involved in movies. I was making someone else's dream come true. Not mine."

Yet she went on fine-tuning her skills—or as she put it, "sullenly, dissatisfied and unhappy, I was learning a craft." So that, looking back years later, she could say, "I am proud of the product I developed and sold for so many years, the product called Mary Astor."

Along the way she made a remarkably prescient decision about her career. By the mid-1930s she was highly marketable and highly paid—specializing, she would say, in

> secretaries, princesses, crooks, the wife of, the girl friend of. . . . I was "Sally at the door, waiting for him" or "Pretty girl, that secretary of yours; now about our deal with the mining company." Or (hero to hussy), "Sure, I'm married, but what's that got to do with us?" and there's a dissolve to me, rocking a cradle, or knitting little things.

But when she was offered starring contracts—grander roles, more money, less work—she turned them down:

I was afraid of starring, of being too "successful." It sounds paranoid, but I was practical. Because starring was one hell of a gamble, and I couldn't afford to gamble. I could go on more or less hiding in feature roles, working consistently and not being responsible for the product. "A Joan Crawford picture," "a Norma Shearer picture," "a Ronald Colman picture": If they were bad, it was *their* fault; they were box-office magic or box-office poison. Once you reached their level, you had to stay at the top, for where else could you go except down? I really wanted to stick around, to feel secure. And I did, and I was.

ED SOREL DISCOVERED MARY ASTOR IN 1965, the year after she made her final film. Stripping layers of linoleum from the floor of the kitchen in an apartment he had just moved into, he came upon old newspapers reporting the purple diary scandal. He was hooked. He was besotted. And he remained so until, just over half a century later, he was ready to give us *Mary Astor's Purple Diary*. It's a love letter, which means it's a fan's letter. And why not? If you love a movie star, you're a fan.

It's also a love letter to "the movies," and a love letter from Sorel to himself as a kid and a young man from a poor working-class family in the Bronx. His father was tough—violently opposed to his pursuing art as a career—but so was his mother, who was certain he was talented and fully supported his passion for drawing. Like Mary he changed his name, a further distancing from his father, but while Mary was rechristened by her studio, Ed himself chose "Sorel" to replace "Schwartz" because of his sympathy for Julien Sorel, the doomed hero of Stendhal's *The Red and the Black*. Talk about romantic! Naturally, Eddie Schwartz Sorel would fall in love with a onetime movie star.

Sorel had a slow start as an artist/illustrator/caricaturist. Again and again, in various books and catalogs, he is self-deprecatory about his natural abilities, and he's more or less right: His early drawing, often stiff and crude, barely suggests the triumphs to come. But the wit and intelligence were evident from the start, and the political passion. He was part of the generation of Milton Glaser (best man at his first wedding), Seymour Chwast, David Levine, and Tomi Ungerer, and he went on to work for left-wing venues like *Ramparts, Monocle, The Village Voice,* and *The Nation,* as well as *The New Yorker, Esquire, The Atlantic Monthly, Time, New York,* and many others, including *Penthouse* ("The only mass magazine that allowed me to do anti-clerical cartoons"). Cardinal Spellman was a particularly rich target.

And then there was Nixon, the richest and ripest target of all. The only cover Sorel ever did for *Screw* was one he knew no other magazine would publish: a caricature of Judge John Sirica listening to the Nixon tapes unspool, with a voice saying, "Oh! Oh! That feels so good . . . deeper, Bebe, deeper . . . ohhhh! OH! BEBE! YOU'RE SO BIG!!" And another voice replying, "Thank you, Mr. President."

Yet in a series of children's books Sorel reveals a tender side of his nature, and a deep nostalgia for childhood. Perhaps the most suggestive of them, published in 2000, is *The Saturday Kid,* whose young hero, Leo, closely resembles the young Ed, sharing with him a love of old movies and old movie palaces. Leo triumphs as a boy violinist, is filmed meeting the mayor, and prevails over the bullying classmate who's been tormenting him. It's "dreams of glory" time. Sorel may have been a slow starter, but he was never short on ambition. And like his heroine, Mary Astor, he never stopped improving as an artist, slaving at his drawing until he was in sure command of his pen.

He reached a peak in the art he created for *First Encounters,* a series of actual "memorable meetings" for which his beloved second wife, Nancy Caldwell Sorel, wrote the text: Henry James meets Rupert Brooke; Sarah Bernhardt meets Thomas Edison; Alexander Fleming meets Marlene Dietrich; Willie Mays meets Leo Durocher. . . . You don't want to miss any of them. This is Max Beerbohm turf, and the Sorels don't suffer by comparison.

Mary Astor's Purple Diary goes even further, because it's inspired by love as well as nostalgia. There Mary is: gloriously naked on the endpapers; enraptured by Barrymore, their prominent chins ecstatically dueling; noble and composed while under assault in the courtroom; facing down Irving Thalberg; canoodling with Kaufman in a Central Park horse and buggy.

She may not have wanted to be a star, but Sorel has made her one today, while so many of the supernovas of her time have vanished.

SOREL'S NATURAL TERRITORY is movie-star glamour. For Astor's real history you have to read *My Story*—a book that her priest/therapist had suggested she write and that became a considerable best seller when it was published in 1959. Her third and fourth marriages had failed. Her career had dwindled. She had a full hysterectomy. A long, painful relationship was petering out. Her parents—finally—died; she had gone on modestly supporting them. And after her MGM contract ended she had no steady income; in fact, she was broke. "The market refused to deliver or even sell me any food until I paid something on the bill of about seven hundred dollars."

Friends brought her food, the Motion Picture Relief Fund helped out, she got a scattering of jobs. And her inner strength began to manifest itself. Slowly she found lucrative work in television, where her name and her professionalism prevailed as she gamely mastered a new medium. She did a few shows, including a tour of George Bernard Shaw's *Don Juan in Hell*. And she went on writing. Her first novel, *The Incredible Charlie Carewe*—about a rich, charismatic psychopath—is amazingly assured: derivative, yes, but solid commercial fiction that deserved its commercial success. (Her lifelong passion for reading had paid off.) Other novels followed, as well as her other successful memoir, *A Life on Film*, this one focused on her movies.

Through these ups and downs two things remained constant: her heavy drinking and her search for spiritual and/or psychological succor. It took years before she could acknowledge that she was an alcoholic and learn to deal with this crippling disease, and it took years before she could feel that through her conversion to Catholicism, she had found a sound relationship with God. It also took years for her to come to terms with her grown daughter, Marylyn, and the son, Tono, she had had by her third marriage. What she never became with her children was close.

TO FIND OUT WHAT HAPPENED to Mary Astor in her later years, we have to go to another new book, which, strangely enough, has appeared at the same moment as Sorel's. This one, by Joseph Egan, is called *The Purple Diaries*, and for the most part it retells the life as we know it from Mary herself, only with far more detail from the trial records and considerable quotation from the press coverage. (Huge headline in the *Daily News*: FILM STAR DARES "RUIN" FOR CHILD.) All this will be a treat for completists, of whom I am not one.

But over the decade he spent working on this book, Egan came to know and befriend Marylyn, now in her eighties, a mother of four with forty-three grandchildren and great-grandchildren. Mary, we learn from Marylyn, was a responsible mother, but like her own parents, not a demonstrative one. She was determined to raise Marylyn simply and strictly, with strong values and "no undue pampering." As Egan puts it, "Raised by an inflexible tyrannical father, as a mother, Astor was also inflexible," one who "needed to have the final say on everything." Marylyn had some good times with her, but Mom was mostly off at work, and servants substituted. Then she spent years at boarding school—a relief. (Her younger half brother, Tono, whom she adored, spent years at military school.) At eighteen, she married—a not very happy marriage that nevertheless lasted fifty-seven years: no four husbands for Marylyn. And no children raised coolly at a distance.

There's a very long interview between Marylyn and Egan that can be found online (TheMaryAstorCollection.com), and from which he distills the mother/daughter relationship and the story of Mary's final decades. She went back to her drinking. She drifted away from her Catholicism. For years she lived in a private cottage at the Motion Picture Country Home, taking her meals by herself—she was happiest as a loner. She went on writing, and occasionally made public appearances—after all, she was an articulate survivor of Hollywood's "golden" period—but she wasn't really interested in either Marylyn's life or her children. Marylyn and her husband only rarely made the three-hour drive to see her, nor were their meetings comfortable.

Yet Marylyn loved her mother, and Mary loved her, to the extent that she was capable of loving. What she couldn't be was nurturing. Or approving. What Marylyn had to deal with, Egan writes, "was a mother who believed there was something wrong with her daughter, who was a constant disappointment to her mother." In other words, Mary behaved to her daughter the way Otto had behaved to her.

Throughout Mary's career, she always preferred unsympathetic roles, the sleazier the better: a moll here, a prostitute there, the selfish mother of *The Great Lie*, the killer Brigid O'Shaughnessy in *The Maltese Falcon*, the tough, domineering Fritzi Haller of *Desert Fury*, owner of a gambling club always ready for a fight. "I needed a target," Astor wrote about this role in *A Life on Film*; "I needed to fight with somebody." Fritzi, said Marylyn, was the part that most closely resembled Mary in real life. "*Desert Fury* was really her."

The last time the two women met was four months before Mary's death, at eighty-one, in 1987. When "I told her I had missed her," Marylyn said, "she told me 'not to get too sentimental' about it. I'd had it . . . and I asked her why she would never let me love her like I wanted to. . . . Mom looked at me for a few seconds as only she could and then looked at me again, and just told me, 'GO.' . . . I never saw her alive again."

Yet long afterward Marylyn could say, "Warts and all I still wouldn't have changed her for anyone else. She was the only mother I had. She was the best mother I had." Not a ringing endorsement, but Marylyn emerged more or less intact from her childhood, and has had a good life. And so did Tono. Mary Astor may not have been nurturing, but she was reliable and she had rigorous standards. Somehow her kids survived and prevailed.

Ed Sorel doesn't tell us about these later years—the Mary Astor he cherishes and celebrates is written in his heart in purple ink. But then he isn't Mary's daughter.

Liquid Asset

ESTHER WILLIAMS

THERE ARE MOVIE ACTORS and there are movie stars, and then there are performers who are entire genres in themselves: Their films could not have existed without them. Without the dimpled Sonja Henie, 20th Century Fox's ice-skating musicals could never have been made. And when MGM decided to trump Fox's ace with swimming extravaganzas—"'Melt the ice, get a swimmer, make it pretty!' cried Louis B. Mayer"—it was Esther Williams who made them possible. MGM knew it, too. As Williams tells it in her fresh and convincing autobiography, *The Million Dollar Mermaid*, after she became a swimming champion at not quite seventeen and a hit in Billy Rose's Aquacade in the 1940 San Francisco World's Fair, the studio practically hijacked her from her steady and congenial salesgirl job at I. Magnin.

Esther Williams was not only a terrific swimmer; she had pinup proportions and the perfect 1940s all-American look. She couldn't act, she couldn't dance, she couldn't sing. But she had what it takes in the water; and the qualities of character that had made her a champion in a highly competitive sport—self-discipline, strength of will, clearheadedness—were the qualities essential for survival in the studio system. She stood up to her treacherous swimming coach, to the rascally Billy Rose, to the priapic Johnny Weissmuller in the Aquacade (where "everyone seemed to be in heat" and where "under the stage, he'd whip off his trunks so I could see that he was beautifully equipped").

She stood up to her swindling agent, to Louis B. Mayer's tantrums, to Howard Hughes ("Don't even try, Howard, I'm too athletic"), to tyrannical directors and egomaniacal co-stars. Even the secretary of the Navy didn't daunt her. Modeling her Cole of California Esther Williams

Esther Williams in *Million Dollar Mermaid*

bathing suit, she asks, "Mr. Secretary, could you make this the official swimsuit of the U.S. Navy?" "Consider it done."

You can enjoy Esther Williams musicals (I do) and you can find them ludicrous (I do), but you can't dispute her determination. No star ever worked harder, often under perilous conditions ("I think Esther Williams is dead," her wardrobe lady shouted once. "She can't get out of the pool"). And her hard work paid off; quickly she became a top ten box-office attraction. The formula of her movies was cut and dried—what she calls the mismatched-lovers plot punctuated by gigantic aquatic production numbers. Sometimes she had fun—appearing often opposite that other all-American, Van Johnson. Sometimes it was hell, as when Gene Kelly tormented her during the making of *Take Me Out to the Ball Game*. The problem was that "as much as Kelly resented the fact that I was not a dancer, he resented my height even more." Typically, when things got really bad, she laid it on the line: "Gene . . . I have perfect proportions in a swimsuit, and that's why I'm here making movies at MGM. I'm sorry that my physique doesn't fit in with your plans."

So how did it happen that this formidable professional led such a disastrous personal life? She begins her book by revealing that in 1959, following the example of Cary Grant, she took LSD to "find some answers." She was thirty-seven years old. Her second marriage—to the alcoholic and compulsive gambler Ben Gage—was over, but he had left her owing $750,000 to the IRS. And with MGM crumbling, nobody was going to make multimillion-dollar aqua-musicals ever again. The LSD helped explain her to herself by making her relive the moment—she was eight—when her adored sixteen-year-old brother, Stanton, the pride and hope of the Williams family, died without warning. "Suddenly . . . a revelation hit me, and I knew what my life was all about. . . . His talent, his good looks, his ambition had been our only chance to break out of poverty. . . . Now that he was gone, somebody had to take his place or we would all be lost. . . . I looked about me and realized that . . . I would have to be that rock. . . . If my shoulders weren't strong enough as yet, then I would make them strong."

She proved strong enough to survive being raped repeatedly by a sixteen-year-old boy her parents had taken into the family (this began when she was thirteen and went on for two years). She survived a foolish early marriage. She even survived Ben Gage; she had to—they had three children, and he certainly wasn't going to provide. Luckily, her mother was a source of unsentimental common sense. ("I heard the voice of my mother, Bula, in the back of my mind. 'Esther,' she asked, 'what part of the problem are you?'") Nor did it hurt that she was healthily sexual—enjoying romps with at least two of her leading men, Victor Mature and Jeff Chandler, although the latter relationship ended when he cheerfully revealed himself as a confirmed cross-dresser. Even then, she kept her sense of humor and her cool, explaining to him, "I can't be married to a matron," and leaving him with a useful fashion tip: "Jeff, you're too big for polka dots."

Yet this is the point when her story takes a deeply disturbing turn. In 1960, Fernando Lamas, her leading man seven years earlier in *Dangerous When Wet*, re-enters her life. For the next twenty-two years, she lives in total submission to him—it would be fair to call it bondage. Their deal is simple: She will stop being "Esther Williams"; only "Fernando Lamas" matters. She will recede from public view, be a housewife, have no wishes or will of her own. And no other man must look at her—in fact, it's better when she gets fat, so that no man will want to. In return, he will be faithful.

Lamas's peculiarities apparently stemmed from immense vanity covering profound insecurity, and some of them can be seen as amusing. "He absolutely hated wrinkles. If we were driving to a party, he often would get behind the wheel nude from the waist down, with his perfectly pressed English gabardine pants on a hanger behind him. When we got within a couple of blocks of our destination, he'd find a secluded spot, leap out into the bushes and put on his trousers." (Why didn't I ever think of that?) But no one could find amusing his refusal to have anything to do with his wife's three children. They were not welcome in the Lamas household, and chillingly Williams relates how she spent years surreptitiously cooking for them and driving the food to where they were staying, helping them with their homework, and scurrying nervously home. Only in 1982 does she turn back into the Esther Williams we thought we knew, defying Lamas by insisting on going to her daughter's wedding. And at this very juncture, he is stricken by the cancer that swiftly killed him.

This is a dreadful story, and Williams tells it honestly. But does she really understand how and why it happened? She insists that she made a sacred pledge to care for Lamas until death, to make up to him for the traumas of his childhood. ("I have always been a person of my word, and only death could set me free from the vows I took.") But surely there is more to it than that. Perhaps this was the price she paid for being the family rock. Perhaps she found psychic advantages to being trapped in a pumpkin shell. Happily, since Lamas's death she has regained her energy and drive, making a good fourth marriage, re-emerging as a successful businesswoman and becoming, as she puts it, "godmother to a sport"—synchronized swimming.

And she has written, with the help of Digby Diehl, this interesting and engaging account of her life, and of the Hollywood she knew.

Her account is peppered with anecdotes about the great and the near-great—Dietrich, Crawford, Bette Davis, Lana Turner, even the Windsors. She describes a dinner in Spain where the Duke was passing out from drink until "finally the Duchess took him into a bathroom upstairs and emerged with him on her arm. He wasn't steady by any means, but at least he was vertical. 'I used your favorite thing,' Wally shouted to me proudly ... 'I threw water in his face!'" Water had certainly carried Esther Williams a long way.

The New York Times
OCTOBER 3, 1999

Tame Jane

JANE EYRE IN THE MOVIES

THE NEW FILM VERSION of *Jane Eyre* isn't all bad, but it's all wrong. The story, despite a confusing flashback structure, is coherent. The dialogue is satisfying. The look is convincing. What's lacking is *Jane Eyre* itself—Charlotte Brontë's feverish inner world of anguish and fury. Instead, everything is pallid and sedate. Only the landscape projects some feeling: The director (Cary Joji Fukunaga) and the cinematographer (Adriano Goldman) are far more at home looking at moors than at people.

Some viewers find the classic 1944 version over-melodramatic: Joan Fontaine too beautiful for plain Jane, Orson Welles's Rochester over-the-top with his flaring cape and piercing eyes and ultra-resonant voice. Well, he *is* over-the-top—but that's true to the nature of Brontë's imaginings. And if Fontaine is too classically beautiful, her perfectly chiseled features more Hollywood than Yorkshire, her screen presence has the right eager masochism for Jane—as it did for her two most triumphant earlier films, Hitchcock's *Rebecca* and *Suspicion*. The black-and-white photography, all deep shadows and swirling mists, ups the windblown stakes, and we're in a recognizable projection of what the novel feels like. *Jane Eyre* the novel is operatic; the new movie is what opera never should be: tame.

There have been many previous adaptations, including an early sound version from the "Poverty Row" Monogram studio, with the stolid and moribund Colin Clive as a bloodless Rochester and a too-handsome Virginia Bruce as a Jane with a Southern accent. Various television attempts have been livelier, though it would be hard to identify a more miscast Rochester than George C. Scott or a more irritating Jane than Susannah York in Delbert Mann's 1970 version. But they all suffer from the same syndrome: *Jane Eyre* is too highly charged, too febrile, for the small screen, and for TV-type acting.

And now it turns out that it's also too highly charged, too febrile, for this latest large-screen attempt by Fukunaga and Moira Buffini, a not very experienced director and screenwriter who have no problem with pictorialization but shy away from high emotion. Can they be embarrassed by all that passion, all that lack of good taste? The acting is careful and small-scale. Michael (*Inglourious Basterds*) Fassbender's Rochester is standardly handsome rather than rough-hewn, and he speaks well, but his performance is tender rather than threatening or even edgy; he's a post-feminist lover. Jane is Mia Wasikowska, who was exceptionally moving in HBO's *In Treatment* as a suicidal teenage gymnast, but whose portrayal of the young daughter in *The Kids Are All Right* was no more than capable, and whose Alice in Tim Burton's *Wonderland* was conventional and dull. (If you're looking for real acting in that movie, don't take your eyes off Johnny Depp's wild and daring Hatter.)

Michael Fassbender and Mia Wasikowska in *Jane Eyre* (2011)

Orson Welles and Joan Fontaine in *Jane Eyre* (1944)

Wasikowska is talented, certainly, but she's yet to show that she can create a character; what she does instead is be herself: serious, sensitive, occasionally breaking out her lovely smile. She's nowhere near intense enough for this iconic nineteenth-century emotional extravaganza that's thrilled generations of young women (and men). As Jane she gamely goes through the paces, but no sparks fly—certainly not the crucial ones with Rochester. When their eyes first meet, they're cautious and reflective. When Orson Welles's glare meets Joan Fontaine's instant surrender, stand back!

What we have here is the usual result when the movies take on a famous book with a singular voice. They hold on to the plot, the furnishings, even the language, but they lose the essence. It's the problem with all the *Vanity Fair* adaptations—they give us Becky, they give us the Waterloo ball, but they can't give us Thackeray's sardonic vision of *Vanity Fair*. No filmed *Moby-Dick* reflects Melville; no filmed *Madame Bovary* suggests Flaubert. The current *True Grit* is a sad case in point: It reproduces Charles Portis's story—but ploddingly. The special charm of the book lies in the earnest, humorless voice of its girl heroine, and how do you convey that on film? The utterly affectless Hailee Steinfeld, playing Mattie Ross, hasn't a clue. But the Coen brothers don't have one either: Their movie is about Jeff Bridges wearing an eye patch. (I feel particularly strongly about this one, maybe because I was the book's editor.)

The great exception to the rule is Dickens. *David Copperfield, Great Expectations, Oliver Twist* have made terrific movies, and there are acceptable television adaptations, too. But as everyone has noted, Dickens was a cinematic writer; they only had to follow along, they didn't have to reinvent. No, it's likely to be second-rate novels that make good movies, ones with exciting stories and clearly etched characters but no particular vision of life, no unique authorial voice. These latter qualities are what books are for. Back to Charlotte Brontë.

Monstres Sacrés *in Love*

STRAVINSKY AND CHANEL

ALL BIOPICS ARE BY DEFINITION RIDICULOUS, since their subjects have to be manifestly unique people—why else would the movie be made?—while what makes them unique is exactly what's so impossible to convey. (Creativity is invisible, hence unfilmable.) At best, what you get is the kind of superior impersonation Meryl Streep is so adept at, from Isak Dinesen to Julia Child, or that motored not one but two faux-Capotes a few years ago. (The best such recent effort was Marion Cotillard's Oscar-winning turn as Edith Piaf. The movie itself was standard stuff, but Cotillard's performance seemed less like an impersonation and more like the real thing—or *a* real thing.)

Hollywood once majored in stuff of this kind. Through the decades geniuses suffered (the uplifting stories of Louis Pasteur, Madame Curie, and Dr. Erlich—and his Magic Bullet) and artists suffered (the tormented trajectories of Chopin, Van Gogh, Michelangelo). Later came the entertainment icons—Al Jolson, Billie Holiday, Ray Charles, and their endless spawn of Lifetime TV specials. And then there's the world of Classica—Alexander, the Macedonian who's had the distinction of being portrayed by a Welshman (Richard Burton) and an Irishman (Colin Farrell); Cleopatra—you know who played *her*; and—still around in a few obscure and empty theaters—that renowned early-fifth-century Alexandrian astronomer and mathematician Hypatia, in a Rachel Weisz ego-trip titled *Agora*. (She's murdered by a Christian mob.)

The latest stab at showing us how genius operates is *Coco Chanel & Igor Stravinsky*, a swanky re-enactment of the supposed flaming affair between two of the major creative forces of the last century. (In real life, they did—or didn't?—share a brief moment.) Why and for whom was this movie made? There's no big name attached to it—it was never

Mads Mikkelsen and Anna Mouglalis in *Coco Chanel & Igor Stravinsky*

headed for your local Cineplex. One possible clue: Anna Mouglalis, who plays Chanel, has worked for the fashion house for eight years, and remains a "muse" for Karl Lagerfeld's Chanel products. Is this what's meant by "synergy"?

Mouglalis is a great beauty—the closest thing we've seen to Ava Gardner since Ava Gardner. And beauty is the main thing the movie offers—every approving review gloats over the opulence and glamour of the period sets and costumes; it's *Masterpiece Theatre* meets *The Rite of Spring.* Which is indeed how the movie opens: with a meticulous and convincing re-enactment of the famous "scandal"—the boos, the catcalls—of the 1913 premiere of that Stravinsky/Nijinsky/Diaghilev *cause célèbre.* Coco, elegantly strapless, is on hand, coolly approving while taking note of the hunky young composer (Mads Mikkelsen). Here, to anyone who knows the Stravinsky iconography, is where a willing suspension of disbelief had better start kicking in: Stravinsky was many extraordinary things, but at five feet three inches and with his owl-like visage he was no hunk. In the last few years, Helen Mirren, in a burst of verisimilitude, sported Her Majesty the Queen's signature hairdo and Nicole Kidman proudly asserted Virginia Woolf's nose. *Coco Chanel & Igor Stravinsky* is much too busy with the verisimilitude of the furniture and the drapery to bother with what its iconic protagonists really looked like.

World War I comes and goes, and the Stravinskys are on their uppers, needing a place to perch while the great man Creates. Coco has not forgotten him, and offers Igor and his little woman and their four littler ones her country estate to live and work in. (Cozily, she'll be there, too.) Madame S, who's suffering from jealousy as well as tuberculosis, is understandably miserable, but *tant pis*—what must be, must be, when two voracious geniuses are living under one roof, particularly when they're so well dressed.

Despite all its pretensions, *C & I* is just the same old Hollywood story: A selfish and tormented hero is torn between a ruthless Joan Crawford and a self-sacrificial Lillian Gish. Poor Catherine Stravinsky (Elena Morozova, in the film's only convincing performance) confronts Coco: Think of the children. Have you no heart? And you'll be stunned to hear that beneath her coldness, her ruthlessness, her straplessness Coco *does* have a heart, and subtly engineers a quarrel with her lover, so that the Stravinskys are forced to decamp with the family more or less intact. But not before we've been treated to a variety of embarrassing sex scenes. It's just plain mortifying to find yourself contemplating Igor Stravinsky's bare buttocks pumping away over Coco Chanel's bare everything. For comic relief, though, we do get Igor teaching Coco how to play the piano in two minutes. (She doesn't reciprocate by teaching him how to sew, although she does stitch on one of his buttons.)

There's been a run on Chanel lately: not only last year's Audrey Tautou movie *Coco Before Chanel* (actually, she was Gabrielle before she was Coco), but a couple of years ago a TV movie with Shirley MacLaine (!) as the mature Chanel. Neither of these films was exactly persuasive. Even so, in the dialogue department the new movie wins hands down. The epic spat between the two *monstres sacrés* goes as follows:

> She: "I'm as powerful as you, Igor, and more successful."
> He: "You're not an artist, you're a shopkeeper."

End of affair.

Well, Chanel *was* a shopkeeper (and what a shop!), and she would undoubtedly have acknowledged it: She was above all else a realist. Diana Vreeland put it this way: "Peasants and geniuses are the only people who count, and she was both." And "Coco was never a *kind* woman . . . but she was the most interesting person *I've* ever met." I just wish D.V. had lived long enough to see her and her equally prodigious lover portrayed not as the earth-shaking revolutionaries they were but as props in a high-toned soap opera.

The New York Review of Books (NYR Daily)
AUGUST 3, 2010

An Actress Like No Other

SETSUKO HARA

W E'RE ALWAYS HEARING ABOUT THE ENDS OF ERAS, but the recent death of the great actress Setsuko Hara really *is* the end of an era—the era of the classic Japanese film, of the directors Mizoguchi, Ozu, Naruse, Kurosawa, and Kinoshita (to name only the best-known here in America), and of the period's dominant actresses—Kinuyo Tanaka, Hideko Takamine, Isuzu Yamada, Machiko Kyō, and Hara herself. Her death at the age of ninety-five, more than fifty years after her voluntary retirement from the screen—and from all public life—still comes as a shock. There's now no one left of this astounding constellation of talent; and that she was by far the most emblematic figure of the era makes her disappearance reverberate even more strongly.

In the West, most of us first encountered her in 1972 when Yasujirō Ozu's 1953 masterpiece, *Tokyo Story*, was released here. I had never heard of Ozu, although I had seen and admired international award-winning Japanese films like *Rashomon, Gate of Hell*, and *Ugetsu*. Ozu had obviously been considered "too Japanese" for Western consumption, and it was greatly due to Dan Talbot, who ran the Upper West Side's New Yorker Theater, as well as an important film-distribution company, that he finally emerged here. Beginning with the moment when *Tokyo Story* first reached us, Ozu's international fame and influence have grown and grown to their current towering stature.

I remember reading the *Times*' ecstatic review of it and dragging myself and my wife, Maria, to upper Broadway on the hunch that we would love it. In the seventies the New Yorker was the place to go for the city's trendiest film-lovers, of whom I was not one. My passions were books and dance; I had no background in cinema history or aesthetics. I watched movies the way I read novels, for story and character, and a vision of life. Almost from the first moment, *Tokyo Story* seemed to me different from any movie I had ever seen—as true to life and as moving as Chekhov. By the time the movie was halfway over, I realized that the sophisticated audience was in tears—as I still am when I see it, and I've seen it more than a dozen times.

An old couple leave their distant seaport town in the south to visit their grown children in Tokyo, and return home a short time later, disappointed but not embittered. Their doctor son is preoccupied with his middling career and his family; their daughter, who runs a beauty parlor, is grasping and callous. Only their daughter-in-law—whose husband, their middle son, died in the war—welcomes them with a full heart. She lives alone in a respectable but shabby room and supports herself with an ordinary office job, casually taken advantage of by her late husband's family.

Her name is Noriko, and she is played by Setsuko Hara—a classic grave beauty with huge eyes and an exceptionally wide smile, and an actress of extraordinary restraint, across whose mobile face flicker emotions that reveal a woman of deep feeling and extraordinary generosity. Noriko's nobility of character, together with her unbreachable modesty and tact, make her final revelation of loneliness and unhappiness—and her unvarnished perception of humanity—all the more anguishing. She embodies Ozu's vision: People die, families dissolve, life disappoints. Accept it and endure.

Noriko is the quintessential Hara character, and in her other Ozu roles the actress suggests the same spiritual yet down-to-earth qualities. She worked for other directors as well, of course (including, atypically, for Kurosawa in his unsatisfactory version of *The Idiot*), yet nearly always within a narrow range of roles. She is inescapably refined, sensitive, well-born, and almost always modern—she's the archetype of the post-war young woman. Yet she also embodies the virtues of the *traditional* Japanese woman: loyalty, self-sacrifice, suffering in silence; she's the perfect daughter, wife, mother. She was utterly real, yet she represented an ideal ... *the* ideal. It was the revered novelist Shūsaku Endō who said of her, "Can it be possible that there is such a woman in this world?"

Setsuko Hara and Chishu Ryu in Ozu's *Tokyo Story*

Hara was born in Yokohama in 1920, and it was an uncle, a director, who eased her way into the movies when she was fifteen. Two years later she was playing central roles, her fresh beauty and charm irresistible. But it wasn't long before her inner depth and strength had manifested themselves. There would be no hiccups or longueurs in her thirty-year career.

She was famously and completely private about her life, never marrying, never linked with anyone romantically, although many people believe that she and Ozu had an affair: He, too, never married, living with his mother until she died only two years before his own death on his sixtieth birthday, in 1963. He was buried in the seaside resort town of Kamakura, just outside Tokyo, and it was to Kamakura that Hara, in her early forties, retired shortly after his death, living out her long life in her family house, making no public appearances, shunning interviewers and photographers, mostly seeing family and her old classmates from school. The one thing she did reveal to her countless admirers, in her final press conference, was that she had never enjoyed making movies, and had only done it to help her family financially. Then, fifty-odd years of silence. To avoid fuss, she had arranged that her death, which occurred on September 5, not be made public until more than two months had gone by.

Setsuko Hara has frequently been called the Garbo of Japan not only because of her unique beauty and mysterious spiritual quality but because of her early withdrawal from public life. Garbo, however, flirted with the idea of a comeback, and her retirement to the Upper East Side of Manhattan was hardly equivalent to Hara's ruthless self-imposed isolation. Hara really *did* want to be left alone. (If she resembles any Western star it is Lillian Gish, whose radiant beauty also masked indomitable strength, whose ambiguous relationship to D. W. Griffith echoes Hara's to Ozu, who never married and was hardly ever the subject of gossip and speculation—a foreshadowing of Hara's renown as Japan's "eternal virgin.") And yet she retains her powerful grip on those of us who have been under her spell from the start. I remember Dick Cavett telling me that on a trip to Japan he had found out where she lived, made a pilgrimage to Kamakura, left a bouquet of flowers on her doorstep, rung the doorbell, and then scurried away, chagrined at the idea that he had trespassed on her privacy.

And to Susan Sontag she was a sacred icon—whenever a Hara film was being shown at Japan Society (on East Forty-Seventh Street), Susan was there in the front row. I had arranged for a private screening at MoMA of one of her greatest films, *The Ball at the Anjo House*—a postwar version of *The Cherry Orchard* that was the Japanese critics' choice as the finest movie of 1947—and Susan, of course, was on my list, and overjoyed to be seeing it. Unfortunately, she had to leave halfway through: It was opening night at the Met and she was due there. But we had found out that the following week *Anjo* was going to be shown, once only, at a film festival in Boston, and Susan made her own pilgrimage. How not?

On a more personal note: In the fifty-odd years that I've been seeing movies, plays, operas, and ballets with Maria, the screening at MoMA was the only time she ever broke into audible sobs. As for *Tokyo Story*, in 2012 it was the number-one choice of the world's leading directors as the greatest film ever made. It has my vote, too.

The New York Review of Books (*NYR Daily*)
DECEMBER 15, 2015

·⦗ OBSERVING DANCE ⦘·

The Magic of Ashton

FOR TWO WEEKS THIS SEASON, ballet came back to life in New York as something you could love without hesitation or reservation. American Ballet Theatre, after floundering so long in search of plausible repertory, found it where they should have been looking all this time—in Frederick Ashton. By staging so beautifully two of his greatest works—*La Fille Mal Gardée* and *The Dream*—the company not only revitalized its dancers but revitalized an audience that's spent far too long dutifully trying to find pleasure in duds like *The Snow Maiden*, superduds like *The Pied Piper*, and the Crankotrash of *The Taming of the Shrew* and *Onegin*. Gallant stabs at Martha Graham's *Diversion of Angels* and Balanchine's *Symphony in C* haven't measured up to these masterpieces. But Ashton suits ABT—and if the company perseveres, he will come to suit the big Met audience, too. As a friend of mine remarked after the cheering at the end of *Fille* had died down, "You'd have to be dead not to love it."

This is not the conventional *Fille* that ABT was trotting out in the 1970s, a production that had nothing to recommend it but the star power of Makarova, Baryshnikov, and Gelsey Kirkland. This is Ashton's great reinvention of 1960, in which the traditional French tale of young lovers triumphing over parental disapproval is transmuted into an enchanting English pastoral, reflecting, as Ashton wrote, an "eternally late spring . . . of perpetual sunshine and the humming of bees—the suspended stillness of a Constable landscape of my beloved Suffolk, luminous and calm." Above all, it's a ballet about love: Lise and Colas's love for each other, of course, but also the love that is so touchingly indicated between Lise and her mother, the Widow Simone, who is determined to marry off her daughter to the zany, rich simpleton Alain; the love of the strutting cockerel for his four hens, of Alain for his red umbrella, and underlying the entire ballet, the love of dancing which redeems everyone and everything. Even when the Widow is at her crossest with her wayward daughter, she can be coaxed into her joyful clog dance or will snatch up a tambourine to get Lise up on her toes. And poor abject Alain, disdained by Lise, will brighten at the sound of a flute and burst into his brilliant parody of classical dance. He may be a fool, but he's a dancing fool. As for the chickens, they were born to dance.

Ashton, I suspect, was partly drawn to *Fille* by his lifelong adoration of Anna Pavlova, in whose repertory it was featured for many years. But it was that other great Russian ballerina, Tamara Karsavina, who in her old age taught him the touching mime passage from the Petipa version in which Lise, believing herself alone, acts out her dream of being married, being pregnant, and having babies—one, two, three! Ashton's *Fille*, then, is a French story told in an English spirit with Russian connections.

There was one Russian Lise in the four casts ABT presented—the formidable Bolshoi star Nina Ananiashvili—and although she's somewhat mature to be playing the very young Lise, in the rapturous pas de deux that brings the love story to its climax, she demonstrated the command of a true ballerina, dominating the audience rather than appealing to it. But the success of *Fille* ultimately depends on the degree of sympathy between the lovers. First-cast Ashley Tuttle and Ethan Stiefel are both impeccable classical dancers but, as they used to say, they come from two different worlds: She's delicate, romantic, womanly; he's a horny kid. The best-matched couple were Xiomara Reyes and Angel Corella, at first childlike and shy in their feelings for each other, then growing—like a Romeo and Juliet for whom things work out happily—from puppy love to tender and satisfied passion. Where Stiefel was randy, Corella was ardent.

The final pairing gave us Gillian Murphy—at last promoted to principal rank—and Maxim Beloserkovsky, and what they projected was glowing youth. The intricacies of the ribbon dances were easily dealt with by Murphy's rock-solid technique, and the barnyard high jinks—churning the butter, sampling the porridge, trying to sneak out the gate to get to the boyfriend—allowed her to relax into her open American niceness. Beloserkovsky is good to look at, with his endlessly long legs and handsome features—think Cyd Charisse—but he's an under-energized dancer and not what you'd call an actor. It was Ananiashvili's partner, Carlos Acosta—ABT's latest Hispanic import—who caused the biggest stir. He's big, strong, centered, accurate, engaging—a black Cuban with lots of experience and charisma. In *Fille*, though, his acting was limited to The Shrug and The Grin.

All three of the Widows—Victor Barbee, Kirk Peterson, and Guillaume Graffin—were funny and touching; the drag is good-natured, not campy. The Alains were more variable: Joaquin De Luz dancing up a storm but too relentlessly chipper; Carlos López unformed; only Herman Cornejo subtly identifying the sadness as well as the goofiness in this glorious creation. But although Alain is a disappointed suitor, won't he really be happier with his umbrella than he would have been with Lise? So there's a happy ending for everyone—except for those like me who, after five performances, were left pining for more. This production, staged by Alexander Grant (the original Alain), Christopher Carr, and Grant Coyle, is markedly superior to the Royal Ballet's. Well, London's loss is our gain. Ashton's *La Fille Mal Gardée* is a great work of art. In its generosity of spirit, its belief in the power of love and the power of dance, its humanity and decency, its innocent sexuality, it shines like a good deed in a bad world.

In the years immediately following *Fille*, Ashton went on expressing his love for love—in the enchanting *The Two Pigeons* (1961), the overwrought *Marguerite and Armand* (1963), and, in 1964, the radiantly beautiful *The Dream*, the first ballet made on Anthony Dowell and Antoinette Sibley. Dowell (now Sir Anthony) worked with Christopher Carr on staging and coaching *The Dream* for ABT, and the result is another miracle of re-creation, authentic but not slavish. When the curtain goes up on David Walker's exquisite forest glade and the sixteen fairies rush on in their beautiful bell-shaped skirts, their hair piled up behind their coronets, you're in enchanted territory. The choreography here is so fluent, so charged, so natural, that even before the entrances of Oberon and Titania and Puck, of the star-crossed lovers, of Bottom and his gang, you know you're in the hands of a master.

Balanchine's *A Midsummer Night's Dream*, choreographed two years before Ashton's version, is about contest: The battle between the king and queen of the fairies over her little page is prolonged and serious, and Oberon practically gloats over his victory—this is a relationship in trouble. (The misunderstandings among the humans also cut deep.) In Ashton's *Dream*, Oberon never ceases to love his queen; you can sense his rueful ambivalence over the trick he's played on her. Their quarrel is only a pretext: Its real function is to serve as foreplay to the ecstatic duet at the end that signals their passionate and melting reconciliation. In contrast, the squabbling humans are close to caricature in their Victorian costumes and posturings—Lysander and Demetrius in their velvet frock coats and pugilistic stand-offs, Hermia and Helena with their tiffs and makeup kisses—while putting the transformed Bottom on pointe underlines what an oddball donkey he is, not a semi-tragic one, like Balanchine's.

It was gratifying to see how this *Dream* gave nourishment to so many of ABT's dancers. Oberon seems to me Stiefel's finest role: It accords with his somewhat arrogant demeanor and gives him plenty of opportunities to show off his transparent classicism—those whip-clear turns and elegant jumps—without demanding the kind of realistic acting he can't pull off. Beloserkovsky's technique and strength weren't up to the job—and why expose a non-turner to this role so dependent on fast turns? But the nature of Acosta's technique matches the fierce demands on Oberon, and he helps Julie Kent, so bland usually, reveal a new sexiness and playfulness as Titania. She's generally partnered by the slightly built Corella; Acosta's massiveness brought out an appealing delicacy. Amanda McKerrow was underpowered as Titania (opposite Beloserkovsky), but Alessandra Ferri, also approaching the end of her career, has retained enough of her ballerina strengths to make a satisfying pairing with Stiefel.*

As for the fiendishly demanding role of Puck—darting, crouching, leaping, spinning—it gave further opportunities to the company's two brilliant little guys, De Luz and Cornejo. ABT has now what practically amounts to a monopoly on first-rate male dancers—it's almost unfair of them to add Acosta to the mix. But he's of a different breed from a Stiefel or a Corella; like José Manuel Carreño, whom he's presumably being groomed to spell, he's a grown-up.

For these two weeks of Ashton we can forgive ABT their dopey Tchaikovsky-snippets program and even the pernicious *Onegin*. I don't know why they chose to invest this heavily in Ashton at this moment; I only know he's made them a powerful contender.

The New York Observer
JUNE 24, 2002

The Triumph of the Trocks

WITH THEIR EXQUISITE TIMING, Les Ballets Trockadero de Monte Carlo—the Trocks, to you—have bourréed into the Joyce. It was only weeks ago that the Kirov got out of town, and two of the ballets they were featuring—*Swan Lake* and *Don Quixote*—are also featured by the Trocks in performances that are looking less and less like outright parody. As the level of technical accomplishment among the Trock guys has skyrocketed, the idea of their actually *dancing* Odette or Kitri has become more alluring. Yes, it's fun to camp it up as a Russian ballerina with a funny name—Sveltlana Lofatkina, Elena Kumonova—or a danseur from hell like Igor Slowpokin. And at least one of the Trocks,

---

*The finest of all pairings would eventually be Murphy with David Hallberg.

Ida Nevasayneva, is still relying far too heavily on mugging: last season, in *The Dying Swan*; this year, swathed in yellow tulle and prancing around with a watering can, in Agnes de Mille's 1928 *Debut at the Opera*. But though the Trocks stubbornly persist in their tedious tradition of repeated pratfalls and outlandish exaggerations, they're also seriously stretching toward *Swan Lake* and *Don Q.* Indeed, their recent *Paquita* and *La Vivandière* are creeping up on being straight.

It's the tension between the over-the-top slapstick, the ruthless ambushing of the ballets we most love, and the disturbing yet moving vision of men striving to conquer ballerina roles that gives the Trocks their distinction and makes them more than a high-camp joke. The best of the guys are first-rate dancers who are happily at home dancing these prima roles. Robert Carter (Olga Supphozova), hurtling around the stage as Liberty Bell in the big slam-bang pas de deux from Balanchine's *Stars and Stripes*, or tossing off triples in *Paquita*, would be triumphing in those very roles in "normal" ballet companies if he'd only bothered to be a girl. He's wonderful—polished, musical, commanding; he's got style, not just attitude, so he registers less as a man in drag than as a somewhat hefty ballerina. Yet because he is a guy in a tutu, he's also very funny. Carter and several of his colleagues, with their rock-solid pointe work, masculine power in turns and fouettés, and dynamic traversals of the stage, actually make a kind of case for men in women's roles: They give us an alternate universe of the ballerina in which force takes the place of beauty. It's tantalizing—at least until the lights come up.

The Trocks' *Swan Lake* Act II is a happy corrective to those dreary productions we're constantly being subjected to. The eight corps swans peck away when they're not breaking into the breaststroke. The world's tiniest Benno (Mr. Slowpokin) collapses under the weight of the formidable Odette (Madame Lofatkina). Prince Siegfried (Pepe Dufka) may have very little elevation, but his wig is even more ludicrously golden than those sported by so many Soviet and post-Soviet danseurs. And the whole gang gets hopelessly lost trying to decode all that undecipherable mime. (The Kirov version just leaves it out; the Trocks make Harpo look contained.) But through it all glimmers a real *Swan Lake*—of sorts.

As for the company's new *Don Q*, Fifi Barkova (Manolo Molina), with her Hitler hair-comb and grimly flirty Spanishisms, takes center stage and fights to keep it. There's a killer parody of a Petipa vision scene with the corps in bright blue, waving fairy wands, and of course the inevitable *Don Quixote* pas de deux, carried off with panache by Barkova's Kitri and her Basil (R. M. "Prince" Myshkin), until she breaks his spirit. Don't mess with Kitri!

The big event of the season is the return to the Trocks of choreographer Peter Anastos after a quarter century of disaffection. His signature pieces for the company—*Go for Barocco* and *Yes, Virginia, Another Piano Ballet*, parodies of Balanchine and Robbins—are probably the Trocks' best-known works, and rightly, because they don't simply mimic the mannerisms of their targets; they stand, as it were, as seditious new works by these masters.

The new Anastos piece, *La Trovatiara Pas de Cinq*, is relatively minor, because its target is less challenging, but it's a real comic ballet, not just a joke. The giant and gorgeous Nadia Rombova (Jai Williams), with her far-flung extensions and the softest toe shoes ever seen—she's all knuckled over—dominates as a kind of harem or pirate girl, swirling her skirts and beaming her relentless grin. Two other big wild hussies and two teensy guys flashing teensy swords fill out the pas de cinq with the help of Verdi. It's all pure fun and games in the backwash of *Le Corsaire*, a spoof by a true choreographer who knows how to put a ballet together.

The New York Observer
AUGUST 26, 2002

Twyla Tharp Takes Over Broadway

TWYLA THARP once said to me, "George Balanchine is God." She herself doesn't seem interested in being God; the universe, the nature of man and love, the future of the art—these aren't the things that concern her. On the other hand, she's just accomplished something that God clearly hasn't had time for: With *Movin' Out*, she's revitalized Broadway. Call it a musical, call it a show, call it a ballet, call it a dance extravaganza, call it the story of America from pre- to post-Vietnam, call it a tribute to Billy Joel, call it an act of megalomania—why not just call it a hit? Hits are what Twyla Tharp has always been about, even as she's also been about expanding what dance can do and what *she* can do. Yes, she's ambitious, both for herself and for her art, and yes, her reach on occasion exceeds her grasp. But so what? Who else has her reach? And who else has her authority? *Movin' Out* has dozens of first-rate dancers and musicians, plus a brilliant backup team of designers, but—trust me—it's a one-woman show.

A lot of print has been expended on the story Tharp is trying to tell here—the story of Eddie and Brenda and Tony and Judy and James, pals back in high school, whose lives are shattered by Vietnam and then, slowly, repaired, except for James, who is killed in battle at the end of Act I. (He makes a comeback appearance in a visionary scene in Act II, and a good thing, too, considering how compelling Benjamin G. Bowman is both as a decent young kid and as a dying grunt.) For the record: Eddie and Brenda break up, Brenda and Tony fool around, James and Judy get married (there's a wonderful touch when he gets down on one knee to propose and one of his hands flutters for a moment against his heart), Vietnam, post-war degradation—dope, orgies, panhandling, disco—and finally healing and reconciliation, with Tony and Brenda back together and friends reunited.

I call this a story, but it isn't one, actually, and it certainly isn't a plot; it's a series of generic situations linked by the sensibility and sound of Billy Joel's songs and the fecundity of Tharp's dance language. The dances don't illustrate the songs as much as embody them—and, at times, leave them behind. Yet the songs give Tharp a chance not only to return to her lifelong obsession with American youth as expressed in the way it dances and moves, but also to extend her range into war, death, and regeneration. The initial Vietnam sequence is harrowingly effective, all tracer bullets and explosions, bravado and terror; no one has done this better. The orgy scene is much less original; it seems to be just going through the motions (which include shooting up, humping, and the odd whip).

The more storylike moments of renewal—Judy and Eddie run into each other while jogging, everyone gets together at a reunion in the final scene—are far less convincing than what is the real climax of *Movin' Out*, a tremendous outburst of joyous dance energy from Eddie and the ensemble to "The River of Dreams," "Keeping the Faith," and "Only the Good Die Young." From the opening words—"In the middle of the night"—this number blasts the theater apart, not only through its daredevil lifts and throws and slides, the nonstop propulsive excitement of all these terrific dancers going all-out, but because Tharp makes us accept that in her world—and, for the moment, in ours—what really heals is dance itself. The jogging, the reunion, the hugs, the uncorked bottle of champagne—these are sentimental clichés that are Tharp's accommodations to the genre she's embracing, the Broadway show.

She goes really wrong only once, when she has Judy—in an ugly black dress with little slits in it and an even uglier hairdo—bourréeing and jetéing through the Vietnam vision scene while tormented soldiers convulse around her. This is not only mawkish and pretentious, it's the one place where the marriage of Tharp's modern-dance vocabulary and classical-ballet vocabulary fails to work: The two styles fight each other, and ballet loses. Judy's trajectory from official Nice Young Girl to tragic emblem—that is, we might say, from jitterbugger to ballerina—isn't earned. I suspect it has to do with the casting of Ashley Tuttle, a core member of Tharp's regular company, who happens to be an exquisite classical dancer (she's a principal at American Ballet Theatre—an exemplary Giselle). You can put Tuttle in a cute teenage outfit and have her hanging out with the local grease monkeys, but the Giselle comes through; beneath the hip-hop, her movement is irredeemably refined.

You can also spot the classicist beneath the prole in the performance of the two lead men, John Selya as Eddie and Keith Roberts as Tony. Both are refugees from ABT, and both are the beneficiaries of Tharp's unerring intuition about what a dancer's strengths may be—in this, she does resemble Balanchine. In the last several years, she's

revealed these two as tremendous technicians and profound interpreters of her kind of dance. The same is true of her leading woman,
Elizabeth Parkinson, a red-haired beauty who can be both dominating and lyrical. These three are so powerful, so secure, so convincing
as they toss off the wickedly demanding feats Tharp requires of them
that you wholly accept them as the characters they're meant to be
portraying.

And yet when you watch the alternate dancers who perform the
leading roles at matinees, something interesting happens to the show.
They don't have the total dance authority of the first cast, and that may
be why they seem closer to the actual world of Billy Joel—you can
imagine them emerging from a youth of broken-down convertibles,
cheerleaders, jukeboxes, acne. William Marrié, the excellent substitute
for John Selya, is a little less convincing as a dancer and a little more
convincing as an Eddie. Karine Bageot (Alvin Ailey, *The Lion King*,
currently on the screen in *Frida*) softens Brenda—she's all smiles and
sex appeal—whereas Parkinson is as spiky, as tough, and as demanding
as . . . Twyla Tharp herself. Ron De Jesús, the substitute Tony and another first-rate dancer, could have come out of the projects, while Keith
Roberts, with his all-American good looks and impeccable technique,
could only have come out of ballet school. So although it would be a
serious loss to miss Selya, Roberts, Parkinson, and Tuttle (luckily,
Bowman plays every James), don't feel cheated if you find yourself at a
matinee. And in one regard, you'll definitely come out ahead: Good as
Michael Cavanaugh is as the piano-and-song man in charge of the music
side of things, Wade Preston is better—the voice is deeper, more emotionally charged, more affecting. He even looks more like Billy Joel.

Movin' Out, then, is a landmark Broadway event, though it may also
prove to be a dead end. There are no other Twyla Tharps out there—just
compare her work to, say, Susan Stroman's in the insanely overpraised
Contact, which serves up one cliché after another without mercy or
remission. Tharp's only competition is her friend and onetime collaborator the late Jerome Robbins (years ago, they made a piece together,
Brahms/Handel Variations, for City Ballet). Like Robbins, Tharp has large,
ambitious concepts; and, like him, she's not only an obsessive worker

but a tyrant, demanding the best out of everyone, starting with herself, and usually getting it. You could say that *Movin' Out* is the first real successor to *West Side Story*, although that show had the advantage of a clear and powerful story line—*Romeo and Juliet*, remember? But watching this new show, I thought of Robbins more specifically in relation to his *Dances at a Gathering*. There's a famous moment at the end of that ballet when the central male dancer—Edward Villella, originally—bends down and reverently touches the floor, which is where all dancing begins. Toward the end of *Movin' Out*, Tharp—in homage? going Robbins one better?—has Keith Roberts bend down and seem to *kiss* the floor. I guess the stakes are higher these days. But then, with Twyla Tharp, the stakes are *always* high. Like all real artists, she's a gambler, and this time she's hit the jackpot.

The New York Observer
NOVEMBER 11, 2002

Robert Altman at the Ballet

THE COMPANY, Robert Altman's new ballet film, is a sharp reminder of how one can forget to be grateful for small blessings. In the years since the Joffrey company has given up its New York seasons, I had managed to forget just how trite and dated the basic repertory of this company is; how slick and empty the work of its artistic director, Gerald Arpino; how numbing the sight of all those earnest young dancers trying to make art out of straw—or do I mean bricks out of sows' ears? Thank you, Robert Altman, for reminding us of what we've been spared—although a world that's come up with Boris Eifman on an annual basis (and at the City Center, the very place where the Joffrey reigned long before it became the Joffrey Ballet of Chicago) is not a world we can really be thankful for.

What a bizarre movie this is! Unlike most ballet movies, whose plots are relentlessly predictable (a Rocky in tights or a tutu making it against all odds), *The Company* has no plot at all. Although the story is credited to Barbara Turner and Neve Campbell (who also stars and co-produces), there is no story; instead, there are slices of ballet life (the physical hardships, the pain, the anxiety, the camaraderie, the ex-ultation) and yards and yards of dancing, almost all of it bad. There are characters who are never characterized, situations that are never resolved. It's often hard to tell who is who. Or why.

And then, of course, there is Altman's famous darting camera, shooting through, around, above the dancers. Clearly, he's in love with the world of ballet. And there's Neve (*Scream*) Campbell herself, who's bravely got herself back into shape years after abandoning ballet for acting. She's worked hard, and is rewarded by looking no more or less adequate than her colleagues. It's fortunate that this is the repertory she's being seen in: As with much of what the Joffrey dances, it really doesn't matter who does what as long as everyone just keeps going.

At least two of the works on view are new. The first is a lugubrious and pointless duet set to "My Funny Valentine" by the ubiquitous Lar Lubovitch. Campbell, equipped with a pushy ballet mother and a nice smile, is on her way up the company ladder and lands this plum role. The ballet itself is so forgettable that you've forgotten the beginning before you get to the end, but it does provide two bits of amusement. First, the way the great choreographer is greeted when he arrives at the studio: "Do you know how long this company has waited for a Lar Lubovitch ballet?" (My guess is that it didn't have to wait more than ten minutes after asking.)

Then there's the premiere. It's at an outdoor Chicago theater, and a storm is whipping up. The audience sits there hypnotized by the genius of Lubovitch and Campbell while lightning and thunder gather. Then, up umbrellas when the deluge strikes! But nobody thinks of leaving. How gratifying to see so many dedicated balletomanes in Chicago, a city that has famously withstood every attempt to make it available to ballet.

The other new work is by Robert Desrosiers, and it's a hoot. It's called *The Blue Snake* because it features a giant blue snake. Dancers cavort around in costumes designed to reduce them to special effects. Desrosiers, like Lubovitch, is shown in the Act of Creativity, and he can make fun of himself, so I don't have to bother. This work is closer to Cirque du Soleil than to ballet, and it's harmlessly silly. Poor Neve Campbell falls and hurts herself during the premiere, but hunk interest James Franco is on hand with flowers to cheer her up. (He's some kind of chef in a fancy restaurant—and he's creative, too; with shrimp, if I remember correctly.)

We get a second-rate ballet by Alwin Nikolais, a snatch of Laura Dean, and three helpings of Arpino, whose endless parade of cheap, trendy works has held the Joffrey back for decades. He inherited the company from his friend and partner, Robert Joffrey, none of whose work, by the way, turns up in this film. There's a moment from the company's reconstruction of Saint-Léon's *La Vivandière* pas de six—suddenly, real steps. But it's over before any permanent damage can be done to the reigning aesthetic.

Why movie and dance critics are taking *The Company* seriously, I can't imagine. Are they impressed by Altman's reputation and naive sincerity? By the fluid semi-documentary approach? Are they enjoying Malcolm McDowell's fakey but enjoyable performance as Mr. A (for Antonelli), the egotistical and cowardly stand-in for Arpino? Or are they just relieved to see a ballet movie in which the heroine neither dies (*The Red Shoes*) nor has an overnight sensational success (most of the others)? *The Company* certainly does propose that dancers have a hard time of it. It's true that Neve Campbell's character has a largish, habitable place to live in, but it's right next to the El, with trains roaring past. That's hardship.

I enjoyed a couple of short scenes in which a steely senior ballerina stamps her pretty little toe shoes and gets her way. And, of course, the moment when someone says, "Margot Fonteyn—she was a dame." (It's the only reference I can recall to any ballet name or subject not connected to the Joffrey. Talk about product endorsement!) And finally there's Gerald Arpino's remark in the press release: "Robert Altman really directs the way I choreograph." That says it all.

The New York Observer

JANUARY 5, 2004

The Disgrace of New York City Ballet

BORIS EIFMAN'S *Musagète* may not be the worst ballet ever put on by New York City Ballet—the last twenty years have offered it lots of competition—but its premiere last Friday was without question the lowest point in the history of the company (and I've been following its fortunes since the beginning, in 1948). Forget the fact that Eifman is unmusical and vulgar, and that his dance-dramas are overwrought exercises in hysteria; these things can come as no surprise to anyone who, lured by the hyperbole of the daily press, has attended his psychosexual assaults on the great ballerina Olga Spessivtseva (*Red Giselle*), Dostoevsky's famous brothers (*The Karamazovs*), Tchaikovsky (*Tchaikovsky*), et al. In fact, *Musagète* is comparatively tame compared to those flights of high garishness—no dry ice, no flashing red lights; no suicides, no rapes. The only rape was of the memory of George Balanchine, whose centenary *Musagète* was commissioned to celebrate.

Was it naïveté or deliberate effrontery that led Eifman to choose as his subject Balanchine himself? He writes in a program note, "This ballet is dedicated to George Balanchine. It is an expression of my admiration of him. . . . It is not a biographical ballet, but there is the personality of the choreographer. . . . I was absorbed in the world of Balanchine's ballets and, fascinated by the personality of the choreographer, was unable to free myself from this spell." It's all nonsense: The subject of an Eifman ballet is inevitably the Anguish of the Tormented Artist—and it doesn't take much stretch of the imagination to figure out who that tormented artist really is. (Oddly, in person Eifman emits a cherubic, untormented sweetness.) As for Balanchine, in real life there was never a less anguished artist; he just got down to whatever job was at hand and did the necessary, with a total absence of agony or ecstasy.

Eifman's Balanchine suffers, suffers, suffers. He's impersonated by the affectless Robert Tewsley, who is new to the company and possibly unaware of the presumption involved. We see him in a white polo shirt and black pants. He's at the end of his rope, or his tether, or his life, looking back. There's a lot of business with a straight-backed chair—he's either sitting in it (a wheelchair? a hospital chair?) or being pushed around in it by a grim attendant, or lying on the floor and manipulating it with his foot. Chair play is replaced by cat play: Wendy Whelan is Mourka, the cat famously owned by Balanchine and his wife Tanaquil Le Clercq (she published a book about Mourka). There are a few ingenious moments in the man-cat duet—the only bearable moments in the proceedings. Whelan, a dancer (and person) of integrity, has been quoted as saying she was relieved to be playing a cat rather than any of the people represented in this ballet, and how right she was!

There's a large corps who dart in and out in various changes of costume, but everything they do is generic and pointless. Balanchine-Tewsley thrashes around in distress—arching his back, collapsing to the floor. And then we're shown Le Clercq herself, in the person of Alexandra Ansanelli, who must be aware of the mortifying position Eifman and the company have put her in.

Le Clercq, a much-loved dancer of incomparable wit, style, and glamour, contracted polio in Copenhagen, in 1956, while the company was on tour. At first it didn't seem that she would survive; eventually she recovered, but was confined to a wheelchair for the rest of her life. Balanchine essentially abandoned the company for a year, to tend to her at home. To dramatize this horrible and traumatic episode involving two people who were as intensely private and dignified as Le Clercq and Balanchine, to show Le Clercq suddenly staggering and lurching around the stage and then being dragged off on a long piece of black cloth, and to do this on the stage of Balanchine's own theater, under the auspices of his own company, and with the excuse of celebrating him, can only be described as disgusting. People in the audience whom I recognized as old Balanchine hands were gasping in disbelief; one man was murmuring, "Oh no!" I found it as painful a moment as I've ever spent in the theater.

But that was not all. We had yet to survive watching Maria Kowroski impersonate Suzanne Farrell and, with Tewsley, act out the complicated relationship between Farrell and Balanchine. Again, the Artist in Torment, but by this time who could care? The worst had already happened. It should be noted, though, that although Kowroski bears a certain physical resemblance to Farrell, and appears to advantage in certain Farrell roles, when she attempted to *be* Farrell, the disparity between her real but unformed talent and Farrell's genius was all too blatantly underlined.

An even greater disparity was revealed when Eifman chose to end his ballet with a rip-off (sorry, a pastiche—sorry, an homage) of Balanchine's *Theme and Variations*, itself a tribute to Balanchine's great predecessor Marius Petipa. (Get it? The torch is passed down from Petipa to Balanchine to Eifman.) Here Eifman attempts a classical ballet, tutus and all, that despite its pilferings from *Theme*, and its pathetic allusions to other Balanchine formal works (the last moments of *Symphony in C*, for instance), makes it clear that he has no talent whatsoever for serious ballet. He lacks musicality, he lacks vocabulary, and he lacks any sense of how to deploy groups of dancers in stage space. You don't get to be a Balanchine by sampling his work, as Eifman does here and, indeed, throughout *Musagète*: If what was going on wasn't so offensive, you could amuse yourself by checking off the quotations from *Apollo, Serenade, Agon,* et cetera.

Assuming Eifman were capable of being humiliated, he surely would have been by the cosmically disastrous scheduling of his piece directly after *Theme and Variations* itself. It would be nice to think that the pairing was a comment on Eifman's talent by the head of the company, Peter Martins, who is, I believe, quite capable of this kind of mischief, but the likelihood is that the program was conceived well before City Ballet knew that Eifman planned to end *Musagète* with his variation on *Theme and Variations*. The larger question is why Martins brought this disgrace upon himself and the company he runs.

However one may disagree with many of his choices, and regret the diminution of his own considerable talent, he is a savvy and serious figure—he certainly knew what he was getting when he hired Eifman. When the commission was announced, there was a lot of speculation about Martins's motives: an attempt to attract the Russian émigré audience that, with its cigarettes and cell phones, flocks to the City Center to applaud the Eifman seasons there? An attempt to flatter *The New York Times*, which is so greatly responsible for his success?

I wish it were that simple. But for Peter Martins to choose to celebrate George Balanchine with a choreographer so much his polar opposite, and with a work that would have wounded him to the heart, goes beyond opportunism or cynicism. To encourage—even to allow—the appearance of *Musagète* on the stage of the State Theatre suggests an unconscious impulse of parricide or regicide. Or both. Sophocles knew what he was writing about in *Oedipus Rex*, and Freud understood him perfectly.

The New York Observer
JUNE 28, 2004

Farrell and Don Q

GEORGE BALANCHINE'S *Don Quixote*—that ambitious, mysterious work that fascinated and confused us all back when it was made in 1965—has just been restaged, by Suzanne Farrell, for the first time since it disappeared from the repertory in 1978. When it was made, Balanchine was sixty-one, Farrell, his newest muse, was nineteen, and this extraordinary dance-drama was taken by everyone to be his unequivocal tribute to, and surrender to, her powers. Now forty years have gone by.

Balanchine, of course, is dead. Farrell is approaching sixty. And an entire generation has never seen it. Once it was retired, not many people can have believed they'd ever see it again. (I certainly didn't.) But Farrell, for whom it naturally has profound significance and to whom Balanchine left it in his will, has against all odds resurrected it for us. Combining her own small company with dancers from the National Ballet of Canada, she's presented it at the Kennedy Center in Washington (it will later be performed in Canada), and she's done it admirably. With very little time to mount this elaborate production, and with dancers not many of whom approach the first rank, she's made the most plausible case possible for *Don Quixote*, as spectacle and as art.

From the start, *Don Quixote* was seen as a problem, most of all by Balanchine himself—he was always fiddling with it: adding music, moving sections around, creating new dances. Audiences were perplexed by its unique and unexpected combination of drama, pageantry, religiosity, formal divertissement, and the heightened passages he created for Farrell, as well as by the central character being a non-dancing role. The music, by Balanchine's old friend Nicolas Nabokov (they went back almost forty years, and had been discussing this ballet for almost that long), took much of the blame for what was generally seen as a flawed effort. And yet *Don Quixote* was compelling, especially when on occasion Balanchine himself took the central role.

Act I is the weakest. The servant girl Dulcinea, who lovingly ministers to the Don, also appears to him in the guise of the Virgin Mary. The hero, with his befuddled grasp of reality, sets off on his quest to vanquish injustice, accompanied by the faithful Sancho Panza. There's some generic peasant dancing in a town square, a juggler, a puppet show with children, a horse, a donkey, and a remarkable solo for Dulcinea, who at this point appears as a young girl accused of complicity in a murder.

Act II takes place at the court of a duke and duchess who maliciously welcome the mad Don as an honored guest only to encourage their courtiers to torment him. Here we witness the bitter cruelty of Cervantes's Spain, but also the Don's courtesy, innocence, and generosity. His innate chivalry keeps him from grasping that he's being made a fool of. There's an extended divertissement—a suite of ingenious formal dances (flamenco, Mauresque, Sicilienne, et cetera)—and finally an orchestrated assault on the Don by the masked courtiers, who prod him with their rapiers, blindfold him, leap on his back, pummel him, and leave him almost dead, after a surreally horrible final moment when one of them smears his eyes with a gout of whipped cream. During this powerful and deeply disturbing passage, Dulcinea appears as a vision of tenderness and consolation.

It's the third act that explodes into brilliance. Surrounded by a formal group of maidens led by two demi-soloists and their cavaliers, Dulcinea—now divorced from any direct responsibility to the plot—performs one of the most intense and thrilling dances in all Balanchine. At first she's grave, but soon she erupts in a galvanic outpouring of ardor and despair. And now it becomes almost impossible to speak about "Dulcinea" rather than about Farrell. Here, perhaps, was Balanchine's most indelible presentation of her astounding qualities; here, almost at the start of their unprecedented collaboration, she was fully and magnificently identified.

Fortunately, there's a murky film, unavailable to the public, of the first performance of *Don Quixote*. It features Balanchine and Farrell, and to watch it is to experience the miracle of his total grasp of her potential genius. If this were the only documentation of Farrell, you could infer her entire artistic life from it—it's as valuable as the famous filmed passages from the first act of *Giselle* that give us our only glimpse of the legendary Olga Spessivtseva.

Farrell's performance is heart-stopping—the amazing off-balance lunges, the ravishing back-bends, the absolute fearless abandon, the total commitment to the gesture and the moment. Yes, she's still a baby, but she's also, already, a peerless ballerina, in complete charge of her body, her role, and Balanchine.

This dance is beautifully constructed, the solos and the material for the corps effortlessly integrated, and for once Nabokov's music is appropriate—romantic and exciting in the right way. (At other times, it's pure movie music, and second-rate movie music at that.) The two dancers Farrell chose to portray Dulcinea carried things off with admirable aplomb and to good effect, despite the light-years disparity between their talent and Farrell's. Sonia Rodriguez is accurate and hardworking—she's an excellent executant—but she's essentially un-exciting: a ballerina, but a provincial one. Heather Ogden, second-cast, is younger and freer—both more innocent and more involving. How odd that Farrell, of all people, cast her second. After all, if Balanchine had stopped to consider status or age, he wouldn't have made *Don Quixote* on her in the first place.

After the climactic third-act pas d'action, the ballet returns to its story—the final degrading assaults on Don Quixote; his famous delu-sional attack on the windmill; his grotesque journey home in a pig cage. His last fevered vision is of an ominous procession of church dig-nitaries, and then of Dulcinea, once again seen as the Virgin, welcom-ing the hero in his martyrdom. When he dies, she reappears as the simple peasant girl, placing two wooden sticks in the shape of a cross on his body.

Balanchine, as seen in the film, keeps the ballet from veering into self-pity—his Don is vigorous in his old age, bewildered rather than distraught or loony, aristocratic without being proud. Farrell's Momchil Mladenov is tall and thin (Balanchine's preference for the role), but at the start his body and movement style give him away as inappropri-ately young. He recovers, though, through focus and intelligence, and creates a credible Don.

Farrell has handled the complicated stage business impeccably—scene flows into scene, the transformations and other special effects work easily, and the sets (by Zack Brown) are an improvement on the heavier aesthetic of Esteban Francés.

The weakness in the production lies in the secondary perform-ers. Although there are several pleasing dancers in the second-act divertissement and in the third act—Natalia Magnicaballi, Erin Ma-honey, Shannon Parsley—they can't compare with Balanchine's 1965 company: dancers of the caliber of Patricia McBride, Suki Schorer, Mimi Paul, Patricia Neary, Marnee Morris, Gloria Govrin, Arthur Mitchell, and on and on. It's a dazzling honor roll. That Farrell succeeded as well as she did with dancers considerably below this level of talent is a trib-ute to her teaching and coaching skills—no surprise to anyone who has watched her guide dancers over the past several years. One of the many things she learned from Balanchine is to cheerfully and honorably make the best of whatever resources are available, and her respect for her dancers has been repaid with their obvious devotion to her, and to him.

Just as it did forty years ago, *Don Quixote* leaves us fascinated, moved—and puzzled. Back in the 1960s and '70s, it was less easy to see it as a link in a chain of related works—related not because they're all dance-dramas but because they all center on a certain kind of male figure. Yes, Balanchine has given us the male glorious—Apollo, Oberon, the "Rubies" boy—and the male humorous and the impersonal cavalier. But surely we sense a more direct connection between him and a parade of men in extremis which begins with the Prodigal Son, debased by the vicious Siren, and proceeds through the romantic Poet undone by the fatal dazzle of the *Sonnambula*, the tragic Orpheus destroyed by Eurydice's importunities, and the desperate Schumann, succumbing to madness. Don Quixote, despite the loyalty and solace offered by his fantasy Dulcinea, is humiliated like the Prodigal, maddened like Schumann, and driven to death like the Poet and Orpheus.

What sets *Don Quixote* apart from these other ballets is that there isn't a great deal of distance between Balanchine's own pain and the pain suffered by his hero: He's so personally affected by the buffetings life inflicts on the Don—so obviously identifying with him—that he seems to be saying, "I don't deserve this." And then he rewards himself with heaven.

We're not used to a Balanchine so humanly exposed, and Farrell, at nineteen, could hardly have understood what *Don Quixote* was revealing. Her devoted reconstruction of it makes it clear that now she understands.

The important practical question raised by her production is whether such a large-scale, problematic work can become a permanent part of the Balanchine repertory. Certainly it will stay alive as long as Farrell has the opportunity to present it, and perhaps there are major companies—the Kirov, say—who might take it on. It's even possible, I suppose, that Farrell and New York City Ballet might eventually accommodate each other. But is *Don Quixote* worth preserving? After all, other important Balanchine works have vanished—*Cotillon*, the full-length *Le Baiser de la Fée*, the early versions of *Mozartiana, Balustrade, The Seven Deadly Sins.*

None of these works, however, was as meaningful to him, or as revealing. The lesson we just learned in Washington is that although we didn't realize we've been missing it since it vanished almost thirty years ago, *Don Quixote* does still matter, both for its own sake and because of its unique place in the Balanchine canon. When you're dealing with a supreme master—a Shakespeare, a Mozart—you need to be able to revisit his entire corpus of work. You need *King Lear* all the time, but every decade or so you also need *Timon of Athens.* Otherwise your understanding of a genius like Shakespeare—or Balanchine—is diminished, and so are you.

The New York Observer
JULY 11, 2005

Cunningham's Boundless Ocean

WE KNOW HOW Merce Cunningham works and how he thinks—we've been told, over and over again, by him and by others. We know that the dance is a thing apart from the music; that elements of the dance have been determined by chance procedures, often involving the I Ching; that we're meant to concentrate on the moment, on the human body doing certain things that may be disconnected from the previous moment, or the next. No choreographer has been more explicit about his goals and methods, and Cunningham seems to believe that his theorizing is what makes it possible for him to do what he does.

What it doesn't do, alas, is help me watch him. I just don't care—or haven't the intelligence to absorb—that he's "mapped out the space, dividing it into 19 sections, each with 8 sub-areas," as my friend Nancy

Dalva recently reported in *The New York Times*; or that "he made the 128 movement sequences." If you're caught up in the dance, you're not counting; and if you're counting, you're not caught up in the dance. (It's the same with the notorious 32 fouettés in *Swan Lake*.)

Cunningham has just revived a very long piece, *Ocean* (1994), at the new Rose Theater, whose performance area was reconfigured into a circle, the audience seated all around—with the 112 (!) orchestral musicians, in the top balcony, also ringing the stage. At four points around the circle were placed digital monitors, counting off the seconds. (*Ocean* lasts exactly ninety minutes.) No doubt this device was of help to the dancers in keeping track of where they were in the piece, since the sound (a layer of orchestral music by Andrew Culver and a layer of electronic music by David Tudor), although at times exciting and certainly ocean-suggestive, was hardly something the dancers could hold on to.

But the monitors performed another function as well: They gave *us* something to hold on to. Since Cunningham long ago dismissed narrative from his work (although he danced enough of it with Martha Graham) and also dismissed music as the basis of dance (although he studied at Balanchine's School of American Ballet), the countdown provided a badly needed chronometric structure for the viewer—or at least for this viewer.

Which isn't to say that I didn't take pleasure from innumerable ravishing passages among the outpourings of invention that Cunningham always provides. Clusters of dancers ran on from behind recessed curtains, sometimes working in twos, threes, fours, sometimes working alone. On occasion, a large group would be hectic with activity while a single couple across the circle would pose in absolute stillness, the woman in an endless supported arabesque; at other times, a couple would take a ravishing sculpted position on the floor, in contrast to the buzz of motion surrounding them. Twice, all fourteen dancers claimed the space together—climaxes we welcomed, even if we didn't understand why they were there. (Maybe just because they're crowd-pleasers? Cunningham, despite his purity, is also a showman.)

The Cunningham vocabulary, with its tilts and nestlings and crooks of the limbs, provides him with endless opportunities that satisfy both viewer and dancer—his dancers never look less than happy and fulfilled in what they're doing. And in this very long piece, the constant flow of events moved—yes—like an ocean tide. But we know why the ocean's tide comes in and goes out; we're not meant to know why Cunningham's does, we're only meant to accept. It's hard, though, to break the habit of a lifetime, as he requires us to do. Perhaps animals, birds, and butterflies really do live only in the moment; people, for good or ill, are stuck with both memory and anticipation.

Through *Ocean*'s ninety minutes, the pale unitards worn by the dancers at the start are exchanged for brighter ones; at the end, they're all dark purple. That's a straightforward progression. But it's the only one I could identify, other than the inexorable flashings of the digital monitors, reminding me that this, too, would pass.

The New York Observer
JULY 25, 2015

The Bolshoi Wows Its Fans

IN 1874, the great Danish choreographer August Bournonville traveled to St. Petersburg, where, as he tells us in his memoirs,

> I saw in turn *Le Papillon, La Fille du Pharaon, Don Quixote, Esmeralda*, and *Le Roi Candaule*. . . . I did justice to the richly imaginative arrangement of the settings and transformations as well as the magnificent appointments; acknowledged the considerable advantages that lay in the use of a *corps de ballet* consisting of more than *two hundred* partly young, pretty, and clever people; and was not blind or indifferent to the superb talent that displayed itself especially among the female members. . . . I sought in vain to discover plot, dramatic interest, logical consistency, or anything that might remotely resemble sanity. And even if I were fortunate enough to come upon a trace of it in Petipa's

Don Quixote, the impression was immediately effaced by an unending and monotonous host of feats of bravura, all of which were rewarded with salvos of applause and curtain calls.

No, no—Bournonville can't be reporting from Petersburg one hundred thirty years ago; he must have been at the Met these past couple of weeks, watching the Bolshoi's current versions of two of those ballets, *Don Quixote* and *La Fille du Pharaon* (*The Pharaoh's Daughter*). True, the corps didn't have two hundred members. It didn't even have the seventy-two dancers in *Pharaoh* who, the historian Krasovskaya tells us, "bore flower baskets on their heads from which small children emerged in the finale." But it had everything else, from a prancing monkey to a dead lion to a giant killer asp to coffins that suddenly tilted up, revealing the mummies inside, as in a Dracula movie. And it certainly had the same applauding audience, presumably transported intact across time and space to cheer the same feats of "bravura."

Pharaoh was the turning point in Petipa's career—it stayed in the repertory for more than half a century after its triumphant premiere in 1862. But who knows what such great dancers as Kschessinska and Pavlova were actually dancing when they appeared in it? The original ballet has been more or less lost, and the version we've just been exposed to is the recent creation of Pierre Lacotte, who has performed the same disservice for *Paquita* and *La Sylphide*. Ignoring the few existing clues to what Petipa actually did, he has started from scratch, or rather (as the program puts it) has based his work on "motifs from the ballet of the same name by Marius Petipa," one of those motifs being the story itself: English explorer in Egypt falls into an opium trance and finds himself back in Ancient Times transformed into Ta-Hor, in love with Aspicia, the Pharaoh's Daughter. And then—hours later—he wakes up and, guess what, it was all a dream!

I would state categorically that Lacotte's *Pharaoh's Daughter* is the dopiest classical ballet I've ever seen, but it's possible I've wiped potential rivals from my memory, the way we're told (though I don't believe it) women forget labor pains.

Monsieur Lacotte, imported from Paris, would seem to believe he's improved on Petipa, but all he's got going for him is his chutzpah. He can't choreograph for the corps—everything's confused and clichéd; important action is blocked (could anyone actually see Ta-Hor shooting that mangy lion?); he's completely lacking in dance invention; he doesn't characterize—Aspicia and Ta-Hor are the blandest couple in all balletdom; there's no urgency (or coherence) to the narrative—it's just endless stretches of generic dance, with constant changes of costumes. And speaking of costumes, they (as well as the pathetic sets) are also by M. Lacotte, and they make the dancers look like those imitation-Erté figurines that live in the windows of going-out-of-business stores.

At the first performance, the beautiful Svetlana Zakharova, newly defected from the Kirov, was Aspicia—as beautiful as ever, with those amazingly arched feet, those endless limbs, that small, perfect head, that strong technique. Luckily, she couldn't sneak her outrageous hyperextended kicks into ancient Egypt, but she made up for it with her relentless smile, her calculated wooing of the audience (this tendency was even more pronounced in *Don Quixote*). Her best moments came in the underwater vision scene, in a simple, lyrical solo, with no Ta-Hor to get in the way. As for poor Ta-Hor, the role lacks any defining characteristic other than a bare chest, but Nikolai Tsiskaridze's touchingly naive effeminacy gave him (and us) something to hold on to.

What can the Bolshoi have been thinking? On top of the rest, the ghastly score, by Pugni, only pointed up the vast superiority of Ludwig Minkus's *Don Quixote*. (Those who deride Minkus got what they deserved.) I suppose the powers-that-be were thinking box office, and they were right: There was standing room only at the Met and the usual bravos, bravas, and bravis from a largely Russian-émigré audience.

It's to the credit of the Bolshoi's new artistic director, Alexei Ratmansky, that this ersatz resurrection of *The Pharaoh's Daughter* was taken aboard before he was. Far more important: Ratmansky himself choreographed the one unclouded artistic success of the company's season, a brand-new version of an ill-fated ballet from the 1930s, *The Bright Stream*. It sounded ominous—fun and romance on a Soviet collective farm—but it turned out to be sunny, funny, modest, *pleasing*.

The heroine is young Zina, "the Bright Stream Collective's morale officer," living contentedly among the wheat sheaves with her husband, Pyotr. A troupe of performers arrives from Moscow to entertain The Workers (you see their little train passing by, puffing smoke). Among the performers is The Ballerina, and it turns out that she and Zina were at ballet school together! What's more, Zina—not even her husband knows she was a dancer—is just as good as she ever was, whipping off fouettés and matching The Ballerina jeté for jeté. (So much for dancers having to keep in shape.) Pyotr is quickly flirting with his wife's old friend, and the rest of the plot deals with his mild comeuppance— there's a touch of *La Fille Mal Gardée*, a touch of *Coppélia*, a touch of *The Marriage of Figaro*, yet it adds up to its own charmingly realized world.

You'd have to know more than I do about the Soviet Union in the mid-1930s to understand why Stalin shut down this ballet, with its amiable Shostakovich score. Perhaps collective farms were too serious a matter to be made into comic ballets. But Stalin's loss is our gain. With its generous array of character roles—the schoolgirl, the milkmaid (who jauntily milks the five fingers of the faux-cow), the "Anxious-To-Appear-Younger-Than-She-Is Wife" and her put-upon husband, the tractor driver (who doubles as a doggy), the accordion player, et al.—*The Bright Stream* rushes along on its merry way, its individual bits of schtick perhaps too extended, but all of them cleverly carried out and amusing.

I won't try to explain why The Ballerina's partner gets himself up like a Sylphide, or why The Ballerina turns up in male drag—the important thing is that Ratmansky has made a cohesive whole out of drag and cow and ballerina and the Toonerville Trolley. And unlike Lacotte, he understands his corps and knits it joyously into the fabric of the ballet. Although there's nothing Bournonville-like about the manner of *The Bright Stream*, Bournonville might well have approved: Like his own ballets, it creates a real world with real people who are believable as lovers, friends, and members of a community.

The first Zina was the ravishingly charming, fragile-seeming Svetlana Lunkina, whom Ratmansky promoted to principal dancer during the curtain calls—a highly popular move. But the second Zina, Anastasia Yatsenko, was also entrancing—the company's depth is formidable. The two guys who took the drag role were both brilliant on pointe and wildly funny—our old friend Tsiskaridze could melt into the Trocks at a moment's notice. *The Bright Stream* isn't in the same league as Ashton's *La Fille Mal Gardée*, but arriving unheralded in the middle of the Bolshoi's boom-boom season, it was precious balm, particularly coming, as it did, after the unspeakable *Spartacus*, a very different kettle of Soviet kitsch.

Spartacus has always been a smash success, with its unspeakably vulgar Khachaturian score, its agitprop posings and posturings, its noble slaves and wicked Romans, its endless opportunities for the most blatant kind of heroics: Stalwart men leap and leap and leap, brandishing swords and muscles. There's a loving, long-suffering heroine, a vicious vamp of a villainess, a nasty Roman general, and, of course, the quintessential Stalinist hero, Spartacus, who manages to destroy all his followers as well as himself. The Kremlin has always liked this one, New York has always cheered its pyrotechnics, and the fans from Brighton Beach were in seventh heaven.

As for the *Don Q*, it made almost no sense, but there were so many terrific character dancers flaunting their fans and swirling their ruffled skirts that it hardly mattered. So what if you couldn't tell who was who, or why all those gypsies were carrying on, or why Kitri, the innkeeper's daughter, and Basil, the barber, were getting married in a palace, or why the ballet had no big climax but ended with the famous pas de deux. You were looking, maybe, for narrative integrity? We did get Petipa's beautiful vision scene, replete with dryads and a thrilling short variation by a very young new girl, Natalia Osipova, whose body is problematic but whose open, flying jumps and eager spirit were electrifying. Zakharova, in the lead, did all the right things—her technique doesn't falter, except (like that of most of her colleagues) in supported turns—but she's really not a Kitri; her flamboyance is pasted on, not natural to her: She's at her best in more lyrical ballets like *La Bayadère* and *Swan Lake*. Far better suited to the role is the company's splendid workhorse, Maria Alexandrova, who has the necessary push and thrust and—yes—bravura, tearing through space with her tremendous jeté.

You can't really familiarize yourself with a major company by watching half a dozen performances of four ballets—you only get a superficial sense of who's who and what's what. On the basis of the

Bolshoi's two-week visit, I see a company with a split aesthetic, trying to decide what it wants to be. How many more obscure Petipa ballets can be exhumed and tarted up? How much Soviet-period stuff is worth reviving? Can Ratmansky build on his success with *The Bright Stream?* (His *Cinderella* has had a mixed reception abroad.)

There's a basic problem here. With the exception of the sublime Ulanova (like Zakharova, imported from the Kirov), the Bolshoi's stock in trade has long been its explosive *Übermensch*, with ballerinas to match—the consummately flamboyant Maya Plisetskaya, after all, was for years its emblematic dancer (and the greatest of all Kitris). Now, in a post-Soviet world, the company has begun catching up—to Balanchine, in particular. What will happen if good taste, long its missing ingredient, begins to manifest itself? Will the company lose its innocence— and its doggedly retro-Soviet audience? Cautiously, Ratmansky is feeling his way. Who would have believed that the Bolshoi would ever be giving us guys got up as Sylphides? Meanwhile, despite its schizophrenic repertory, it's in excellent shape and well worth looking at: It's got strong dancers, conviction, pizzazz—and lots of beautiful girls.

The New York Observer
AUGUST 8, 2005

The French on a Vivaldi Spree

Question: What's an hour and a half long (without intermission), driven by Concept, and set to Vivaldi's *The Four Seasons?*
Answer: Either of two ballets that have just had their Paris premieres.

NICOLAS LE RICHE's *Caligula,* in fact, has just had its *world* premiere— though I doubt it's going to see much of the world beyond the Paris Opéra.

You might think it was either a daring idea or a crackpot idea to set a ballet about Caligula to Vivaldi, but it's neither: We're just too accustomed, in our post-Balanchine world, to ballets that are motored by their music. As it turns out, *The Four Seasons* is there for a *historical* reason. You see, Caligula reigned for almost four years, and each year gets a Season of its own—his inevitable death coincides with darkest winter. Otherwise, the music is of minor relevance: Yes, it keeps things going, but like the set and the costumes, it's an extra—subordinate to the Big Idea.

And what is that Big Idea? It's that Caligula was not just your ordinary young psychopathic tyrant, murderous, treacherous, caring only for the great mime Mnester and the horse Incitatus (who had his own palace and may even have been made a Senator); no, he was a kind of poet. "The Caligula who interests me," says M. Le Riche, "is the creator who pursues his dream to its utmost limit." In other words, he's a French intellectual.

The very extensive, informative program notes bear this out. Suetonius is on hand to provide a few hard facts, but the big guns are Roland Barthes and Nietzsche. And Racine: Guillaume Gallienne, the dramaturge, explains that *Caligula* is structured like a Racinian tragedy, obeying the fundamental rules of the classical stage: the unities of time, place, and action. Caligula, you see, is a tragic hero—"He is fundamentally alone."

There's no disputing the intelligence at work in all this, but it's all in the head. On the stage is an ordinary, thin spectacle, undistinguished by any choreographic originality and conveying nothing. There are eight Senators in *Planet of the Apes* getup (two of them are women, a touch that doesn't come from Suetonius), and eight female "followers," two of whom are men. When Caligula comes slowly, slowly down a giant set of stairs in his tight, brief red costume with white markings on the front, you can tell there's something wrong. Everyone's scared, and you would be, too, if your Emperor were making horrible faces at you and pushing you around.

Caligula was performed by a handsome young dancer named Jérémie Bélingard, and he's as delicious a Roman tidbit as we've encountered since Tony Curtis in Kubrick's *Spartacus*. (He should be careful, though:

Hunky can quickly turn to chunky.) Most of his long role is taken up with gesturing, posturing, and emoting, punctuated by extended off-center balances, a few bursts of explosive movement, and several intimate pas de deux with La Lune (The Moon, to you), who invades Caligula's imagination and "stands for his vision of inaccessible love." She's danced convincingly by Clairemarie Osta, but there's not much for her to do except tangle with him on the floor and be wafted on high in a few ballet lifts that are so standard they're beyond banal. Steps are not M. Le Riche's strong point.

The scene with the horse (Gil Isoart) has some charm, as Caligula tenderly leads him around the stage at the end of a long ribbon (there's a metal bit in his mouth). At one point, the young emperor drags the two female Senators up the stairs and out of sight, and when he brings them back, they're much the worse for wear—now we understand why Le Riche has planted women in the Senate. One of the Senators is casually murdered and left lying on the stage for quite a while. You don't know why until you read in the program notes that Caligula, when he killed people, liked to smell the odors of their decaying bodies—he'd only let them be carted off when the air around them grew suffocating. Oh, those poets!

Eventually, the Emperor himself is assassinated, though even here the drama is dissipated. A lot of people stab him upstage and run away, and after standing there apparently unscathed, he staggers downstage and collapses. Blackout. Curtain.

The group dances are dance-by-numbers; the solos are oy vey. Most interesting are the extended passages for Mnester, all in white, who comes on with other mysterious figures in the breaks between the four seasons (to some "*création électroacoustique*" by Louis Dandrel) and performs very deliberate and slow gestures, interrupted by a single, sudden double air turn—who knows why?

Because Mnester is performed by the Opéra's finest dancer, Laurent Hilaire, your attention is held. This is an artist of the first rank—slim, elegant, focused, intense; there's a little Anthony Dowell in him, a little Peter Boal, but the sharp mind is his own. Under the inexplicable rules of the Opéra, Hilaire has "officially" retired now that he's forty-two.

Luckily, he's already working as a ballet master, and we can hope that he'll be able to pass along to the next generation his exemplary dedication and comportment.

It's easy to poke fun at all this overthink and underdance, but credit should be given where it's due. *Caligula* is without value, but it's not vulgar Eurotrash; its creators just mistake intelligence for talent and concepts for ballets. But where would someone like Le Riche—he's a popular young star of the company, and this is his first work of substance—have learned otherwise? There's no recent choreographic tradition here to build on—no Balanchine, no Ashton, not even a Robbins, a Tudor, or a MacMillan. And so the Opéra alternates between this kind of expensive, efficient, meaningless story-concept ballet and the predictable imports: Forsythe, Trisha Brown, and, like just about every serious ballet company in the world today, Balanchine. A revival of *Jewels* premieres this week.

As for the second new ballet to *The Four Seasons*, at the Théâtre de la Ville, it's by Angelin Preljocaj, and it's actually *called The Four Seasons*. It's also far more interesting and alive than its rival. Preljocaj is an experienced choreographer, and although he also lives and dies by The Concept, his current work doesn't rest on an intellectual concept but a visual one. For more than ninety minutes, a succession of outré costumes and objects comes into view—most of them surprising and many of them witty. There's a hail of sponges from above, and a weird pair of dancers got up as porcupines—or are they hedgehogs? There are two fellows in cellophane, and a group covered from head to toe in Kermit green. ("Hi, Greenie," one of them says—in English, "it's me." "Oh, you're so green! You're the greenest!") There's a pair of black stiletto pumps that falls to earth, and Spongeman, and a couple in white masks that are attached to each other at the nose, and a girl in a bikini—you get the picture.

None of this would be more than decoration if Preljocaj wasn't also demonstrating a certain gift for actual choreography, for meaningful encounter through expressive movement. Again and again, people confront each other, sometimes in naked antagonism, plucking at each other's flesh, sometimes in amity. The dancers have strong, individual looks and personalities—like Mark Morris's, say. You get interested in them. There's not much sense of structure to this *Four Seasons*, but even when things get complicated, they don't get confused. And good old Vivaldi seems to be on hand for a reason: Preljocaj isn't the most musical choreographer of our day, but he's listening. As for his chief collaborator, Fabrice Hyber, who provides the *"chaosgraphie"* as well as the décor and most of the costumes and props, he has an inventive mind and a goofy sense of fun.

Preljocaj, at least in this work, and in the context of French ballet as a whole, is a solid plus. And he's come a long way. The Opéra has just been showing his well-known piece from the early nineties, *Le Parc* (it's been seen in New York), and it's in the *Caligula* tradition: no rotting corpses or Senatorial horses, no Vivaldi (it was Mozart's turn), but intellectual concept all the way. It's handsome, it's suggestive, but it's dull, dull, dull—again, Laurent Hilaire saved the day, to the extent that it was savable. The fact that Preljocaj has grown more interested in movement and less in thinking is the healthiest thing I can tell you about the state of ballet in Paris today.

The New York Observer
OCTOBER 31, 2005

Peter Martins's Efficient Swan Lake

PETER MARTINS's *Swan Lake* does its job—it gets people into the theater (*all Swan Lakes* get people into the theater), and then it gets them out of the theater in only two and a half hours. In other words, it's efficient, and if efficiency is what you look for in ballet, this is the production for you. If your taste runs to beauty, feeling, resonance, stay home and listen to your favorite recording of Tchaikovsky's great score. At least you won't be distracted from it.

What to make of Act I? In traditional *Swan Lakes*, it's Prince Sieg-fried's twenty-first-birthday celebration, his coming-of-age. The en-tire court, from his mother the Queen on down, is on hand. We see the formal world he inhabits—his old, affectionate tutor; the courtiers and peasants who dance to amuse him; his friend Benno, who leads a charm-ing pas de trois for his pleasure; the Queen, who presents him with a crossbow and reminds him that it's now time for him to marry, as a prince must. There are pretty girls who would be happy to dance with him, if only he wanted to dance with them.

But we sense that despite the happiness of the occasion, Siegfried is not content or at peace—he's restless, he's disaffected, he's yearning for something beyond all this formality; he's yearning for a profound love, not one commanded by his mother. And when he hears the first strains of the famous swan theme, he's off to meet his fate, and his doom.

For Martins, all this is reduced to a mere divertissement—a series of dances, ably staged, with no content whatsoever. The party, if that's what it is, is populated by eight couples—"villagers," the program tells us, though if they're villagers, why are the men's costumes in the same style as the Prince's? And where's the court? And why are sixteen horribly self-conscious and smirking children trotted on, other than to elicit *oohs* and *aahs* from the audience? The indescribably ugly set—dreary colors leaking down a charmless beige background—and the corrosively bilious costumes in rancid greens and oranges add to the general gloom. I think we're meant to be in some kind of arcade. To cheer things up, there's a single dark-brown wooden chair for Sieg-fried. And how to tell that he's restless, disaffected, yearning? He has absolutely nothing to do or to respond to. The central figure in this act is a totally irrelevant jester, endlessly leaping and cavorting, leeching all possible seriousness from the enterprise.

And so Act II, the first lakeside act—with more Danish expression-ist décor, which as it happens doesn't really show the lake—comes out of nowhere. There's been a moment back at the arcade when Siegfried vaguely senses something out there calling, calling. We're given a quick, untraditional glimpse of the villain, Von Rotbart, luring him on, so that it's not Siegfried's own longings that lead to the tragedy but something out of a monster melodrama. Then clunk, clunk, clunk, the arcade disman-tles itself and we're ready for the hunters, the swans, and Odette her-self. But since she doesn't answer to any internal urgency in Siegfried, there's no emotional content to their meeting, nor is there any mime to explain why she's there, who she is, or, for that matter, who that nasty creature is, darting around getting in the way. He's Mr. Orange Cape, that's who he is, and that's what Von Rotbart's entire performance is reduced to.

Act III, the "black act," is set in what half a dozen years ago I de-scribed as a look-alike for the waiting room of the Poughkeepsie train station—I've been back to check, and I got it right. Again, there's not much of a court to welcome the six princesses on display for the Prince to choose among, and the courtiers on hand are no more interested in them than Siegfried is. On comes Odile, she and Siegfried hurry off, and we're into the endless divertissement, beginning with a very effective Martins pas de quatre: He's always good at this kind of classical pastiche, and we soak it up like parched earth. Then the national dances: Hungar-ian, Russian, Spanish, Neapolitan—it's like the "Small World" boat ride at Disneyland. They're mostly standard and well crafted, except for the studiedly "sexy" Russian one, which is endlessly long and tedious and features the unforgettable male costume of little black bolero over bare chest, brocaded tea cozy on the head, and violet skirt above the knee. Who will join me in a class-action suit to rescue the poor guys who have to appear in this ludicrous getup?

The Black Swan pas de deux rolls in, climaxed by the famous fouet-tés that everyone's counting on (and counting): Some ballerinas get through all thirty-two of them, others stop (wisely) at twelve or so. There's a strange little moment when Rotbart keeps patting and stroking his daughter's arms and shoulders. What are we meant to think? And then the deed is done: Siegfried pledges himself to the wrong swan, Odile's per-fidy is revealed, and the wicked pair make their (botched) exit. Despair.

The final act is the closest Martins comes to an imaginative ap-proach to *Swan Lake*. Siegfried rushes to the lake after Odette, but she makes it clear that they can never be together. Yet somehow their love, though doomed, is enough to destroy Rotbart, and he collapses in a puddle of orange cloak. (I found myself whispering, "What did he die of?" A colleague nearby muttered: "Boredom.") There's no struggle between good and evil, there's no apotheosis, but there's an exciting mass exit of swans, enveloping Odette and leaving Siegfried behind. It's far closer to the end of *Giselle* than of *Swan Lake*, but the lovers' being thwarted and the sentencing of Odette to eternal swanness suits Peter Martins's cynical vision of a *Swan Lake* that values a jester and an orange cape above the profound claims and dangers of romantic love.

Is the Martins *Swan Lake* worth seeing? No. But it's worth performing, because it gives so many chances to so many demi-soloists, and there's a big new crop of very capable young girls—and even a few potentially good boys. And in fairness to Peter Martins, I should report that the audience whooped it up for all the jesters. Never underestimate the power of cute.

The New York Observer
JANUARY 23, 2006

A New Sleeping Beauty, *a Great Aurora*

A NEW *GISELLE*? A new *Swan Lake*? Another day, another dollar. But a new *Sleeping Beauty* is always an event, and for many reasons. Its score is Tchaikovsky's greatest, which means ballet's greatest. Its demands on a ballet company are enormous: huge cast, opulent sets and costumes, a special brand of ballerina, a rigorous and exposed style, a complicated and demanding tradition . . . and imagination.

Beauty isn't like any other ballet. It isn't, of course, a tragedy or a melodrama, but it's also not a boy-meets-girl comedy—a *Coppélia*, a *Fille Mal Gardée*; those works present their heroines with simple domestic problems, which get predictably resolved. And it's not a wish-fulfillment fantasy like *Cinderella*. *The Sleeping Beauty*, rather, looks at the cycle of life, involves a brush with malignity and death, and gives us a heroine who must awaken to love and sexual experience, and whose trajectory to emotional fulfillment implies the restoration of the entire world to harmony.

This is no small order, and many—most—productions falter on their way to achieving it. How many great *Beauty*s can we recall? Hardly a man is still alive (can there be any?) who remembers Diaghilev's extravagant London production of 1921—the production that more or less bankrupted him. Balanchine never attempted a complete *Sleeping Beauty*, much as he loved it (and referred to it constantly in his work); no Ballet Theater *Beauty* has ever done the trick; Peter Martins's compact version misses the glory. There were lovely Kirov performances in the 1960s (with Kolpakova), but the Kirov is now giving us its painstaking and glacial reconstruction of the 1890 original. And the two most recent Royal Ballet attempts have been failures.

It was the Sadler's Wells/Royal staging—conceived in 1946 for the post-war reopening of Covent Garden—that became the benchmark for *Beauty*s in the West. In a new book celebrating the Royal's seventy-fifth anniversary, the British dance critic Zoë Anderson describes it: "The production, designed by Oliver Messel, was a vision of splendour at a time of bitter austerity. Paint and canvas were scarce, rationing was still in force, coupons had to be found for fabrics, gloves and boots. The Queen's train was made from somebody's velvet curtains. . . . Messel's sets combined airy architectural fantasy with a sense of place. The soft colours set the dancers off, surrounding them with light and space. . . . Groupings looked marvelous . . ." And, of course, it starred Margot Fonteyn in her greatest role.

It was this same production that three years later, in 1949, opened the famous Sadler's Wells season in New York, earned the company its international reputation, crowned Fonteyn as a prima ballerina assoluta, and—to be a touch fanciful—kissed classical ballet back to life in America. It's not only memory, often so treacherous, that keeps it so dear to us; what we have on film confirms its beauty, its style, its musicality, and Fonteyn's greatness. For years the company toured it in America, until finally it was gone. And nothing on its level has come along to replace it. The Royal's style eroded; the company's focus was more and more on the far-from-classical dance-dramas of Kenneth MacMillan; even Frederick Ashton, the company's great choreographer, was neglected—a pattern that has been reversed in recent years, first under Anthony Dowell, now under Monica Mason.

As for *Beauty*, there was a new production in 1968; another (by MacMillan) in 1973; another in 1977; another (by Dowell) in 1994; another (by Makarova) in 2003. Now, only three years later, Monica Mason has brought to America the company's latest attempt to restore its signature work to its former resplendence.

Here's how the credits run: "Choreography by Marius Petipa. Additional Choreography by Frederick Ashton, Anthony Dowell, Christopher Wheeldon. Production by Monica Mason, Christopher Newton after Ninette de Valois and Nicholas Sergeyev. Original Designs by Oliver Messel. Realization and Additional Designs by Peter Farmer . . ." What does all that mean? That Mason has decided to go backwards in order to progress. The key decision was to "realize" the Messel sets and costumes—to restore to *Beauty* the lovely atmosphere it once exemplified.

I saw this new *Beauty* at the Kennedy Center in Washington, and it was immediately apparent that it was too big for the stage—or the stage was too small for it. Everything looked cramped. There should have been more room in the Prologue for the wicked fairy Carabosse and her scampering rats to wheel about in. Aurora's thrilling first entrance through the arcade upstage was partially blocked by the courtiers; they had nowhere else to stand. The Lilac Fairy's boat, by which she conveys the Prince to the sleeping castle, was not only especially ugly but also too big in this context. One would have to see the production on a stage suited to it to know whether it's a keeper.

Some questionable decisions have been made. Why has Ashton's "Garland Dance" been thrown out and replaced by a fussy mishmash by Wheeldon? Why do we have a sketchy and feeble drop curtain at the start, in such contrast to the regal Messel look? Why, if you're out to preserve and conserve, do you have to put your personal and irrelevant stamp on things?

But none of that constitutes the main issue. Alas, for all its earnestness and prettiness (and the costumes, at least, are very pretty), this

Beauty is strangely wan: The "Realized" sets seem dutiful (the third act looks positively skimpy), and there's far more here of Farmer himself, and less Messel, than we've been led to believe. The classical approach to the fairy variations appeared to have been carefully learned for the occasion, not an expression of an inbred company style. The Carabosse (I saw Genesia Rosato) was less than menacing, at her best when emitting a soundless shriek of laughter. (You may prefer Carabosse *en travesti*, as I do, but we don't have to go back further than Merrill Ashley or Lourdes Lopez in the Martins version to recall chilling performances by women; Mason herself was a superb Carabosse.) The Bluebird pas de deux was underpowered. The fairy-tale characters were game but limp. The Lilac Fairy was strongly danced by the talented Lauren Cuthbertson, but she lacked the magical womanly grace and authority with which Lilac rights the wrongs of the world.

And yet . . . the crucial element was there. Makarova once said, "*Sleeping Beauty* is a triumph of academic virtuosity, permeated with a youthful charm which a ballerina has to radiate." The Aurora of Alina Cojocaru radiated youth, natural charm, and—so important—ease. And her technique is solid. But there's nothing solid about the way she dances: She's light, quick, confident, both delicate and strong. Like Fonteyn, she's instantly lovable—you see at once why her parents, the suitors, her friends, the courtiers, the fairies all care about her. And because you love her, it's unbearable when Carabosse poisons her, even though you know that rescue, in the form of the Lilac Fairy, is on the way. Her Rose Adagio started wonderfully—the first turn relaxed and sure. There were one or two shaky moments, but they didn't detract from the serene glow of happiness that she emanated. This, after all, is the moment when she's taking her place in the world—it's a birthday party, it's an engagement party, it's a celebration of the first step of a girl into womanhood. If the Rose Adagio is only a technical triumph, it's empty, and *The Sleeping Beauty* is dead; Cojocaru makes us experience it as a burst of joy, not a challenge.

Her variation was pure and unforced, her *danse vertige* moving, her Vision Scene romantic and alluring: Of course the Prince would fall instantly in love. And in the profound third-act pas de deux she was assured and brilliant, flinging herself into the famous fish-dives with gleeful abandon. What she lacks, for me, in this climax to the entire ballet is a new gravity and depth. A century has gone by, and she's been wakened by the man she loves—she *is* a woman now. And she's not only being married, she's being crowned. Her world—our world—has been through an ordeal and survived, and she is the emblem of that survival. But she's been reawakened to a new life, not her old one. If her "death" and rebirth don't lead to a new understanding, a new maturity, it's been a waste of a hundred-year sleep.

I don't as yet sense in Cojocaru an understanding of all this, but it will surely come. She is, with Diana Vishneva, one of the two most satisfying classical ballerinas in the world today. She has the looks, the talent, and the opportunity—the company knew what it had from the start. We know that envy is one of the deadliest of the sins, but how can we not envy the Royal this enchanting Beauty?

The New York Observer

JULY 17, 2006

Romeo+Juliet *Stripped Clean*

PETER MARTINS'S *Romeo + Juliet* is now in the midst of a two-week run at the State Theater. Let's look first at one of its pluses: the plus sign in the title that replaces Shakespeare's unwieldy "and." What can it mean? Is it an advance warning that Martins is going to trim all excess fat from this weighty drama? Certainly, his take on the tragic goings-on in old Verona is thin. Consider some of the things that are missing.

1) Verona. This town is seriously underpopulated. In the big public scenes—those meant to show us how the ugly feud between the Montagues and the Capulets is tearing the city apart—there's no one to be seen except six Montague couples (in green) and six Capulet couples (in red). And, of course, the three young lads—Mercutio, Benvolio, and

Romeo—and their mortal foe, Tybalt. I take it back: At one point, five little harlequin boys wander over from the School of American Ballet to provide a touch of the cutes.

2) Sex. The main innovation of this production, we've been hearing, is that everyone's young, young, young. Romeo plus Juliet are meant to be real teenagers—in fact, the original first-cast Juliet (she dropped out) is still in the school. But unlike the teenagers in the famous Zeffirelli movie, City Ballet's teenagers are boyish and girlish but not sexish. They yearn, they hug; Juliet flings back her head in ecstasy, Romeo billows his cloak around the stage when he isn't straining to hold her aloft in every conventional swooning lift you've ever seen; but they just don't seem to have the hots for each other. Maybe they're meant to be so young they're prepubescent?

3) Inventive choreography. The story of Romeo and Juliet is an easy one to tell, since it's linear and since everyone in the world knows it already. Martins, who's always had a gift for narrative, has the bones of the story sturdily in place, ready and waiting for a resonant dance approach. It doesn't come. There are several effective dramatic scenes—for instance, the final confrontation between Juliet and her parents. And the interminable dueling is well handled (although the fatal thrust to Mercutio is awkwardly blurred). But the actual dance passages are purely generic. The quarreling factions, the guests at the Capulet ball, the antics of the lads, are all flavorless, except for some amusing virtuoso stuff for Mercutio; the duets between Romeo and Juliet are flat and derivative. This is the great disappointment: I had hoped that Shakespeare's heart-tugging story together with the ballet's swelling Prokofiev score might bring out a more expressive side of Martins's temperament, but no. The choreography, although always professional, is just slapped on to keep the plot going, not to evoke a world or a tragedy.

4) Taste. Martins's commitment to his compatriot the Danish artist Per Kirkeby is beyond my understanding. His notoriously inappropriate designs helped to wreck Martins's *Swan Lake*, and his *R + J* is just as counterproductive. The curtain goes up on a stubby construction that looks like cinder block, against a violent backdrop of abstract reds, blacks, and ochers. Is this *Romeo* or is it *Le Sacre du Printemps*? The cinder block structure opens

up and moves about to become Juliet's bedroom, Friar Laurence's cell, the ballroom, the tomb, et cetera—at its most ridiculous when the balcony scene becomes the battlement scene. (Are the two Danes confusing Verona with Elsinore?) And the costumes are equally off-putting. Tybalt's canary-yellow outfit may be the most egregious, but Paris's lavender tights are in the running. The ball costumes are fussy and cheap, and in rancid colors. Yet for all the in-your-face visuals, the overall effect is ultra-minimal. There's no physical surround for the action to inhabit.

It wasn't a bad idea to trim Prokofiev's long score, which was conducted with welcome nuance by the company's new music director, Fayçal Karoui. Compressing the score certainly helped Martins collapse the action into two acts for additional speed and efficiency, as he did with both *Swan Lake* and *The Sleeping Beauty*. But are speed and efficiency what we look for in *Romeo and Juliet*?

The Martins *Romeo + Juliet* just doesn't add up. It's lacking in passion and tragedy; there's no sense of period or place; the poetry and color of the play aren't even suggested. However, the bottom line of all *Romeo*s is the bottom line: Like *Swan Lake*, it's a surefire box-office winner. When ABT's overstuffed, overheated MacMillan version turns up soon at the Met, you'll be able to compare it to this thin, cool new one. I myself prefer whichever one I'm not seeing at the moment.

The New York Observer
MAY 8, 2007

Can Martha Graham Be Kept Alive?

FOR THOSE OF US WHO CARE about Martha Graham, it's been a bumpy ride.

I got on board in 1958, the year of Graham's full-evening dance-drama *Clytemnestra*, the first work of hers I ever saw. To some Graham purists it was suspect—"a bit Hollywood," as Arlene Croce put it. To me it was a revelation of what theater could be. And what dancers could be. Graham herself, in the title role (of course), was clearly diminished in strength—she was almost sixty-four. But every gesture was so full, so powerful, so telling that it didn't matter; all she had to do was lift her arm and it was thrilling. And, just as exciting, every one of the principals had the powerful presence of a star, in no way outshone by the star of stars, Martha herself.

Given the consistent quality of repertory and performance, who could imagine then that the great days were drawing to an end? Nineteen sixty-two saw the last really satisfying new work: *Legend of Judith*, with Martha as the Old Judith looking back over her life while Linda Hodes as the Young Judith dealt with poor Holofernes. After that, every season showcased an eagerly anticipated new work: *The Witch of Endor* (David and Saul), *Cortege of Eagles* (the Trojan Women), *A Time of Snow* (Abelard and Heloise), *Mendicants of Evening* (Marian Seldes intoning the poetry of Saint-John Perse while bolts of cloth were flung across the stage). Every one of these pieces was a disappointment—a formulaic imitation of the kind of dance-drama Martha had invented.

By the mid-1970s (and that's being generous), the whole Graham experience was deflating. The new works were more and more lackadaisical and perfunctory, although the loyalists pretended otherwise, and a new generation of dancers—dedicated, talented, and hardworking though they were—lacked the charisma of their predecessors. Worse, as Martha herself aged and became embittered (and alcoholic), unable to reconcile herself to her enforced retirement from dancing, the famous Graham technique began to erode.

And so we arrived at the substitution of chic for art: the Halston years; the Blackgama ad years (Martha in furs); the Margot-and-Rudy years; the Betty Ford–Woody Allen gala years. And the years (until her death, in 1991) dominated by Martha's young protégé, Ron Protas, and characterized by the abrupt dismissal—the massacre—of the leading dancers of the golden period who were the logical successors to carry on the great work. Finally, there were the catastrophic legal entanglements that followed Martha's death, threatening the existence of the company and the repertory.

IT'S TO THE ETERNAL CREDIT of the band of believers who persevered against the formidable odds that we have today a functioning Graham enterprise—that we're in the midst of a two-week season at the Joyce that's attracting an enthusiastic audience. But the inevitable questions arise: What is this audience seeing? Or, more directly, are these performances reasonable facsimiles of what Graham intended and achieved? To a large extent, the unfortunate answer is no. The fact that pleasure can still be taken in certain works is a testament to their inherent merits—their compelling concepts, their immaculate structure, their striking imagery. Others are, at least for now, gone with the wind.

The most distressing example is *Embattled Garden*, the garden in question being Eden, the characters Adam and Eve, Lilith and the Stranger. This work, like *Clytemnestra*, was mounted in 1958, when it was obviously intended to be taken as a wry and wicked sex comedy—a jaundiced but sympathetic commentary on what fools these lovers (us) be.

Today it's an overwrought melodrama of lust and betrayal. I was so confused opening night that the next morning I called Paul Taylor for a reality check (he danced the Stranger for years). "Yeah," he said, "it was definitely tongue-in-cheekish back then." There were no tongues in cheeks at the Joyce performances.

Almost as endangered is the rhapsodic *Diversion of Angels*, a pure-dance work that has inspired audiences since its creation almost sixty years ago. Today's company approaches it with diminished technique and exaggerated piety. Of the three lead women, the imposing Katherine Crockett was not much more than adequate as the one in white, and Blakeley White-McGuire was a disaster as the one in red, her character's thrilling rushes across the stage reduced to zero effect, the signature contractions in midflight almost imperceptible. (More perceptible was the signature narcissism of her partner, Maurizio Nardi.) Only the young Atsuko Tonohata, in yellow, projected the simple, happy ardor that brings *Diversion* to life.

THERE WERE UNFORTUNATE CIRCUMSTANCES this season. Most serious was the absence of Fang-Yi Sheu, an extraordinarily talented and beautiful dancer who illuminated the repertory these past few years. There's no one in the current company at her level. Miki Orihara is an elegant, lovely dancer, but her Medea, in *Cave of the Heart*, doesn't sear you. (Sheu ripped your heart out.) Two of the five women listed in the program as principals aren't on view at all, and there's only one principal male listed, the exemplary Tadej Brdnik. He's a persuasive Oedipus in *Night Journey*, the kind of hunky guy Graham liked to cast opposite her. ("Me Martha, you Tarzan.") The Jocastas of both Crockett and Elizabeth Auclair were subpar, the power of the chorus of seven has been diluted, and with the departure of the company's senior men, the blind seer Tiresias pounding across the stage with his heavy staff has been reduced to a boy with a pogo stick.

As a result, no doubt, of all these absences, the entire season's casting looks thin, dominated as it seems to be by Jennifer DePalo, a soloist who is certainly competent but who lacks sufficient inner life to ignite Graham's highly personal art. In sum: This is a repertory that demands stars being performed by a company that lacks them.

Much is being made of this being the Graham Company's eightieth anniversary. There's a series of special events, beginning with a single performance on opening night of *Lamentation Variations*, an effective tribute by three current choreographers (Aszure Barton, Richard Move, and Larry Keigwin) to Martha's most famous solo. Saturday afternoon we were amused, charmed, moved, and irritated by a ninety-minute tightly choreographed speakathon called *From the Horse's Mouth*, featuring a roster of almost thirty Grahamites, old and young, telling anecdotes about her, doing some modest steps, parading her spectacular costumes. Most welcome were a few famous old-timers: Pearl Lang, Mary Hinkson, Stuart Hodes. Most missed were other famous old-timers who have to go nameless because there were so many of them. A gala is upcoming. In other words, the season has been cleverly orchestrated by the company's new artistic director, the praiseworthy Janet Eilber.

But what was she doing exhuming *Acts of Light*, a totally meretricious piece of work from 1981? How shamelessly Graham pieced together bits and pieces of her past, demeaning them in the process! Worst is the endless Part III ("Ritual to the Sun"), with eighteen or so dancers in Halston's clinging faux-nude body-stockings doing floor exercises and other gymlike things before massing for a faux-ecstatic faux-climax. Some works deserve to die the death, and this one should be buried once and for all with a wooden stake through its heart.

Luckily, two Graham masterpieces will be added to the repertory in the season's second week: *Errand into the Maze* and *Appalachian Spring.* Will they serve as an antidote to *Acts of Light?* Hope springs eternal. . . .

The New York Observer
SEPTEMBER 18, 2007

Bourne's Male Swans Are Back at the Lake

I DISLIKED MATTHEW BOURNE'S *SWAN LAKE* a dozen years ago when it hit Broadway, transfixed the critics, and swept the Tonys. Since then it has played on and on all over the world, and now it's back (at the City Center) in a new and improved version, which I don't like much more than the original.

Everyone knows its "shocking" premise: The poor Prince hates the falsities of the Court (the usual adolescent anti-establishment angst); loathes yet lusts for the Queen Mom (there's a near-rape—not only incest but lèse-majesté); is uncomfortable with sexy girls in general and in particular with a pushy girl in pink; and finds comfort only with his dear little toy bird. He's a mess—not only gender-confused but species-confused, as we discover when he encounters a dozen or so big he-swans with gleaming bare torsos and rippling muscles and thick white shag from their navels to their shins. One of them is . . . Him! Odette himself! And they get it on.

But not until we've been dragged through some introductory scenes that look like skits from a bad revue, the first of them an interlude in an opera house in which four butterflies, three monsters, and a parody huntsman do a parody dance that comes straight out of British panto. Then the Freudian bit with Mom. Then our boy in "A Seedy Club" that evokes every conceivable nightclub cliché. Then he's out on the street, roughed up and miserable. And finally, he's down at the lake, near suicide . . . when up pops the Swan.

Actually, there are a dozen of them, sexy, scary, and aggressive. (No surprise to me, having read in an English newspaper half a century ago—and never forgotten—not only that "swans have been known to attack Scotties" but that "one blow from a swan's wing can break a man's leg." I've kept my distance ever since.) The Prince, though, is enthralled, ecstatic. Is it real? A fantasy? A wet dream?

Following (vaguely) the outline of the original ballet, the next act takes place in a ballroom, where the Queen, now alerted to her son's . . . peculiarities? . . . parades a covey of elegant ladies for him to choose among. And, bang, Odile—the false Odette—barges in (he's in leather now) and is all over every woman in sight, beginning with the Queen. You could call this scene "The Triumph of Rough Trade." With that busy pelvis action that's his specialty, the Swan is pure catnip, and the Prince is in an agony of humiliation and jealousy.

This "black act"—everyone's in black except the Queen, who's in red—is the only part of the ballet that has some genuine appeal to it: It's cleverly staged and it's energized; there's a witty dance with the "Princesses," and the choreography for all the national dances—Spanish, Magyar, et cetera—is original and amusing. The dance vocabulary is still thin here, but it's more various than that of the bird sections, in which the guys clomp and thump around with stylized swan gestures.

Act IV: The Prince collapses, is taken to the hospital, medicated, and put to bed, where in his tortured dreams he rushes back to the lake (as in the standard version) only to see the real Odette being pecked and thrashed to death (those powerful wings!) by her co-swans—I'm not clear why. In the morning, his mother finds him dead, but don't worry—there's an apotheosis, and we see Prince and Swan united forever up in the sky. In other words, it's the same old story: boy meets bird, boy loses bird, boy gets bird.

That this is all a homosexual retelling of a work we know so well is not a problem—*Swan Lake* has survived other provocative concepts—but to portray Odette as the aggressor and the Prince as passive is to violate Tchaikovsky's great score. What's really disturbing isn't that the Bourne version is just another iteration of that worn-out trope of a boy waking up to his true sexual identity; it's that the underlying emotional dynamic is so infantile. It's not only the toy bird in bed with the Prince, but also that he's clearly happiest when being picked up and cuddled.

All of which seems to fit smoothly with Bourne's misogyny: Both of the prominent female figures—the sexually voracious Queen and the sexually voracious bimbo in pink—are presented as threatening. They're caricatures of women, and so, too, are the predatory ladies in black in the ballroom scene. Only adolescent boys and menacing swans are allowed real sexual feelings.

This *Swan Lake* is startling and at times effective; it's also coarse and at times risible. Overall, it's as infantile as its hero. I hope that's not why it has enjoyed so huge a success, but I suspect it may be.

The New York Observer
OCTOBER 27, 2010

A *New* Nutcracker *Hits BAM*

THE PROBLEM with getting Balanchine's *Nutcracker* out of your head while watching other versions isn't just that it's so familiar; it's that it's so perfect. He knew the Tchaikovsky ballet inside out, of course: As a boy, at the Mariinsky, when the ballet was barely twenty years old, he had been the Mouse King, the Prince, and later the Candy Cane. More important, for him Tchaikovsky was a god—and, he said, *The Nutcracker* was Tchaikovsky's masterpiece. What he took from the score, above and beyond everything else, was that it was intended as a celebration of Christmas—a child's Christmas.

Balanchine also emphasized that the original scenario was based less on the famous tale by E.T.A. Hoffmann than on the lighter French version of the story by Dumas père. "Everything that appears in the second act of *Nutcracker* is a candy or something tasty," Balanchine told Solomon Volkov in their book of interviews. "Or a toy . . . The Sugar Plum Fairy is a piece of candy and the dewdrops are made of sugar. The Buffon is a candy cane. It's all sugar!" And spectacle. Stravinsky agreed: He once remarked to Balanchine that he particularly liked Tchaikovsky's *Nutcracker* "because there is no heavy psychology in it, just an entertaining spectacle, understandable without tons of words."

Balanchine shows us an instant grave connection between his little heroine and the polite boy who in the first act Drosselmeyer brings to the Christmas party. It's a moving suggestion of how children can be drawn to each other—a touching foreshadowing of sexual attraction. But his children remain children throughout their dream experience, from the nightmare of the battle with the mice to their joyous visit, as Sugar Plum's guests, to the Kingdom of the Sweets. They have an adventure but they don't have a story.

There are countless other versions that do center on a story— a story of a girl's psychological growth from preadolescence to young womanhood, and of the children's awakening feelings for each other and their eventual adult union. The ultra-talented Alexei Ratmansky, in ABT's new production which premiered before Christmas at BAM, both sticks to the basics and steps out into a modest story line. Early on, his young Clara and her Nutcracker boy are pointedly shown echoing their adult avatars, the Princess and Prince, who perform a classical duet that does get the principal dancers onstage in Act I but blunts their eventual big pas de deux. We don't need young Clara imagining her future this explicitly. And it seems gratuitous when at the end of the ballet we're shown the Prince and the Princess getting married.

This is not the kind of happy ending *The Nutcracker* demands. When Clara goes home to bed, she should have visions of sugarplums dancing in her head, not visions of wedding veils.

Ratmansky gives us the conventional Christmas party, but before we get to it there's an introductory kitchen scene that all too cutely establishes the mice as major players. Seen once, it's charming; seen again and again, it suffers the fate that cuteness inevitably brings upon itself. The party scene amusingly deploys the usual naughty Fritz, but the interplay between the boy and the girl children is strangely lifeless. The growth of the Stahlbaums' tree is also underexploited. It sort of grows, sort of tilts, sort of inches forward, and then is awkwardly replaced by gigantic frail and unconvincing boughs that lumber on from the stage-right wings. Meanwhile, our minds can't help recalling the magic of Balanchine's tree. It's not just nostalgia that makes us miss it now: A great coup de théâtre has been replaced by a humdrum device.

Even so, Ratmansky delivers many happy effects here. His dances for Drosselmeyer's puppets are ingenious and appealing. When the boy Nutcracker is felled by Fritz, the four puppets rush back on and stand over him in frozen poses of concern. An immense storybook chair glides onto the stage, from which Clara flings her slipper and conquers the Mouse King. Things aren't helped by a Drosselmeyer whose characterization lacks focus, but Ratmansky's Clara—the extraordinarily sensitive half-child, half-adolescent Catherine Hurlin—holds everything together with her believable and blessedly unadorable performance.

And then a dazzling triumph. The Snowflake scene turns into an electrifying pas d'action, Clara and the Boy darting through the snow, sliding and flopping on the ice, being normal, happy kids at play—until the sky darkens, the snowflakes grow threatening, the cold turns to chill, and danger is only averted by the arrival of Drosselmeyer with a sleigh to carry them off to the Kingdom of the Sweets. Here we don't miss Balanchine's brilliant abstractions because Ratmansky has come up with such a felicitous substitute. Unlike so many other talented choreographers, he's completely comfortable with ballet on the largest scale.

In the second act, his other great strength emerges: endless inventive detail, from the flick of a foot to the toss of a head. His take on the obligatory scenes that make up the divertissement is mostly original and entertaining—what a relief, for instance, to take a break from Balanchine's sinuous Coffee arching her back and clapping her little bells. Instead, bare-chested Arabian Sascha Radetsky tries to cope with his four importunate wives in their harem pants and beads—a witty reimagining. The Chinese dance is traditional yet all Ratmansky's own. The three bouncy Russians are the three bouncy Russians we've seen in a dozen ballets, but they're especially invigorated and invigorating. Only the five girls listed as the Nutcracker's Sisters (an unexplained and unrealized conceit) have nothing of interest to do to the music Balanchine uses for Marzipan.

As for the great Waltz of the Flowers, Ratmansky has eliminated the Dewdrop—no doubt wisely: Who could compete with Balanchine here? In her place we have four busy bees (in orange and black, with antennae) buzzing among the girls and doing for them what bees do for flowers. At times, the overall effect of the waltz is diminished by these apian pranksters, but this is acceptable fun.

The divertissement as a whole, however, doesn't lead up to and prepare for the supposedly climactic grand pas de deux; it's not a culmination. First-cast Gillian Murphy and David Hallberg are the company's supreme classicists, and they handled the tricky steps flawlessly. As usual, Paloma Herrera was pleasing if surfacey, and Cory Stearns handsome and half-baked.

Most startling were Veronika Part and Marcelo Gomes. As always, he's grand and generous, sympathetically dealing with her sometimes overwrought effects—the head flung back, the voluptuous smile. (They'll work out their partnership problems.) Part has outdone herself in this role. For all her large-scale dark beauty, she's usually phlegmatic, but here she was rapturous, ecstatic-orgasmic! More Anna Karenina than Nutcracker Princess. I don't know what this has to do with *The Nutcracker*, but it was gratifying to see her come so vividly alive.

At the very end, Clara is back in bed, clutching her toy nutcracker and drifting off to sleep. Yes, it was all a dream.

This *Nutcracker* wouldn't be worth dissecting if it weren't so intelligent and inventive, and Ratmansky will surely refine it over the years. It doesn't really challenge Balanchine, but it can stand on its own beside him.

The New York Observer
JANUARY 5, 2011

The Glory of the Young Paul Taylor

THE TREMENDOUS ACHIEVEMENT of the Paul Taylor season that just ended was the revival of his 1966 masterpiece *Orbs*. It must be his longest work—it's in two parts, split by an intermission—and it's been revived only once before, in 1982. This is a magisterial piece, an astounding summing-up by a choreographer barely in his mid-thirties, set to his most daring choice of music: the late Beethoven string quartets. Only a supremely confident young man could have embraced this daunting challenge.

Orbs also provided Taylor with one of his greatest roles. His character is the Sun (in a white unitard, decorated with silver stars), and around him revolve the planets and moons. He presents them—the planets in two male-female couples, the moons four ravishing girls in shimmering Alex Katz costumes—and proceeds to instruct, nurture, discipline, and cherish them.

The four sections of *Orbs* represent the four seasons, beginning with "Venusian Spring," in which he demonstrates the ways of sexual love to his celestial brood. (They learn fast.) On to the confrontational "Martian Summer"—set to the formidable *Grosse Fuge*.

When, after the intermission, we find ourselves down on Earth and among mere humans, it's at an autumn wedding. Everyone's in brown. The Sun is now the solemn, yet occasionally sly, minister. The bride and her bridesmaids and her conventionally weeping mother are our old friends the female planets and their moons. We recognize the male planets in the groom, frantic with nerves—obsessively checking his hair, his tie, his fly—and his best man. The wedding takes place, there's a nutty outdoor feast with an outlandish roasted bird flung about, and there's much fluttering from the women, with their affectionate homage to and parody of the girls at another wedding, the one in Graham's *Appalachian Spring*. (Graham at this period was never far out of Taylor's mind.)

And then we're back in the heavens, for the most beautiful and resonant passage in the entire work—"Plutonian Winter." The orbs are deadened, life has drawn to a halt. Here we're reminded of the plangent sadness that informs another of Taylor's finest works, *Sunset*. The planets, their moons at their feet, are isolated in their separate muted spotlights. (Exceptionally striking in her desolation is the magnificent Amy Young, holding the most beautifully posed and poised balance I've ever seen. She's frozen in her stillness—secure beyond secure.) The now-dimmed Sun presides.

Paul Taylor may be a pessimist, but he's not a sadist, at least not here. Winter, too, passes, and he brings the Sun and its satellites back to life and harmony in a reaffirming whirlwind of a coda. It's like the coda to *Don Giovanni*, when normal existence resumes after the Don's descent into hell.

The outpouring of invention in *Orbs* is endless, its felicities countless—no wonder Arlene Croce referred to it as "perhaps the most charming work in the modern dance repertory." Because the Taylor season was cut from three to two weeks this year—the City Center is again shutting down for repairs, and nothing can be allowed to interfere with the Encores! series—*Orbs* was presented only twice. Let's hope we don't have to wait another thirty years to see it again.

The New York Observer
MARCH 9, 2011

Thirty Years of Peter Martins

PETER MARTINS has been making ballets for thirty-six years now, ever since *Calcium Night Light*, in 1977. As I remember it, City Ballet's orchestra was on strike, the company was shut down, and somewhere in Brooklyn Martins previewed this startling duet (to Ives) for Heather Watts and Daniel Duell. Everyone trooped out to see it, everyone was knocked out by it, and soon it was in the company's repertory. Arlene Croce described its climax as "a staccato, nonstop, seriocomic pas de deux in which limbs become hinges and handles, bodies are clamped together, then slid apart." She went on to say that "the choreography makes not one superfluous gesture, everything stands out with bright-edged clarity, and the flatly factual tone communicates an instantaneous emotion." Balanchine liked it enough to insert it into his own *Ivesiana*, where it didn't belong, but the compliment to Martins was immense.

Calcium was a fortuitous debut, and Martins's ballets through the next several years confirmed this happy first impression: *Sonate di Scarlatti*, *Eight Easy Pieces*, *Lille Suite* were less personal statements than serious attempts to master his craft, under the eye and influence of the greatest of all teachers and exemplars. These works were all fluent and pleasing, and they added up to a convincing apprenticeship. When Balanchine chose Martins as his successor, he knew he was getting a hard-working, competent, and eager dance-maker.

In the immediate years after Balanchine's death, with the entire responsibility for the company on his shoulders, Martins focused more on that responsibility than on his own creative ambitions, but he went on developing new works—eventually, scores of them. Who can remember them all? Who would want to? Far too many seemed to be by the numbers, and the numbers weren't distinctive. Can we really distinguish one of his ballets set to the music of Michael Torke from the next? They all seemed flashy, trendy, empty. He made works to offer opportunities to his younger dancers; he made works to explore the limits of partnering; he made works for his ballerinas, in particular his wife, Darci Kistler, at first to rejoice in her marvelous talents, later to veil her diminishing powers. He made his versions of the classics. He mounted Festivals, Homages, Projects. He went in for desperate, gimmicky collaborations—with Paul McCartney, the architect Calatrava, the designer Valentino. He raised money.

Now he's been in charge for thirty years, and the company is securely afloat—his single greatest achievement. And he's celebrating with a new version of his 1988 American Music Festival, which had been a good idea that unfortunately led to paltry results. He's also celebrating by putting forward his own work with uncustomary boldness—Martins has always been modest. This past week, however, was notable for two things: an all-Martins evening, and a total absence of Balanchine. In all the years going back to 1948, I can't remember a week in which not a single Balanchine ballet was performed, apart from those weeklong runs of Martins's *Swan Lake*s, *Romeo*s, et cetera. An accident of scheduling? Perhaps.

The focus on Martins's ballets has been instructive, occasionally gratifying, and ultimately saddening. His Rodgers and Hart pastiche, *Thou Swell*, shows him at his exploitative worst. (On second thought, the mercifully brief *Sophisticated Lady*, to Ellington, may be even worse.) His *Fearful Symmetries*, to John Adams, is sound and fury signifying nothing—and signifying it for a long time. *Barber Violin Concerto* is a valiant but unsatisfactory response to that overwrought piece of music (it was more interesting when, originally, the second couple was performed by two Paul Taylor dancers).

But. *River of Light*, to a dense but powerful score commissioned from Charles Wuorinen and with ravishing lighting by Mark Stanley, has depth and resonance. I can't remember having seen it before, and would happily see it again. The duet *The Infernal Machine*, to Christopher Rouse, is a fascination of gnarly partnering (it was good to see Ashley Laracey in a prominent role), and another duet, *Purple*, to Torke, at least gave us a chance to watch the enigmatic, elusive Janie Taylor.

The oddest Martins event was the return of *Calcium Night Light*. This piece has never lost its provocative appeal, but it came close the other night, due to suicidal miscasting. Martins is relentlessly pushing Sterling Hyltin, and she's a lovely dancer. But *Calcium* isn't lovely; it's feisty and abrasive. Her silky smoothness is antithetical to the thorny nature of the piece, just as Robert Fairchild's wholesomeness is; there are half a dozen women in the company more suitable for the role. Only Peter Martins's psychiatrist, if he has one, could explain why he would sabotage one of his best ballets this way. Even so, the originality and cheekiness of *Calcium* could be detected through the weak miscasting. We were right back in 1977—this guy had talent. And by the end of the season, Hyltin had found herself in the role—she's a fanatical worker, and an intelligent one.

Martins's talent comes through most powerfully in *Hallelujah Junction*, a really exciting work made a dozen years ago and set to a really exciting two-piano score by John Adams. (Its title refers to a truck stop near the California-Nevada border.) Two grand pianos, beautifully lit, are raised high above and behind the dance area; we can see the two excellent pianists, Cameron Grant and Susan Walters, preside unobtrusively over the dancing. There's a couple in white—Hyltin and Gonzalo Garcia—and a man in black, Daniel Ulbricht. There are four couples in black. Hyltin is lithe and sinuous—not as expansive as Kistler, the original, but radiant. Garcia is stalwart and gracious. Ulbricht shows us his formidable technique without showboating. What's so remarkable about the piece is the excellent structure: The principals, the four couples, come and go in a rapid and inevitable flow, everything exhilarating and natural, everything stimulating, in contrast to the febrile hokeyness of *Fearful Symmetries*. *Hallelujah Junction* is Martins's finest ballet, and why it isn't in the repertory of more companies is one of the mysteries. But the biggest mystery—the sad mystery—is why, if he could make this good a piece, he hasn't made more on its level. Like Marlon Brando in *On the Waterfront*, he coulda been a contender.

The New York Observer
MAY 21, 2013

One Big Bug

DOWN AT THE JOYCE, we've just been treated to *The Metamorphosis*, the much-heralded dance-drama (or something) from England's Royal Ballet, starring principal dancer Edward Watson. Yes, Gregor Samsa wakes up one morning turned into a giant bug, but not until we've seen him going again and again through the dreary motions of his salesman's job. Is it the deadening routine of bourgeois life that brings on the transformation? Not in Kafka's great novella, in which the metamorphosis just . . . happens, in the first line.

This entire elaborate piece, created by Arthur Pita, is a pretext for Watson's tour-de-force performance. He thrashes, he spasms, he crawls and climbs and clambers. He slides and slips through the brown ooze he's been secreting. At times, he seems more simian than insectoid, but who's counting? Watson is terrific, but enough is enough. His family feels the same way, as their initial repulsion/sympathy morphs into irritation. At first, the young sister—in Kafka, an aspiring violinist; here, an aspiring ballet dancer—tries to protect Gregor, but she gets fed up. The sensitive, conflicted mother is helpless. The angry father is alternately belligerent and pathetic. Three men in beards and black hats stomp around. (In the story, they're lodgers; here, they're apparently refugees from *Fiddler on the Roof*.)

We also have a brusque, no-nonsense maid who deals with the bug with neither repulsion nor sympathy. Her job is to clean, and she sweeps, scrubs, and mops, shooing Gregor aside whenever he gets in her way. In Kafka's tragic denouement, he wastes away in shame and guilt— and his family's negligence. In the Pita version, the maid solves everybody's problem by deliberately leaving open the high casement window, and we last see the wretchedly obliging Gregor preparing to defenestrate himself—he knows he's not wanted. Poor bug!

But what a maid! You just can't find help like that these days.

The New York Observer
SEPTEMBER 24, 2013

Paul Taylor's Diamond Jubilee

AT SIX IN THE EVENING on Sunday, March 23, the Koch Theater was filled to the (metaphorical) rafters for an extraordinary event. To celebrate the sixtieth anniversary of the Paul Taylor Dance Company, the great choreographer had decided to add to his three-week season a single performance of his 1965 satiric phantasmagoria *From Sea to Shining Sea*, a work he described in his memoirs as "old Miss America's wrinkles, patriotism past its prime." It has been revived before but not with a cast of thousands, or anyway more than fifty, including a few current dancers, a bunch of recent retirees, and—most precious to the clued-in audience—a group of real old-timers. Senta Driver as "Sweeper"? Roars of welcome. David Parsons (looking great and adorably funny) as the welcoming "Indian Chief" exterminated without a second thought by the Pilgrims? Gales of loving laughter. Eileen Cropley, Renée Kimball Wadleigh, Elizabeth Walton, Sharon Kinney. Everybody's favorite, Carolyn Adams (one of the "Performers in Bathrobes" and doubling as one of the "Tooth Brushers").

Here were heroes like Thomas Patrick, Thomas Evert, Andy Le-Beau, Andrew Asnes (both "Super Mouse" and "Bossy Chair Remover"), Patrick Corbin ("Iwo Jima" and "Motorcyclist"). Three wonderful women who left the company only recently and are still mourned: Lisa Viola, Annmaria Mazzini, Amy Young. Linda Kent, tapping away. Rachel Berman, looking great, as "Streaker." And first, last, and eternally, Taylor's right-hand woman: tall, imposing, enchanting Bettie de Jong—"Big Bertha" herself, anchorwoman in *Esplanade*, and here, at the very end, poor Miss Liberty, slumped in a chair, dangling her crooked crown.

All the characters are played by a dispirited, exhausted gang of performers, dressed in bathrobes, hand-me-downs, cast-offs. Iconic images flash by—Iwo Jima, Betsy Ross, Al Jolson—all drained of life and significance. It's mordant, wicked, funny, distressing. It was the time of Vietnam. Taylor makes no direct reference—he's nonpolitical—but he's clearly unhappy for his country. In his book *Private Domain*, he says, "I viewed the U.S.A. backwards, sideways and askance."

And when the cheers died down and the audience of what seemed like the entire dance world settled in after an intermission, we were knocked out all over again by *Esplanade* itself, Taylor's signature work, as fresh and revelatory as it was in 1975. Yes, the old dancers are gone, but the new ones are sensational. Michelle Fleet has perfected her central role as the skittering solo girl, hopping and back-pedaling her way around the stage when not leaping into someone's arms—and taking for granted that he'll be there. It must have been inspiring and challenging for her to be dancing this in front of Carolyn Adams, the originator and by coincidence another African American. Fleet had nothing to worry about. Neither did redheaded Heather McGinley, a relative newcomer, in the central de Jong role, but then de Jong is the company's rehearsal director, so McGinley learned from the source.

By the time *Esplanade* was into its amazing climax—what Arlene Croce called its "paroxysm of slides and rolls across the floor"—the audience was once again ready to explode with joy. Once more, Croce nailed it: "The dancers, crashing wave upon wave into those slides, have a happy insane spirit that recalls a unique moment in American life—the time we did the school play or were ready to drown in the swimming meet. The last time most of us were happy in that way."

Paul Taylor's Americanness more and more seems to me an essential, if not *the* essential, thing that sets his work off from that of most other choreographers, which may be why it seems harder for the English and the Europeans to take him to heart—they're more at home with the abstractions of Cunningham or the mythic realms of Graham. (His heir in this regard is Twyla Tharp, who danced for him until she went off to be her own kind of American.) Dance after dance is situated in our country and its popular culture—from *Company B* (the Andrews Sisters) to *Black Tuesday* (the Depression) to the all-American horrors of *Big Bertha*; from the gangsters of *Le Sacre du Printemps (The Rehearsal)* to the barbershop quartets of *Dream Girls*; from Alley Oop and that girl in the polka-dot bikini in *Funny Papers* to the traumatizing born-again

Christianity of *Speaking in Tongues* to his most recent masterpiece, *Beloved Renegade* (Walt Whitman and the Civil War) to his two new pieces this season—both minor—*American Dreamer* (Stephen Foster) and *Marathon Cadenzas* (dance marathons of the 1930s). And others. He's American to the core, drenched in our decencies and our corniness (anathema to foreigners), deploring our violence and ugliness, and so both celebrating us and lashing out at our decadence. He knows us well, because he knows himself.

The New York Observer
APRIL 3, 2014

The Mariinsky—a Giant Question Mark

THE RECENT SEASON of the Mariinsky (ex-Kirov) Ballet at BAM inspired a number of questions, to most of which, alas, I don't have the answers.

1) Who is in charge of this great St. Petersburg company? The program lists the famous conductor Valery Gergiev—the Putin of Russian culture—as general and artistic director of the Mariinsky Theatre, but no one at all is listed as being specifically in charge of ballet. Someone must be making the day-to-day decisions about casting, promotions, commissions, but who?

2) So who, then, decided to bring us the 1950 Sergeyev version of *Swan Lake*? Was it a political decision? Let's face it—this iteration of the world's most famous ballet doesn't make a lot of sense. Alas, that's true of many other *Swan Lake* productions, but they err on the side of trendiness: They're Oedipal, all-male, soulless.

This one errs on the side of dogma. There's no mime, so we never understand Odette's predicament; in the first act, the "Reigning Princess" doesn't instruct her son, Siegfried, to get married; Siegfried himself doesn't seem particularly moody or psychologically different from any of the other boys, so why is he drawn away from the castle to the mystical lake? There are no hunters, so Odette and her swans are never in real danger. And in the end, no tragedy—Siegfried just gets pissed off with Rothbart and yanks off one of his wings: curtains for Rothbart. Why didn't Siegfried do it earlier, since it took so little effort? And why—for God's sake, why—the endless exhibitionism of The Joker in Acts I and III? I suppose the Russians can't help themselves—they have these specialty dancers with comical leaps and splits and nonstop high jinks, and they unleash them mercilessly.

And why give the first performance to a dancer—Viktoria Tereshkina—so utterly unsuited to Odette? She's a powerhouse of technique, but she has no Romantic or lyrical impulse, and she has a stolid face. As Odile her pyrotechnics work wonders, but it's too late to save the ballet. (When you're actually grateful for the national dances in Act III you know you're in trouble.) The superb corps and the beautiful, evocative sets are the most distinguished things about this production, but if you find yourself more interested in the Lake than in the Swan, it's curtains for *Swan Lake*, too.

3) Why is *Cinderella* so hard to get right? As its second full-evening offering, the Mariinsky brought us Alexei Ratmansky's 2002 version, which he has since heavily revised (for the Australians). It has strong virtues, even though it's updated to some unspecified Soviet period—the ballroom girls are in inter-war mode, and there's a sketchy big apartment building on a curtain at the start. But even a choreographer as inventive as Ratmansky has trouble filling the endless Prokofiev score, which is as intense as his *Romeo* music, although here it's at the service of a relatively light fairy tale. The ballroom scene is large-scale and pleasing, and Cinderella herself has a variety of interesting passages, but here's what we don't get: the fairy godmother (here she's called the "Fairy-Tramp" and looks like a bag lady); the glass carriage, with or without mice, that magically transports Cinderella to the ball; and the famous climax of the story: the fitting of the slipper on Cinderella's foot. Instead,

the slipper is tossed aside, because True Love does the job instead. Yes, this is a new take, but what a disappointment to the little girls (and some bigger ones) who grew up on that slipper!

First-cast Cinderella was that superlative ballerina Diana Vishneva, who did her best to seem youthful and innocent. But that's not what she is at this stage of her illustrious career. As with *Swan Lake*, seniority rules at the Mariinsky. Gorgeous Ekaterina Kondaurova was the manic stepmother, stealing the show at her all too many opportunities. The young Ratmansky was obviously trying to give us an exciting new consideration of this venerable and rather thin story, but there isn't really enough narrative for three long acts, and he's stuck with a score that goes on and on. A lot here is fresh and amusing, but I'm eager to see what he's done with Cinderella and Prokofiev a dozen years later.

4) Can *Les Sylphides* (here in its original 1908 *Chopiniana* version) still thrill the way it did for most of the twentieth century? Not this boy. The revolutionary Fokine today seems outdated, thin, precious. The Trocks' tongue-in-cheek take on it seems more robust and alive.

5) Who can explain why Benjamin Millepied has been given so many choice opportunities to choreograph? And why he's been given the Paris Opéra Ballet to run? In 2011, he created *Without* for the Mariinsky, and here it was—smaller than life, but an audience hit, with its nonstop artificial turbulence in the near-dark. Chopin piano music, five color-coded couples, lifts and more lifts—does it sound familiar? Yes, and it *looked* familiar. This is a shameless rip-off of Jerome Robbins's masterpiece *Dances at a Gathering.* And don't let anyone tell you it's an homage. The closest it came to outright theft was in the "cute" episode, the only one not almost totally obscured in darkness—when the "orange" couple do all the Robbins adorable things, down to the girl's final smirky shrug at the end.

Dances at a Gathering is about something—about community, love of dance, love of love. No Millepied ballet I've ever seen is about anything at all except putting together a workable piece. The dancers clearly loved dancing *Without*, though, and they gave it their estimable all. Maybe they believe it's avant-garde? *Dances* wasn't even avant-garde when it first saw the light of day, back in 1969.

6) How come the highlight of the Mariinsky's all-Chopin piano music program was Robbins's *In the Night*? At its premiere—in 1970, a year after *Dances*—it looked to me like outtakes from its predecessor (though with only three couples, not five). No longer, at least not in this ravishing performance. The three ballerinas—the lovely young Anastasia Matvienko, also an Odette-Odile and a Cinderella; the magnificent Kondaurova; and the commanding star Ulyana Lopatkina—had all the high Romantic glamour this crowd-pleaser demands, and they were clearly helped by Ben Huys's sensitive staging. But it's Robbins who should get the credit here. *In the Night* is not his finest work, but it's head and shoulders above what we saw of Millepied, Ratmansky, Fokine, and Sergeyev these past weeks. The Mariinsky, like the Bolshoi, always sells out in New York, thanks to that part of the dance audience that thinks being Russian is the ultimate stamp of excellence. Here, in the last performance of the season, they finally got their money's worth— from our own, very American, Jerry Robbins.

The New York Observer
JANUARY 29, 2015

Alice in Love

WITH GREAT FANFARE (and nine tractor-trailers to ferry in its notoriously elaborate production), Christopher Wheeldon's *Alice's Adventures in Wonderland* finally wheeled into New York under the banners of the National Ballet of Canada and the Joyce Foundation (performing at the Koch). This *Alice* is a co-production of the Canadians and England's Royal Ballet, which premiered it in 2011, and it's been making the rounds ever since—Toronto, Japan, Los Angeles, Washington, D.C.— with mixed critical results. But, always, I'm sure, with happy box offices: *Alice* is many things, and potential cash cow is one of them.

How to consider this mammoth undertaking? I can think of three approaches: as a version of Lewis Carroll's masterpiece; as a ballet in itself; as a spectacle. The first is the easiest. Although the incidents of the book are slavishly checked off one by one—as though audiences would picket if anything famous were left out—its essence is instantly obliterated by the decision to turn Carroll's tough-minded, inquisitive, no-bullshit child into a love-smitten teen. There is no dishy gardener-turned-Knave-of-Hearts in what may well be the least romantic novel in English literature—the one most dependent on wordplay rather than love-play. So what we have here is *Alice in Wonderland* without Alice.

As a ballet, Wheeldon's creation reflects his entire career as a choreographer. I can't think of anyone working today whose results veer so drastically from original and persuasive to slack and vacuous. Because he's giving us a love story, his main artillery is reserved for lyrical pas de deux—and we get them again and again. Or, rather, we get *it*: The same swoony passages turn up in the various lovey-dovey encounters that punctuate the three long acts. Wheeldon's idea of romantic love is the rapturous lift—up goes Alice, again and again, hoisted above by the otherwise gratuitous Jack and arcing through the air. I hope she has her Dramamine with her. Wheeldon was doing exactly this same thing a dozen years ago in *Carousel (A Dance)*, but *Carousel* has romance at its heart.

The choreography for Alice is purely generic throughout, but so is this conception of Alice. First-cast Jillian Vanstone is an attractive, appealing girl, and she's a strong dancer—the entire Canadian company is strong—but she has nothing challenging to do: When she's not overhead she just rushes around, smiling. Of Carroll's wary, skeptical girl she shows not a trace.

The opportunities for the character dancers are somewhat greater. The Queen of Hearts (in the Prologue she's Alice's mean mom) gets to do a comic take on *Carmen* as well as a parody of the Rose Adagio from *The Sleeping Beauty* that would have been a lot funnier if it hadn't been so vulgarly broad. But at least it was inventive. The Queen is a dance-up-a-storm role, and Greta Hodgkinson let herself rip. The White Rabbit (Carroll himself as a photographer in the Prologue and Epilogue) twitched and wiggled his way through the piece with just the right amount of camp from Dylan Tedaldi. The Duchess, the Cook, the Fish, the Frog, the tapping Mad Hatter, the bizarre March Hare, the pathetic Dormouse ("Collar that Dormouse! . . . Suppress him!" cries the Queen in the book, and he's duly suppressed)—they're all recognizable, and some of them are fun.

The group choreography—never a Wheeldon strong point—is without surprises, ranging from a real mess of a Caucus Race (think of what Jerome Robbins might have done with it) to a modestly witty romp for all concerned in the climactic trial scene. The ballet as a whole, though, simply isn't a ballet: It's a spectacle that's been produced, not choreographed.

With spectacle, luckily, Wheeldon and Co. are on surer ground. The sets, the costumes, the special effects—these are the elements that come to life. I don't much like the commissioned score by Joby Talbot— it's large-scale, insistent, literal; danceable, but without any playfulness or delicacy to it. The designs are by Bob Crowley, a seven-time Tony Award winner, and they're consistently ingenious and fun, although the first-scene set—a beautiful painted vision of a stately country home—looks more like *Downton Abbey* than an Oxford deanery. Alice is sweetly pretty in her lavender dress and the de rigueur Alice headband. There are touches of real brilliance: the flamingos at the croquet game, each of them with one wing melting persuasively into a mallet; the huge red heart—it looks like vinyl—on which the Queen rides in triumphantly; an endless caterpillar whose segments are prancing girls. And finest of all—a wonderful conceit—the Cheshire Cat, who keeps coming apart and re-forming itself, its many parts maneuvered by people in black in the mode of Japan's Bunraku puppets. His climactic appearance as a gigantic head swaying above the multitude is a fabulous coup de théâtre, just as, in Wheeldon's *Cinderella* last year, the transformation of the tree (a Basil Twist inspiration) was by far the most memorable moment—the *only* memorable moment.

Beggars can't be choosers, and in the spirit of charity I think back over the countless ballets I've seen that have *no* memorable moments.

But this Alice is two hours and forty-five minutes long. I gather that in London it was divided into two acts, the first running for seventy minutes or so, too long for the tot population to hang in there without a break. So it's been restructured into three acts—which means two long intermissions—and it seems interminable. It's just not strong enough to sustain that much audience time. Wheeldon, or the Royal, or the Canadians, should have eliminated some dreary scenes (like the Rajah/Caterpillar number) and shortened the whole thing by twenty minutes while restoring the two-act structure. If they had, I could even imagine seeing it a second time . . . someday.

One of the oddities of the current fashion for retelling children's stories in dance is the echoes from one work to another. In the Prologue to this *Alice*, the heroine is romancing a young gardener—a definite no-no in the pre–World War I world of *Downton Abbey*. (I mean the Deanery.) Jack is thereupon expelled from paradise. In the Prologue to Matthew Bourne's *Sleeping Beauty*, which opened in New York last year in the same week as Wheeldon's *Cinderella*, royal Aurora is having it off with a young gamekeeper. And both ballets end with brief epilogues in which the class-crossed lovers are now modern kids, with no thought of social rank or status. Not only has love prevailed, but so has democracy. Two trendy choreographic minds with but a single formulaic thought?

Are Wheeldon and Bourne the same person? No, but they share the same easy values. Wheeldon is more sophisticated, Bourne more upfront with his populist concepts, yet they reveal a similar emptiness. Bourne wandered, late, into ballet. Wheeldon has less of an excuse— he's had the benefit of the Ashton aesthetic at the Royal, where he grew up (think of Ashton's entrancing *Tales of Beatrix Potter*), and of Balanchine at City Ballet, where he danced and choreographed for fifteen years. For him to prefer orchestrating blockbuster spectacle over advancing the art his talent suggests he was capable of leading is a sad story. We need choreographers, not entrepreneurs.

The New York Observer
SEPTEMBER 16, 2014

The Red Army Assaults Lincoln Center

WHO WOULD HAVE SUSPECTED that right here in New York we're harboring a big cadre of Maoist dance fans, mostly young, full of pep and patriotism, happy to be singing along, tapping their feet, cheering, applauding, as nearly a billion and a half Chinese "artists"—oh no, sorry, that's the entire population of China—rush around the stage, striking poses, crouching, clenching fists, and waving a gigantic Red Army flag while a corps of cute women soldiers with bare knees fire bravely away at . . . well, it's not exactly clear who the enemy actually is. He's called Nan Batian, the Lord of the South, and he's definitely Bad, because he's cruel to peasants—especially to our heroine, Qionghua, whom we first encounter in a dank dungeon, bound to a pillar (in a stylish bright-red outfit), as she awaits being sold into slavery.

But Nan Batian hasn't counted on Qionghua's spunk. She gets away, she's recaptured, she's beaten and left for dead, she's revived in a thrilling rainstorm, and she's rescued by the hero, Hong Changqing, and sent off to the Red Area to join the Red Detachment of Women. All this, and we're only two scenes in.

Spoiler: After numerous battles and frolics (we're by the sea; think "Bali H'ai"), and having observed grateful peasants picking lychees and making bamboo hats for the style-conscious soldierettes, and having mourned the heroic death of Changqing and been buoyed by Qionghua's rise through the ranks, we see her rewarded by being named the Detachment's Party Representative, while (according to the program) "the whole community joins the Red Army and the sound of their combat songs rings out: 'March, march, march, forward for victory!' " If you were hoping for romance, forget it—what's on everybody's mind is liberating the coconut grove. But don't think all is gloom and oppression. Except for the girl soldiers in their snappy gray uniforms, and the dull though well-groomed peasants, everyone's in pinks, turquoises, and scarlets, and very jolly except when dying.

The Red Detachment of Women is the most famous and successful of the propaganda spectacles (aka "ballets") staged by the National Ballet of China, anointed as a masterpiece by Madame Mao in 1964 when the Gang of Four was rampant, and performed to date nearly four thousand times, including the time it was put on for President Nixon when he was in China on his famous 1972 mission. What can Richard and Pat have made of it? You have to feel sorry for them—at least official visitors to Moscow got Plisetskaya in *Swan Lake*.

In fact, what can *we* make of it? What does it spring from? Certainly not from traditional Chinese theater—all that was swept away in the Cultural Revolution. Its roots clearly lie in the propaganda ballets that flourished for decades in the Soviet Union, but those at least were recognizably dance works, however blatant. *Red Detachment* makes *Spartacus* look like *La Sylphide*. The company's dancers are well trained—prima ballerina Zhang Jian has elegantly pointed feet, a punchy arabesque, a good jump. She's won the big competitions, has performed everywhere from Seoul to Copenhagen to Houston, has done all the classics, including *Swan Lake* and *The Sleeping Beauty*, plus *Carmen*, *Onegin*, *Sylvia*, and "many Balanchine ballets," but here she's more like a James Bond sidekick than a classical dancer. The art of ballet as we know it is very thinly pasted onto the whole goofy enterprise. We get a little burst of fouettés here, a sort of *tour en l'air* there, but no one's fooled—this is animated poster art, not ballet.

So why are young Chinese-Americans turned on by this ridiculous propaganda kitsch from a bygone China they presumably deplore? Don't ask me.

And then the National Ballet gave us *The Peony Pavilion*, a much more recent success for the company, based on a late-sixteenth-century play that can take up to twenty hours to perform but here is compressed into two. (You don't have to tell *me* to count my blessings.) Whereas *Red Detachment* is terminally ludicrous, *Peony* is terminally boring. We're told that in China it's often compared to *Romeo and Juliet*, but you wouldn't know it from the stage action. It's all about dream lovers— that much I was able to grasp, with the help of the program notes. "Du Liniang awakes from a deep sleep in which her subconscious has been playing with her emotions" and is joined by two alter egos "who guide her to learn the truth about her body and to enjoy her restless desire." So far, so good, but that's as far as I can take you.

Du Liniang is dressed in beautiful white, the alter egos in bright red and bright blue, there's a platform that goes up and down and tilts, there's a scene in hell, there's death and ghosts and a lovely snowfall. There's a portrait and several intense passages in which a pointe shoe is clutched by the hero. And there's a big wedding. Not exactly *Romeo and Juliet* as I recall it, but maybe the weird caterwauling of the Kunqu opera singing explains everything. The rest of the score is made up of music by Guo Wenjing, relieved by long passages from Debussy (*Afternoon of a Faun, La Mer*), Ravel, Respighi, Holst, and Prokofiev. (The music for *Red Detachment* was by *five* composers, all in a sub-sub-sub-Khachatourian mode, as if Khachatourian weren't sub enough to begin with.)

Again, what *is The Peony Pavilion?* Feeble ballet plus Robert Wilson plus Radio City Music Hall? It's not the spawn of any single recognizable art form—it's pastiche glued together by hardworking, sincere people who have no organic relationship to the elements they're working with. The Russian Revolution stored everything away and brought it out again when the storm had passed. The Cultural Revolution just destroyed. Sadly, the reason these two works have nothing to reveal to us about China and its art is because they're not really Chinese and they're not really art.

The New York Observer
JULY 14, 2015

Michelle Dorrance: Tapping for Joy

ONE OF THE PLEASURES of watching Dorrance Dance—the tap group founded and run by Michelle Dorrance—is registering the contrast between her and the phenomenal Savion Glover, who has dominated the field for so long. Glover has clearly grown to resent what presumably seemed to him the audience's patronizing reaction to his early adorableness, and has come to project a surly aura of go-fuck-yourself-ism that defies his audiences to resist him—difficult to do, given his amazing aptitudes. It has become, for me at least, a trial to watch him: I know when I'm not wanted.

But if Glover has become the Miles Davis of tap, Michelle Dorrance is Dizzy Gillespie—the message is joy. Is she the technical phenomenon Glover is? No, she isn't, and neither is anyone else, but she loves her art form and she wants you to love it, too—not *her*, but what she and her colleagues are up to. The relief! And since she's abundantly talented as both dancer and choreographer, you do indeed love her. Her recent two-week season at the Joyce, which featured nine dancers including herself, and a five-person musical ensemble led by the prodigious Toshi Reagon, had the audience reeling with pleasure.

Dorrance is tall, lanky, angular, and it's not just her tap shoes that sparkle—her legs are everywhere, her body keeps swinging and swaying, her face is animated (sometimes too animated—there's an occasional touch of the smiling sickness). Her two principal co-dancers are also formidable, most strikingly Dormeshia Sumbry-Edwards, a veteran of the honor roll of recent tap history: *After Midnight, Black and Blue, Bring in 'da Noise, Bring in 'da Funk.* She's worked with Gregory Hines and Spike Lee and Michael Jackson (she was his tap coach). She's won countless awards. And when you watch her long solo in the current Dorrance production, *The Blues Project*, you see why. Here is effortless and endless invention as she ranges around the stage, delicate in detail yet accumulating force. You never want her to stop. And you quickly forget you're in the presence of tap virtuosity—this is just remarkable dancing, generous, secure, ego-less, and captivating.

Derick K. Grant is the other powerhouse, also with an immaculate pedigree. He manages to be both dazzling and just so slightly held back, but he too is also all over the place, not locked in one position while drumming his taps. Grant—like Sumbry-Edwards, like Dorrance herself, like all their colleagues—loves to *move*. And Dorrance keeps them all moving, as one burst of activity flows into another: now a couple, now a threesome, now a solo, now the whole gang.

The Blues Project embraces a number of styles, from the hoedown to the Lindy Hop, by no means all of them blues-related, but the overall tone and approach are consistent; this isn't a revue, it's a progress. Nine very individual dancers who complement rather than challenge each other, all of them fully charged and unflagging, create a tumult of joyous excitement. Dorrance is in charge, yes, but she encourages the others to fling in their individual ideas and quirks. And all of them are in constant touch with the astounding Reagon and her fellow musicians performing up on a conspicuous riser at the back of the stage—at times the dancing seems to be accompanying the music rather than the other way round.

What's so gratifying is that despite occasional moments of flirtation with the audience, the overarching impression is of the dancers' pure-of-heart-ness and goodwill—toward each other, toward tap, toward us.

The New York Observer
NOVEMBER 30, 2016

City Ballet: Act III

WHEN GEORGE BALANCHINE DIED, in 1983, it was a tragedy, a catastrophe, the end of civilization, but it wasn't a shock—he had been ill for a year, and more or less out of commission. We had known the end was coming and we knew who the future was: Balanchine and his partner, Lincoln Kirstein, had made it clear that Peter Martins was to run New York City Ballet together with Jerome Robbins. But that was a formality: Robbins, at sixty-four, had no serious interest in performing the kind of administrative labor—and undergoing the stress—that being an artistic director involves.

Through Kirstein, I had become a member of the City Ballet board,

and then had found myself, as a volunteer, deeply involved with programming and marketing. Perhaps a year and half before Balanchine's
death, Kirstein said to me, "Bob, you have to look after Peter. I'm
too old." I didn't know what he meant, and he probably didn't either,
but I always took Lincoln literally—the only person I have ever been
happy taking orders from. In due course I got to know Peter well, and
the dancer Heather Watts, with whom he lived for a decade or so. The
two of them were fired with devotion to Balanchine's art and to the
company—the omens were good.

So Martins became Act II in the history of our great ballet company, and he has kept it thriving, if not always great. But *his* departure,
after thirty-five years, has been abrupt, ugly, and unresolved; there is
no appointed heir, and there is no agreement over whether he deserves
what's happened to him, or even about what *has* happened. He was first
accused of misbehavior in an anonymous letter sent to the School of
American Ballet, and it seems that no one except current members of
the board of directors of the school and of the company knows what
was in that letter.

Martins was then denounced by several ex-dancers, including one
woman who accused him of violent behavior and another of sexual
abuse, who made their allegations to the press. Unhappily, Martins's
history is checkered with instances of violence (toward his wife, the
ballerina Darci Kistler), abuse of alcohol, and romantic relationships with
dancers. An official outside investigation is proceeding, even though
Martins has resigned his posts at the company and the school, but
questions have already been aired about whether the investigation is
disinterested or in some way a board-directed ploy to exonerate him.
I myself have no special information about what did or didn't happen,
and no direct knowledge of his personal behavior these past twenty
years, which is as long as it's been since we were in touch.

All this is anguishing for those who grew up in or around Balanchine's
City Ballet. (Balanchine himself was, to put it tactfully, a ladies' man:
a serial marrier, but also frequently involved with young women to
whom he was not married. Certainly, though, there was never a hint of
violence toward women—he was famously courteous, elegant, appre-

ciative, and loyal.) Nothing excuses the use of violence or the abuse of power, and Peter Martins may have been guilty of both, in which case it's right that he is gone. But his sudden silent departure—after fifty years of service to City Ballet—is dismaying. And the board's reticence about what has happened and is happening is disquieting.

As for City Ballet's Act III, obviously the choice of the next artistic director is crucial, and the board is taking its time before making a move. Its task is not an easy one: As Bette Davis sang in the 1943 movie *Thank Your Lucky Stars*, "The pickings are poor and the crop is lean." Although the company is considerably more than a Balanchine museum, Balanchine ballets—and Balanchine style and technique—are the heart of the enterprise. If the board wants that to continue, and it's inconceivable that it doesn't, it must identify the best Balanchine-inspired person for the job. Among the candidates most frequently mentioned, there are several excellent dancers whose excellence did not lie in Balanchine. There are those with little or no administrative experience, and those who have modest or no choreographic abilities or who are simply not seasoned. And there may well be others whose sense of self-preservation makes them hesitate about wandering into the gladiatorial arena.

So everything's on hold, with the entire serious ballet community unsettled and anxious. As it should be. New York City Ballet is the most significant American dance company, and if it founders, we're all in big trouble.

Meanwhile, the company is dancing. The first two weeks of the current season have come and gone, programmed and cast by Martins, of course, and "supervised" by three ex-dancers plus the resident choreographer, Justin Peck, who is still dancing. As it happens, the repertory has been Balanchine-dominated, apart from some inconsequential leftover new ballets from last season. (The current two weeks, oddly enough, are devoted to Martins's *Romeo + Juliet*.) The heartening news is that the dancers, faced with crisis, rose to the occasion. There was nothing dispirited or slack about what they gave us. Almost everything looked rehearsed and energized. *Cortège Hongrois*, for instance, which a few years ago looked sloppy and limp, was bouncy and convincing—or as convincing as this far-from-top-level Balanchine ballet can be. *The Four Temperaments*, a masterpiece that deserves superb casting, more or less got it, although I'm still not convinced by Anthony Huxley's "Melancholic"—he's more sprightly than it is. Savannah Lowery was vastly improved as "Choleric." Both Sara Mearns and Tiler Peck were dominating as "Sanguinic." And two very different corps girls shone in the first "Theme": composed and strong Lydia Wellington and beautiful Olivia Boisson, whose attack and amplitude are thrilling.

The company's two senior ballerinas were in fine form. Maria Kowroski is dancing with a new refined command—ravishing in *Chaconne* and Ratmansky's *Russian Seasons*. Ashley Bouder was as wonderful in *Divertimento No. 15* as she was last year in *Square Dance*, a welcome relief after Megan Fairchild, who can do the steps but doesn't make anything of them. Both these Bouder roles were made on Patricia Wilde, another phenomenal technician whom she actually resembles.

This season confirmed that Unity Phelan is a major player—a star—with her dark ballerina beauty and her graceful strength. Indiana Woodward is another first-rate talent, bursting with pizzazz. And both Ask la Cour and Adrian Danchig-Waring have broken through—we've been waiting a long time.

There was a premiere: corps member Peter Walker's *dance odyssey*. (Why do young choreographers think that odd spellings or lack of capitalization make things more interesting?) This is Walker's second piece for the company, and it's more ambitious than his first, *ten in seven* (also denied capital letters). The new work goes in for effects—flashing lights, silhouetted dancers across the back of the stage, a neon strip that rises and falls against the backdrop—but they don't add up to anything. Not even appealing music (by Oliver Davis) or colorful costumes (by Marc Happel) could hide Walker's lack of a compelling idea.

And then, pure pleasure. The curtain goes up on Alexei Ratmansky's *Russian Seasons* and you're at once in a complete world—the music (Leonid Desyatnikov), the stylized peasanty costumes of Galina Solovyeva, and most important, an individual and alluring dance vocabulary, combine to create a gripping and seamless work of art full of happy surprises. *Russian Seasons* is a dozen years old and as fresh and impressive as it was when new. Ratmansky unleashes Mearns, enhances Kowroski, respects and nourishes all his dancers. Who can deny that he is the world's leading classical choreographer? If only he were available to run the company! But why would he want to? Running the Bolshoi years ago must have been traumatizing. And as things stand, he can create ballets more or less wherever he wants to—without having to worry about donors and boards.

The New York Observer
FEBRUARY 9, 2018

Note: Several days after this piece was posted, the ballet and school, according to *The New York Times*, announced that the outside investigation "did not corroborate the allegations." But—no surprise—axes are still being ground. Meanwhile, Act III goes on waiting in the wings.

ACKNOWLEDGMENTS

Thanks, to begin with, to the various editors who commissioned these pieces or accepted them for publication—first among them the late Robert Silvers of *The New York Review of Books*. Where would we be without it? Early on, Chip McGrath, and recently Pamela Paul, invited me to write for *The New York Times Book Review*, and I thank them. Corby Kummer of *The Atlantic* took charge of my essay for the magazine on Rodgers and Hart, and since then has cast an unofficial stern but always beneficial eye on what I write.

It's been twenty years since I began reviewing both books and dance for *The New York Observer* (once fondly known as the pink paper). I have had countless editors there, all of them helpful, solicitous, and calming. The crucial one through this entire time has been Adam Begley, who at first was my official editor, and who, years after retiring from the paper, has gone on tormenting me, piece after piece, with his withering—but, alas, essential—interventions. I do the same for him, though of course I am far kinder. By now we've enjoyed two decades of fun together, mostly over the transatlantic phone. And our friendship has deepened.

At FSG, I've again had patient and genial support and encouragement from everyone I deal with, from president and publisher Jonathan Galassi to Lord High Everything Else Jeff Seroy, to devoted (and captivating) editor Ileene Smith and her highly able assistant, Jackson Howard, to the exemplary and endearing Debra Helfand, executive managing editor. Special thanks, yet again, to my production editor, Scott Auerbach, with whom it's always a joy to negotiate semicolons and indents, and to Abby Kagan, a superb designer whose fanatical love of detail and unerring eye make our work together pure pleasure.

As for the illustrations: My decades-long association with Photofest has once more proved invaluable and agreeable, as have my dealings with the terrific group of curators at the New York Public Library for the Performing Arts at Lincoln Center: Linda Murray for dance, Jeremy Megraw for theater, Jessica Wood for music, and Phil Karg for everything. Their Beloved Leader, Jacqueline Davis, sets the tone of benevolent efficiency. Finally, thank you to Condé Nast for the Steichen portrait of Dorothy Parker and to Edward Sorel for his ravishing imagining of the ravishing Mary Astor.

Grateful acknowledgment is made to Photofest for the images from *Heaven Is for Real* (© TriStar Pictures), *Genius* (© Roadside Attractions), *Flesh and Bone* (© 2015 Starz Entertainment, LLC), *Black Swan* (© Fox Searchlight Pictures), *Million Dollar Mermaid* (© MGM), *Coco Chanel & Igor Stravinsky* (© Sony Pictures Classics), and the two versions of *Jane Eyre* (2011: © Focus Features; 1944: © Twentieth Century Fox Flim Corporation); to the Jerome Robbins Dance Division, The New York Public Library for the Performing Arts, for the images from George Balanchine's *The Firebird* and Maya Plisetskaya; to the Billy Rose Theatre Division, The New York Public Library for the Performing Arts, Astor, Lenox and Tilden Foundations, for the images of the Booths and Ethel Merman, and for Martha Swope's image of Elena Tchernichova coaching and the image of Lorenz Hart and Richard Rodgers; to the Music Division, The New York Public Library for the Performing Arts, for the image of Leonard Bernstein; to the Everett Collection for the image from *Tokyo Story*; to Condé Nast for the images of Dorothy Parker and Ethel Waters; to the National Portrait Gallery for the image of Wilkie Collins by Rudolf Lehmann; to Magnum Photos for the Elliott Landy image of Clive Davis and Janis Joplin; to the Archivio GBB / Agenzia Contrasto / Redux for the image of Toscanini; to the William P. Gottlieb / Ira and Leonore Gershwin Fund Collection, Music Division, Library of Congress, for the image of Frank Sinatra; to *The Irish Times* for the image of Sebastian Barry; and to Edward Sorel for the image of Mary Astor.